Frommer's®

W9-AMT-207

P O R T A B L E
Acapulco, Ixtapa & Zihuatanejo

5th Edition

by Juan Cristiano

Here's what critics say about Frommer's:

"Amazingly easy to use. Very portable, very complete."

—*Booklist*

"Detailed, accurate, and easy-to-read information for all price ranges."

—*Glamour Magazine*

BICENTENNIAL
1807
WILEY
2007
BICENTENNIAL

Wiley Publishing, Inc.

Published by:

WILEY PUBLISHING, INC.

111 River St.
Hoboken, NJ 07030-5774

ISBN: 978-0-470-14577-7

Editor: Jennifer Polland
Production Editor: Suzanna R. Thompson
Cartographer: Elizabeth Puhl
Photo Editor: Richard Fox
Anniversary Logo Design: Richard Pacifico
Production by Wiley Indianapolis Composition Services

For information on our other products and services or to obtain technical
support, please contact our Customer Care Department within the U.S. at
800/762-2974, outside the U.S. at 317/572-3993 or fax 317/572-4002.

Wiley also publishes its books in a variety of electronic formats. Some con-
tent that appears in print may not be available in electronic formats.

Manufactured in the United States of America

5   4   3   2   1

Contents

List of Maps   v

1   Planning Your Trip to Southern Pacific Mexico   1

   1   The Region at a Glance 1

   2   Visitor Information 2

        Destination: Mexico—Red Alert Checklist 4

   3   Entry Requirements & Customs 5

   4   Money 8

   5   When to Go 12

        Mexico Calender of Events 13

   6   Insurance, Health & Safety 17

        What to Do If You Get Sick 21

   7   Tips for Travelers with Special Needs 24

   8   Getting There 29

   9   Package Tours for the Independent Traveler 33

  10   Active Vacations in Pacific Coast Mexico 35

  11   Getting Around 37

        Fast Facts: Mexico 42

2   Acapulco   49

   1   Essentials 52

        Fast Facts: Acapulco 55

   2   Where to Stay 56

   3   Where to Dine 64

   4   Activities On & Off the Beach 70

   5   Shopping 77

   6   Acapulco After Dark 78

3   Northward to Zihuatanejo & Ixtapa   82

   1   Essentials 82

        Fast Facts: Zihuatanejo & Ixtapa 86

   2   Where to Stay 87

3 Where to Dine 94

4 Activities On & Off the Beach 97

5 Shopping 102

6 Zihuatanejo & Ixtapa After Dark 103

4 The Oaxaca Coast: From Puerto Escondido to Huatulco   105

1 Puerto Escondido 105

   Fast Facts: Puerto Escondido 110

   Ecotours & Other Adventurous Explorations 118

2 A Trip to Puerto Angel: Backpacking Beach Haven 123

3 Bahías de Huatulco 125

   Fast Facts: Bahías de Huatulco 130

5 Inland to Old Mexico: Taxco, Cuernavaca & Tepoztlán   139

1 Taxco: Cobblestones & Silver 139

   Spanish & Art Classes in Taxco 143

2 Cuernavaca: Land of Eternal Spring 151

   Fast Facts: Cuernavaca 155

3 Tepoztlán 164

Appendix: Useful Terms & Phrases   171

Index   177

   Accommodations Index 181

   Restaurant Index 182

List of Maps

Southern Pacific Mexico   3

Acapulco Bay Area   50

Zihuatanejo & Ixtapa
    Area   83

Downtown Zihuatanejo   89

Puerto Escondido   107

Bahías de Huatulco   127

Taxco   141

Cuernavaca   153

ABOUT THE AUTHOR

A resident of Mexico City, **Juan Cristiano** is a native of Los Angeles who has written extensively about destinations in Mexico and Latin America, the United States, and western Europe.

AN INVITATION TO THE READER

In researching this book, we discovered many wonderful places—hotels, restaurants, shops, and more. We're sure you'll find others. Please tell us about them, so we can share the information with your fellow travelers in upcoming editions. If you were disappointed with a recommendation, we'd love to know that, too. Please write to:

    Frommer's Portable Acapulco, Ixtapa & Zihuatanejo, 5th Edition
    Wiley Publishing, Inc. • 111 River St. • Hoboken, NJ 07030-5774

AN ADDITIONAL NOTE

Please be advised that travel information is subject to change at any time—and this is especially true of prices. We therefore suggest that you write or call ahead for confirmation when making your travel plans. The authors, editors, and publisher cannot be held responsible for the experiences of readers while traveling. Your safety is important to us, however, so we encourage you to stay alert and be aware of your surroundings. Keep a close eye on cameras, purses, and wallets, all favorite targets of thieves and pickpockets.

Frommer's Star Ratings, Icons & Abbreviations

Every hotel, restaurant, and attraction listing in this guide has been ranked for quality, value, service, amenities, and special features using a **star-rating system.** In country, state, and regional guides, we also rate towns and regions to help you narrow down your choices and budget your time accordingly. Hotels and restaurants are rated on a scale of zero (recommended) to three stars (exceptional). Attractions, shopping, nightlife, towns, and regions are rated according to the following scale: zero stars (recommended), one star (highly recommended), two stars (very highly recommended), and three stars (must-see).

In addition to the star-rating system, we also use **seven feature icons** that point you to the great deals, in-the-know advice, and unique experiences that separate travelers from tourists. Throughout the book, look for:

Finds	Special finds—those places only insiders know about
Fun Fact	Fun facts—details that make travelers more informed and their trips more fun
Kids	Best bets for kids and advice for the whole family
Moments	Special moments—those experiences that memories are made of
Overrated	Places or experiences not worth your time or money
Tips	Insider tips—great ways to save time and money
Value	Great values—where to get the best deals

The following **abbreviations** are used for credit cards:

AE	American Express	DISC	Discover	V	Visa
DC	Diners Club	MC	MasterCard		

Frommers.com

Now that you have this guidebook to help you plan a great trip, visit our website at **www.frommers.com** for additional travel information on more than 3,600 destinations. We update features regularly to give you instant access to the most current trip-planning information available. At Frommers. com, you'll find scoops on the best airfares, lodging rates, and car rental bargains. You can even book your travel online through our reliable travel booking partners. Other popular features include:

- Online updates of our most popular guidebooks
- Vacation sweepstakes and contest giveaways
- Newsletters highlighting the hottest travel trends
- Online travel message boards with featured travel discussions

Planning Your Trip to Southern Pacific Mexico

This chapter tells you everything you need to know before you go: Customs and passport requirements, currency details, package tours, getting there, getting around, and more.

1 The Region at a Glance

Though Pacific Mexico may be uniform in its often exotic tropical beaches and jungle scenery, the resorts along this coast couldn't be more varied in personality. From high-energy seaside cities to pristine, primitive coves, this is the Mexico that first lured vacationers around the globe.

Spanish conquistadors were attracted to this coast for its numerous sheltered coves and protected bays from which they set sail to the Far East. Years later, Mexico's first tourists found the same elements appealing, but for different reasons—they were seeking escape in the warm sunshine, and stretches of blue coves nicely complemented the heady tropical landscape of the adjacent coastal mountains.

Time at the beach is generally the top priority for most travelers to this part of Mexico. Each of the beach towns detailed in this book is capable of satisfying your sand-and-surf needs for a few days, or even a week or more. You could also combine several coastal resorts into a single trip, or mix the coastal with the colonial, say, with visits to both Puerto Escondido and Oaxaca City, or Acapulco and Taxco.

The resorts have distinct personalities, but you get the requisite beach wherever you go, whether you choose a city that offers virtually every luxury imaginable or a rustic town providing little more than basic (but charming) seaside relaxation.

Over the years, a diverse selection of resorts has evolved in the area. Each is distinct, yet together they offer an ideal attraction for almost any type of traveler. The region encompasses the country's oldest, largest, and most decadent resort, **Acapulco,** one-time playground of Hollywood's biggest celebrities. Of all the resorts, Acapulco has the best airline connections, the broadest range of late-night entertainment, the most savory dining, and the widest range of accommodations—from hillside villas and luxury resort hotels to modest inns on the beach and in the city center.

The resort of **Ixtapa** and its neighboring seaside village, **Zihuatanejo,** offer beach-bound tourist attractions, but on a smaller, newer, and less hectic scale than Acapulco. They attract travelers for their complementary contrasts—international high-rise hotels in one, plus the local color and leisurely pace of the other. To get here, many people fly into Acapulco, then make the 4- to 5-hour trip north (by rental car or bus), although one can fly directly into Ixtapa/Zihuatanejo, as well.

South of Acapulco, along the Oaxacan Coast, lie the small, laid-back beach towns of **Puerto Escondido** and **Puerto Angel,** both on picturesque bays bordered by relaxed communities. The region's most upscale resort community, **Bahías de Huatulco,** couples an unspoiled, slow-paced nature with the kind of modern infrastructure and luxurious facilities you'd find in the country's more crowded megaresorts. Nine bays encompass 36 beaches—many are isolated stretches of pure white sand—and countless inlets and coves. Huatulco has become increasingly known for its ecotourism attractions; you won't find much in the way of shopping or nightlife, but for most visitors, the clear blue waters and quiet, restful beaches are reason enough to come.

From Acapulco a road leads inland to **Taxco,** a colonial city that clings to the side of a mountain and is famed for its hundreds of silver shops. And verdant **Cuernavaca,** known as the land of eternal spring, has gained a reputation for exceptional spa facilities, while also boasting a wealth of cultural and historic attractions.

The whole region is graced with a stunning coastline and tropical mountains. Outside the urban centers, however, paved roads are few, and these two states remain among Mexico's poorest, despite decades-long influx of U.S. tourist dollars (and many other currencies).

2 Visitor Information

The **Mexico Tourism Board** (© 800/446-3942) is an excellent source for general information; you can request brochures on the country and get answers to the most common questions from the

Southern Pacific Mexico

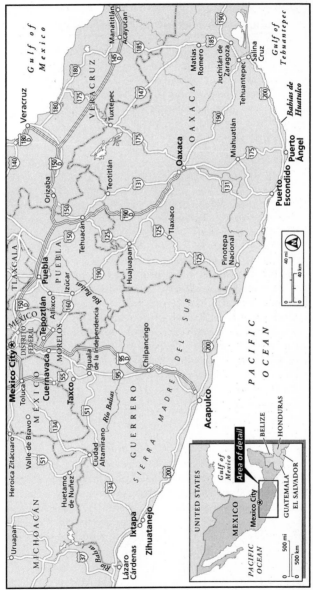

Destination: Mexico—Red Alert Checklist

- Did you check to see if any travel advisories have been issued by the U.S. State Department (www.travel.state.gov) regarding your destination?
- Do you have your passport or official ID? If traveling in a coastal area, did you pack insect repellent? Sunblock? A hat? Sunglasses? A sweater or jacket?
- Do you need to book tour, restaurant, or travel reservations in advance?
- Did you make sure attractions and activities that interest you are operating? Some attractions, such as seasonal nature tours, sell out quickly.
- If you purchased traveler's checks, have you recorded the check numbers and stored the documentation separately from the checks?
- Did you pack your camera and an extra set of camera batteries, and purchase enough film?
- Do you have a safe, accessible place to store money?
- Did you bring emergency drug prescriptions and extra glasses and/or contact lenses?
- Do you know your daily ATM withdrawal limit?
- Do you have your credit card personal identification numbers (PINs)?
- If you have an e-ticket, do you have documentation?
- Do you know the address and phone number of your country's embassy?
- Did you leave a copy of your itinerary with someone at home?

exceptionally well-trained, knowledgeable staff. More information (15,000 pages' worth, they say) about Mexico is available on the Mexican Tourist Promotion Council's website: www.visitmexico.com.

The **U.S. State Department** (© **888/407-4747** or 202/501-4444; fax 202/647-1488; www.travel.state.gov) offers a **Consular Information Sheet** on Mexico with safety, medical, driving, and general travel information gleaned from reports by its offices in Mexico, and consistently updated. The **Centers for Disease Control and Prevention Hot Line** (© **800/311-3435** or 404/639-3534; www.cdc.gov) is a source of medical information for travelers to Mexico and elsewhere. For travelers to Mexico and Central America, the number with recorded messages is (📞 **877/394-8747.** Information is also available at **www.cdc.gov/travel**. The U.S. State Department website (see above) also offers medical information for Americans traveling abroad and a list of air ambulance services.

MEXICAN GOVERNMENT TOURIST OFFICES

Mexico has foreign tourist offices (MGTO) in the United States and Canada. They include the following:

The **Mexican Government Tourist Board** has offices in major North American cities, in addition to the main office in Mexico City (📞 **55/5278-4200**). In the **United States:** Chicago (📞 **312/228-0517,** ext. 14), Houston (📞 **713/772-2581,** ext. 105, or 713/772-3819), Los Angeles (📞 **310/282-9112**), Miami (📞 **786/621-2909**), and New York (📞 **212/308-2110**).

In **Canada:** 1 Place Ville-Marie, Suite 1931, Montreal, Quebec H3B 2C3 (📞 **514/871-1052**); 2 Bloor St. W., Suite 1502, Toronto, Ontario M4W 3E2 (📞 **416/925-0704**); and 999 W. Hastings, Suite 1110, Vancouver, British Columbia V6C 2W2 (📞 **604/669-2845**). The Embassy is located at 1500-45 O'Connor St., Ottawa, Ontario K1P 1A4 (📞 **613/233-8988;** fax 613/235-9123).

3 Entry Requirements & Customs

For information on how to get a passport, go to the "Fast Facts: Mexico" section, later in this chapter—the websites listed provide downloadable passport applications as well as the current fees for processing passport applications. For an up-to-date country-by-country listing of passport requirements around the world, go to the "Foreign Entry Requirements" Web page of the U.S. State Department at **http://travel.state.gov**.

DOCUMENTS

All travelers to Mexico are required to present **photo identification** and **proof of citizenship,** such as a valid passport, naturalization papers, or an original birth certificate with a raised seal, along with a driver's license or official ID, such as a state or military issued ID. Driver's licenses and permits, voter registration cards, affidavits and similar documents are not sufficient to prove citizenship for readmission into the United States. If the last name on the birth certificate is different from your current name, bring a photo identification card *and* legal proof of the name change, such as the original marriage license or certificate. *Note:* Photocopies are *not* acceptable.

Effective January 23, 2007, all U.S. citizens traveling by **air** to Mexico are required to have a valid passport to enter or reenter the United States. As early as January 1, 2008, U.S. citizens traveling between the United States and Mexico by **land** or **sea** may also be required to present a valid U.S. passport or other documents as determined by the Department of Homeland Security.

Safeguard your passport in an inconspicuous, inaccessible place like a money belt, and keep a copy of the critical pages with your passport number in a separate place. If you lose your passport, visit the nearest consulate of your native country as soon as possible for a replacement.

You must carry a **Mexican Tourist Permit (FMT),** the equivalent of a tourist visa, which Mexican border officials issue, free of charge, after proof of citizenship is accepted. Airlines generally provide the necessary forms aboard your flight to Mexico. The FMT is more important than a passport, so guard it carefully. If you lose it, you may not be permitted to leave until you can replace it—a bureaucratic hassle that can take anywhere from a few hours to a week.

The FMT can be issued for up to 180 days. Sometimes officials don't ask but just stamp a time limit, so be sure to say "6 months," or at least twice as long as you intend to stay. If you decide to extend your stay, you may request that additional time be added to your FMT from an official immigration office in Mexico.

Note that children under age 18 traveling without parents or with only one parent must have a notarized letter from the absent parent or parents authorizing the travel.

LOST DOCUMENTS

To replace a **lost passport,** contact your embassy or nearest consular agent (see "Fast Facts: Mexico," later in this chapter). You must establish a record of your citizenship and also fill out a form requesting another Mexican Tourist Permit if it, too, was lost. Without the **tourist permit** you can't leave the country, and without an affidavit affirming your passport request and citizenship, you may have problems at Customs when you get home. So it's important to clear everything up *before* trying to leave. Mexican Customs may, however, accept the police report of the loss of the tourist permit and allow you to leave.

CUSTOMS ALLOWANCES

When you enter Mexico, Customs officials will be tolerant as long as you have no illegal drugs or firearms. Tourists are allowed to bring in their personal effects duty-free. A laptop computer, camera equipment, and sports equipment that could feasibly be used during your stay are also allowed. The underlying guideline is: Don't bring anything that looks as if it's meant to be resold in Mexico. **U.S. citizens** entering Mexico by the land border can bring in gifts worth a value of up to $50 duty-free, except for alcohol and tobacco products. Those entering Mexico by air or sea can bring in gifts worth a value of up to $300 duty-free. The **Mexican Customs** *(Aduana)* website is www.aduanas. sat.gob.mx/webadunet/body.htm.

Returning U.S. citizens who have been away for at least 48 hours are allowed to bring back, once every 30 days, $800 worth of merchandise duty-free. You'll be charged a flat rate of 4% duty on the next $1,000 worth of purchases. Any dollar amount beyond that is dutiable at whatever rates apply. On mailed gifts, the duty-free limit is $200. Be sure to have your receipts or purchases handy to expedite the declaration process. Note: If you owe duty, you are required to pay on your arrival in the United States, either by cash, personal check, government or traveler's check, or money order, and in some locations, a Visa or MasterCard.

To avoid having to pay duty on foreign-made personal items you owned before you left on your trip, bring along a bill of sale, insurance policy, jeweler's appraisal, or receipts of purchase. Or you can register items that can be readily identified by a permanently affixed serial number or marking—think laptop computers, cameras, and CD players—with Customs before you leave. Take the items to the nearest Customs office or register them with Customs at the airport from which you're departing. You'll receive, at no cost, a Certificate of Registration, which allows duty-free entry for the life of the item.

With some exceptions, you cannot bring fresh fruits and vegetables into the United States. For specifics on what you can bring back, download the invaluable free pamphlet *Know Before You Go* online at **www.cbp.gov**. (Click on "Travel," and then click on "Know Before You Go! Online Brochure.") Or contact the **U.S. Customs & Border Protection (CBP),** 1300 Pennsylvania Ave., NW, Washington, DC 20229 (© **877/287-8667**) and request the pamphlet.

For a clear summary of Canadian rules, write for the booklet *I Declare,* issued by the **Canada Border Services Agency** (© **800/ 461-9999** in Canada, or 204/983-3500; www.cbsa-asfc.gc.ca).

For information on U.K. rules, contact **HM Customs & Excise** at © **0845/010-9000** (from outside the U.K., © 020/8929-0152), or consult their website at www.hmrc.gov.uk.

For Australians, a helpful brochure available from Australian consulates or Customs offices is *Know Before You Go.* For more information, call the **Australian Customs Service** at © **1300/363-263,** or log on to www.customs.gov.au.

For citizens of New Zealand, most questions are answered in a free pamphlet available at New Zealand consulates and Customs offices: *New Zealand Customs Guide for Travellers, Notice no. 4.* For more information, contact **New Zealand Customs,** The Customhouse, 17–21 Whitmore St., Box 2218, Wellington (© **04/473-6099** or 0800/428-786; www.customs.govt.nz).

GOING THROUGH CUSTOMS

Mexican Customs inspection has been streamlined. At most points of entry, tourists are requested to press a button in front of what looks like a traffic signal, which alternates on touch between red and green signals. Green light and you go through without inspection; red light and your luggage or car may be inspected briefly or thoroughly. If you have an unusual amount of luggage or an oversize piece, you may be subject to inspection despite the traffic signal routine.

4 Money

The currency in Mexico is the Mexican **peso.** Paper currency comes in denominations of 20, 50, 100, 200, 500, and 1,000 pesos. Coins come in denominations of 1, 2, 5, 10, and 20 pesos and 20 and 50 **centavos** (100 centavos equal 1 peso). The current exchange rate for the U.S. dollar is around 11 pesos; at that rate, an item that costs 11 pesos would be equivalent to US$1. The prices quoted in this book were converted using an exchange rate of 11 pesos to US$1 and US$1.80 to £1.

Getting **change** continues to be a problem in Mexico. Small-denomination bills and coins are hard to come by, so start collecting them early in your trip and continue as you travel. Shopkeepers everywhere seem always to be out of change and small bills; that's doubly true in a market.

Money Matters
The **universal currency sign ($)** is used to indicate pesos in Mexico. The use of the symbol in this book, however, denotes U.S. currency.

Tips **A Few Words about Prices**

The peso's value continues to fluctuate—at press time, it was roughly **11 pesos to the dollar.** Also note that Mexico has a **value-added tax of 15%** (*Impuesto de Valor Agregado,* or IVA; pronounced "ee-vah") on most everything, including restaurant meals, bus tickets, and souvenirs. Always ask to see a printed price sheet and always ask if the tax is included.

Many establishments that deal with tourists, especially in coastal resort areas, quote prices in dollars. To avoid confusion, they use the abbreviations "Dlls." for dollars and "M.N." (*moneda nacional,* or national currency) for pesos.

EXCHANGING MONEY

The rate of exchange fluctuates a tiny bit daily, so you probably are better off not exchanging too much of your currency at once. Don't forget, however, to have enough pesos to carry you over a weekend or Mexican holiday, when banks are closed. In general, avoid carrying the US$100 bill, the bill most commonly counterfeited in Mexico, and therefore the most difficult to exchange, especially in smaller towns. Because small bills and coins in pesos are hard to come by in Mexico, the US$1 bill is very useful for tipping.

Exchange houses (*casas de cambio*) are generally more convenient than banks because they have more locations and longer hours; the rate of exchange may be the same as a bank or only slightly lower. *Note:* Before leaving a bank or exchange-house window, always count your change in front of the teller before the next client steps up.

Large airports have currency-exchange counters that often stay open whenever flights are arriving or departing. Though convenient, these generally do not offer the most favorable rates.

A hotel's exchange desk commonly pays less favorable rates than banks; however, when the currency is in a state of flux, higher-priced hotels are known to pay *higher* than bank rates, in their effort to attract dollars.

The bottom line: It pays to shop around, but in almost all cases, you receive a better exchange by changing money first, then paying for goods or services, rather than by paying with dollars directly to an establishment.

BANKS & ATMs

Banks in Mexico are rapidly expanding and improving services. They tend to be open weekdays from 9am until 5pm, and often for at least a half-day on Saturday. In larger resorts and cities, they can generally accommodate the exchange of dollars (which used to stop at noon) anytime during business hours. During times when the currency is in flux, a particular bank may not exchange dollars, so check before standing in line. Some, but not all, banks charge a service fee of about 1% to exchange traveler's checks. However, you can pay for most purchases directly with traveler's checks at the establishment's stated exchange rate. Don't even bother with personal checks drawn on a U.S. bank—the bank will wait for your check to clear, which can take weeks, before giving you your money.

In most resorts in Mexico, the use of **ATMs** (automated teller machines) is considered safe—just use the same precautions you would at any ATM. Universal bank cards (such as the Cirrus and PLUS systems) can be used. This is a convenient way to withdraw money and avoid carrying too much with you at any time. The exchange rate is generally more favorable than that at a currency house. Most machines offer Spanish/English menus and dispense pesos, but some offer the option of withdrawing dollars. The **Cirrus** (© 800/424-7787; www.mastercard.com) and **PLUS** (© 800/843-7587; www.visa.com) networks span the globe; look at the back of your bank card to see which network you're on, then call or check online for ATM locations at your destination. Be sure you know your personal identification number (PIN) before you leave home and be sure to find out your daily withdrawal limit before you depart. Also keep in mind that many banks impose a fee every time a card is used at a different bank's ATM, and that fee can be higher for international transactions (up to $5 or more) than for domestic ones (where they're rarely more than $1.50). On top of this, the bank from which you withdraw cash may charge its own fee. To compare banks' ATM fees within the U.S., use www.bankrate.com. For international withdrawal fees, ask your bank.

You can also get cash advances on your credit card at an ATM. Keep in mind that credit card companies try to protect themselves from theft by limiting the funds someone can withdraw outside their home country, so call your credit card company before you leave home. And keep in mind that you'll pay interest from the moment of your withdrawal, even if you pay your monthly bills on time.

TRAVELER'S CHECKS

Traveler's checks are something of an anachronism from the days before the ATM made cash accessible at any time. Traveler's checks used to be the only sound alternative to traveling with dangerously large amounts of cash. They were as reliable as currency, but, unlike cash, could be replaced if lost or stolen.

These days, traveler's checks are less necessary because most cities have 24-hour ATMs that allow you to withdraw small amounts of cash as needed. However, keep in mind that you will likely be charged an ATM withdrawal fee if the bank is not your own, so if you're withdrawing money every day, you might be better off with traveler's checks—provided that you don't mind showing identification every time you want to cash one.

You can buy traveler's checks at most banks. They are offered in denominations of $20, $50, $100, $500, and sometimes $1,000. Generally, you'll pay a service charge ranging from 1% to 4%.

The most popular traveler's checks are offered by **American Express** (© **800/807-6233** or 800/221-7282 for card holders—this number accepts collect calls, offers service in several foreign languages, and exempts Amex gold and platinum cardholders from the 1% fee); **Visa** (© **800/732-1322**)—AAA members can obtain Visa checks for a $9.95 fee (for checks up to $1,500) at most AAA offices or by calling © **866/339-3378.** Call © **800/223-9920** for information on MasterCard traveler's checks.

Be sure to keep a record of the traveler's checks serial numbers separate from your checks in the event that they are stolen or lost. You'll get a refund faster if you know the numbers.

American Express, Thomas Cook, Visa, and **MasterCard** offer **foreign currency traveler's checks,** useful if you're traveling to one country or to the euro zone; they're accepted at locations where dollar checks may not be.

Another option is the new prepaid traveler's check cards, reloadable cards that work much like debit cards but aren't linked to your checking account. The **American Express Travelers Cheque Card,** for example, requires a minimum deposit, sets a maximum balance, and has a one-time issuance fee of $14.95. You can withdraw money from an ATM (for a fee of $2.50 per transaction, not including bank fees), and the funds can be purchased in dollars, euros, or pounds. If you lose the card, your available funds will be refunded within 24 hours.

CREDIT CARDS

Credit cards are another safe way to carry money. They also provide a convenient record of all your expenses, and they generally offer relatively good exchange rates. You can withdraw cash advances from your credit cards at banks or ATMs but high fees make credit-card cash advances a pricey way to get cash. Keep in mind that you'll pay interest from the moment of your withdrawal, even if you pay your monthly bills on time, and most banks assess a 2% fee above the 1% fee charged by Visa or MasterCard or American Express for currency conversion on credit charges. But credit cards still may be the smart way to go when you factor in things like exorbitant ATM fees and higher traveler's check exchange rates (and service fees).

In Mexico Visa, MasterCard, and American Express are the most accepted cards. You'll be able to charge most hotel, restaurant, and store purchases, as well as almost all airline tickets, on your credit card. You generally can't charge gasoline purchases in Mexico. You can get cash advances of several hundred dollars on your card, but there may be a wait of 20 minutes to 2 hours.

Charges will be made in pesos, then converted into dollars by the bank issuing the credit card. Generally you receive the favorable bank rate when paying by credit card. However, be aware that some establishments in Mexico add a 5% to 7% surcharge when you pay with a credit card. This is especially true when using American Express. Many times, advertised discounts will not apply if you pay with a credit card.

5 When to Go

SEASONS

Mexico has two principal travel seasons: high and low. **High season** begins around December 20 and continues to Easter, although in some places high season can begin as early as mid-November. **Low season** begins the day after Easter and continues to mid-December; during low season, prices may drop 20% to 50%. In beach destinations popular with Mexican travelers, such as Acapulco, the prices will revert back to high season during the months of July and August, the traditional national summer vacation period.

Mexico has two main climate seasons as well: **rainy** (May to mid-Oct) and **dry** (mid-Oct to Apr). The rainy season can be of little consequence in the dry, northern region of the country. The Pacific coastal region typically receives tropical showers, which begin around 4 or 5pm and last a few hours. Though these rains can come on suddenly and be quite strong, they usually end just as fast and cool off the air for the evening. **Hurricane season** particularly affects the southern Pacific coast, especially from June through October. However, if no hurricanes strike, the light, cooling winds, especially from September through November, can make it a perfect time to more comfortably explore the area. Most of coastal Mexico experiences temperatures in the 80s in the hottest months.

MEXICO CALENDAR OF EVENTS

January

New Year's Day (Año Nuevo). National holiday. Parades, religious observances, parties, and fireworks welcome in the new year everywhere. In traditional indigenous communities, new tribal leaders are inaugurated with colorful ceremonies rooted in the pre-Hispanic past. January 1.

Three Kings Day (Día de Reyes), nationwide. Commemorates the Three Kings' bringing of gifts to the Christ Child. Children receive gifts, much like on Christmas in the United States, and families eat a special *Rosca de Reyes* cake, with a small Christ child doll inside. Whoever receives the doll in his or her piece must host a tamales-and-*atole* party the next month. January 6.

February

Candlemass (Día de la Candelaria), nationwide. Music, dances, processions, food, and other festivities lead up to a blessing of seed and candles in a tradition that mixes pre-Hispanic and European traditions marking the end of winter. All those who attended the Three Kings Celebration reunite to share *atole* and tamales at a party hosted by the recipient of the doll found in the Rosca. February 2.

Constitution Day (Día de la Constitución). This national holiday is in honor of the current Mexican constitution, signed in 1917 as a result of the revolutionary war of 1910. It's celebrated through small parades. February 5.

Carnaval. Carnaval takes place the 3 days preceding Ash Wednesday and the beginning of Lent. Transportation and hotels are packed, so it's best to make reservations 6 months in advance and arrive a couple of days ahead of the beginning of celebrations.

Ash Wednesday. The start of Lent and time of abstinence. It's a day of reverence nationwide, but some towns honor it with folk dancing and fairs.

March

Benito Juárez's Birthday. National holiday. Small hometown celebrations countrywide, especially in Juárez's birthplace—Guelatao, Oaxaca. March 21.

April

Holy Week. Celebrates the last week in the life of Christ from Palm Sunday through Easter Sunday with somber religious processions almost nightly, spoofing of Judas, and reenactments of specific biblical events, plus food and craft fairs. Special celebrations are held in Taxco. Some businesses close during this traditional week of Mexican national vacations, and almost all close on Good Thursday and Friday. Make reservations early and avoid weekend travel. Early April.

May

Labor Day, nationwide. Workers parade countrywide and everything closes. May 1.

Holy Cross Day (Día de la Santa Cruz). Workers place a cross on top of unfinished buildings and celebrate with food, bands, folk dancing, and fireworks around the work site. May 3.

Cinco de Mayo. A national holiday that celebrates the defeat of the French at the Battle of Puebla, although it (ironically) tends to be a bigger celebration in the United States than in Mexico. May 5.

Feast of San Isidro. The patron saint of farmers is honored with a blessing of seeds and work animals. May 15.

June

Navy Day (Día de la Marina), celebrated in all coastal towns with naval parades and fireworks. June 1.

Corpus Christi, celebrated nationwide. Honors the Body of Christ (the Eucharist) with religious processions, Masses, and food. Festivities include performances of *voladores* (flying pole dancers) beside the church and at the ruins of El Tajín. Dates vary.

Día de San Pedro (St. Peter and St. Paul's Day), nationwide. Celebrated wherever St. Peter is the patron saint, and honors anyone named Pedro or Peter. June 29.

July

The Guelaguetza Dance Festival, Oaxaca. One of Mexico's most popular events. Villagers from the seven regions around Oaxaca gather in the city's amphitheater and dress in traditional costumes with "dancing" masks. The celebration goes back to pre-Hispanic times to the fertility goddess for a plentiful corn harvest. Very popular internationally; make advance reservations. Last two Mondays in July (July 21 and 28 in 2008).

August

Assumption of the Virgin Mary. Celebrated throughout the country with special masses and in some places with processions. August 20 to 22.

September

Independence Day. Celebrates Mexico's independence from Spain. A day of parades, picnics, and family reunions throughout the country. The schedule of events is the same in every village, town, and city across Mexico, following that of the capital: At 11pm on September 15, the president of Mexico gives the famous independence *grito* (shout) from the National Palace in Mexico City. People crowd into the central plaza to hear it and to watch the traditional fireworks display that follows. A parade follows the following morning. September 15 to 16.

October

Oaxaca's Ninth Annual Food of the Gods Festival. Oaxaca, Oaxaca. A culinary exploration of the indigenous cultures of Oaxaca. Known globally for its culinary creativity, Oaxaca is the birthplace of chocolate. More information on this weeklong event is available at www.food-of-the-gods-festival.com. October 2 to 9.

Día de la Raza ("Ethnicity Day" or Columbus Day). Commemorates the fusion of the Spanish and Mexican peoples. October 12.

November

Day of the Dead. What's commonly called the Day of the Dead is actually 2 days: All Saints' Day—honoring saints and deceased children—and All Souls' Day, honoring deceased adults. Relatives gather at cemeteries countrywide, bringing candles and food to create altars and sometimes spending the night beside graves of loved ones. Weeks before, bakers begin producing bread formed in the shape of mummies or round loaves decorated with bread "bones." Decorated sugar skulls emblazoned with glittery names are sold everywhere. Many days ahead, homes and churches erect special altars laden with Day of the Dead bread, fruit, flowers, candles, favorite foods, and photographs of saints and of the deceased. On the 2 nights, children dress in costumes and masks, often carrying mock coffins and pumpkin lanterns, into which they expect money will be dropped, through the streets. Cemeteries around

Oaxaca are well known for their solemn vigils and some for their Carnaval-like atmosphere. November 1 to 2.

Revolution Day. Commemorates the start of the Mexican Revolution in 1910 with parades, speeches, rodeos, and patriotic events. November 20.

National Silver Fair, Taxco. A competition of Mexico's best silversmiths and some of the world's finest artisans. There are exhibits, concerts, dances, and fireworks. Check local calendars or call ⓒ **800/44-MEXICO** for details. Late November to early December.

December

Feast of the Virgin of Guadalupe. Throughout the country the patroness of Mexico is honored with religious processions, street fairs, dancing, fireworks, and masses. It is one of Mexico's most moving and beautiful displays of traditional culture. The Virgin of Guadalupe appeared to a young man, Juan Diego, in December 1531, on a hill near Mexico City. He convinced the bishop that he had seen the apparition by revealing his cloak, upon which the Virgin was emblazoned. Every village celebrates this day, often with processions of children dressed as Juan Diego and with *charreadas* (rodeos), bicycle races, dancing, and fireworks. December 12.

Christmas Posadas. On each of the 9 nights before Christmas, it's customary to reenact the Holy Family's search for an inn, with door-to-door candlelit processions in cities and villages nationwide. You may see them especially in Taxco. December 15 to 24.

Christmas. Mexicans extend this celebration and leave their jobs often beginning 2 weeks before Christmas all the way through New Year's. Many businesses close, and resorts and hotels fill up. Significant celebrations take place on December 23. In Oaxaca it's the "Night of the Radishes," with displays of huge carved radishes. On the evening of December 24 in Oaxaca, processions culminate on the central plaza.

Festival of the Radishes (Festival de los Rábanos), Oaxaca. Local artisans and sculptors set up stalls around the main square to display their elaborate pieces of art—made entirely from radishes! Balloons and birds crafted from local flowers add even more color. December 23.

New Year's Eve. As in the rest of the world, you'll find parties, fireworks, and plenty of noise. Special festivities take place at Tlacolula, near Oaxaca, with commemorative mock battles for good luck in the new year. December 31.

6 Insurance, Health & Safety

INSURANCE

TRAVEL INSURANCE AT A GLANCE

Check your existing insurance policies and credit card coverage before you buy travel insurance. You may already be covered for lost luggage, canceled tickets, or medical expenses. The cost of travel insurance varies widely, depending on the cost and length of your trip, your age and health, and the type of trip you're taking, but expect to pay between 5% and 8% of the vacation itself. You can get estimates from various providers through **www.InsureMyTrip.com**. Enter your trip cost and dates, your age, and other information, for prices from more than a dozen companies.

If you'll be driving in Mexico, see "Getting There: By Car" and "Getting Around: By Car," later in this chapter, for information on **collision** and **damage** and **personal accident insurance.**

TRIP-CANCELLATION INSURANCE

Trip-cancellation insurance will help retrieve your money if you have to back out of a trip or depart early, or if your travel supplier goes bankrupt. Trip cancellation traditionally covers such events as sickness, natural disasters, and State Department advisories. The latest news in trip-cancellation insurance is the availability of **expanded hurricane coverage** and the **"any-reason"** cancellation coverage—which costs more but covers cancellations made for any reason. You won't get back 100% of your prepaid trip cost, but you'll be refunded a substantial portion. **TravelSafe** (© **888/885-7233;** www.travel safe.com) offers both types of coverage. Expedia also offers any-reason cancellation coverage for its air-hotel packages.

For details, contact one of the following recommended insurers: **Access America** (© 866/807-3982; www.accessamerica.com); **Travel Guard International** (© 800/826-4919; www.travelguard. com); **Travel Insured International** (© 800/243-3174; www.travel insured.com); and **Travelex Insurance Services** (© 888/457-4602; www.travelex-insurance.com).

MEDICAL INSURANCE

For travel overseas, most health plans (including Medicare and Medicaid) do not provide coverage, and the ones that do often require you to pay for services upfront and reimburse you only after you return home.

As a safety net, you may want to buy travel medical insurance, particularly if you're traveling to a remote or high-risk area where emergency evacuation might be necessary. If you require additional medical insurance, try **MEDEX Assistance** (© 410/453-6300; www.medexassist.com) or **Travel Assistance International** (© 800/821-2828; www.travelassistance.com; for general information on services, call the company's Worldwide Assistance Services, Inc., at © 800/777-8710).

Canadians should check with their provincial health plan offices or call **Health Canada** (© 866/225-0709; www.hc-sc.gc.ca) to find out the extent of their coverage and what documentation and receipts they must take home in case they are treated overseas.

LOST-LUGGAGE INSURANCE

On flights within the U.S., checked baggage is covered up to $3,000 per ticketed passenger. On round-trip international flights originating in the U.S, liability limits are about $1,400 per passenger. If you plan to check items more valuable than what's covered by the standard liability, see if your homeowner's policy covers your valuables, get baggage insurance as part of your comprehensive travel-insurance package, or buy Travel Guard's "BagTrak" product.

If your luggage is lost, immediately file a lost-luggage claim at the airport, detailing the luggage contents. Most airlines require that you report delayed, damaged, or lost baggage within 4 hours of arrival. The airlines are required to deliver luggage, once found, directly to your house or destination free of charge.

STAYING HEALTHY

In most of Mexico's resort destinations, healthcare meeting U.S. standards is now available. Mexico's major cities are also known for their quality healthcare, although the facilities available may be sparser, and the equipment older than what is available at home. Prescription medicine is broadly available at Mexico pharmacies; however, be aware that you may need a copy of your prescription, or obtain a prescription from a local doctor. This is especially true in the border towns, such as in Tijuana, where many Americans have been crossing into Mexico specifically for the purpose of purchasing lower-priced prescription medicines.

Contact the **International Association for Medical Assistance to Travelers** (**IAMAT;** © 716/754-4883, or 416/652-0137 in Canada; www.iamat.org) for tips on travel and health concerns in the countries you're visiting, and lists of local, English-speaking doctors. The United States **Centers for Disease Control and Prevention** (© 800/311-3435; www.cdc.gov) provides up-to-date information on health hazards by region or country and offers tips on food safety. **Travel Health Online** (www.tripprep.com), sponsored by a consortium of travel medicine practitioners, may also offer helpful advice on traveling abroad. You can find listings of reliable medical clinics overseas at the **International Society of Travel Medicine** (www.istm.org).

COMMON AILMENTS

SUN EXPOSURE   Mexico is synonymous with sunshine, with most of the country blanketed in intense sunlight most of the year. Avoid excessive sun exposure, especially in the tropics where UV rays are more dangerous. The hottest months in Mexico are April and May in the south, and July through September along the Pacific Coast, including Baja California. The deserts of northern Mexico are extremely hot during summer months.

DIETARY RED FLAGS   Travelers' diarrhea or *turista,* the Spanish word for "tourist": persistent diarrhea, often accompanied by fever, nausea, and vomiting, used to attack many travelers to Mexico. (Some in the U.S. call this "Montezuma's revenge," but you won't hear it called that in Mexico.) Widespread improvements in infrastructure, sanitation, and education have greatly diminished this ailment, especially in well-developed resort areas. Most travelers make a habit of drinking only bottled water, which also helps to protect against unfamiliar bacteria. In resort areas, and generally throughout Mexico, only purified ice is used. If you do come down with this ailment, nothing beats Pepto-Bismol, readily available in Mexico. Imodium is also available in Mexico and is used by many travelers for a quick fix. A good high-potency (or "therapeutic") vitamin supplement and even extra vitamin C can help; yogurt is good for healthy digestion.

Since dehydration can quickly become life-threatening, the Public Health Service advises that you be careful to replace fluids and electrolytes (potassium, sodium, and the like) during a bout of diarrhea. Drink Pedialyte, a rehydration solution available at most Mexican pharmacies, or natural fruit juice, such as guava or apple (stay away from orange juice, which has laxative properties), with a pinch of salt added.

The U.S. Public Health Service recommends the following measures for preventing travelers' diarrhea: **Drink only purified water** (boiled water, canned or bottled beverages, beer, or wine). **Choose food carefully.** In general, avoid salads (except in first-class

Over-the-Counter Drugs in Mexico

Antibiotics and other drugs for which you'd need a prescription to buy in the States are often available over-the-counter in Mexican pharmacies. Mexican pharmacies also carry a limited selection of common over-the-counter cold, sinus, and allergy remedies.

restaurants), uncooked vegetables, undercooked protein, and unpasteurized milk or milk products, including cheese. Choose food that is freshly cooked and still hot. Avoid eating food prepared by street vendors. In addition, something as simple as **clean hands** can go a long way toward preventing *turista*.

HIGH-ALTITUDE HAZARDS   Travelers to certain regions of Mexico occasionally experience **elevation sickness,** which results from the relative lack of oxygen and the decrease in barometric pressure that characterizes high elevations (more than 1,500m/5,000 ft.). Symptoms include shortness of breath, fatigue, headache, insomnia, and even nausea. Mexico City is at 2,100m (6,720 ft.) above sea level, as are a number of other central and southern cities, such as San Cristóbal de las Casas (even higher than Mexico City). At high elevations, it takes about 10 days to acquire the extra red blood corpuscles you need to adjust to the scarcity of oxygen. To help your body acclimate, drink plenty of fluids, avoid alcoholic beverages, and don't overexert yourself during the first few days. If you have heart or lung problems, talk to your doctor before going above 2,400m (7,872 ft.).

BUGS, BITES & OTHER WILDLIFE CONCERNS   **Mosquitoes** and **gnats** are prevalent along the coast and in the Yucatán lowlands. *Repelente contra insectos* (insect repellent) is a must, and it's not always available in Mexico. If you'll be in these areas and are prone to bites, bring along a repellent that contains the active ingredient DEET. Avon's Skin So Soft also works extremely well. Another good remedy to keep the mosquitoes away is to mix citronella essential oil with basil, clove, and lavender essential oils. If you're sensitive to bites, pick up some antihistamine cream from a drugstore at home.

Most readers won't ever see an *alacrán* (scorpion). But if one stings you, go immediately to a doctor. The one lethal scorpion found in some parts of Mexico is the *centruroides,* part of the Buthidea family, characterized by a thin body, thick tail, and triangular-shaped sternum.

Most deaths from these scorpions result within 24 hours of the sting as a result of respiratory or cardiovascular failure, with children and seniors most at risk. Scorpions are not aggressive (they don't hunt for prey), but they may sting if touched, especially in their hiding places. In Mexico you can buy scorpion toxin antidote at any drugstore. It is an injection and it costs around $25. This is a good idea if you plan to camp in a remote area where medical assistance can be several hours away.

TROPICAL ILLNESSES   You shouldn't be overly concerned about tropical diseases if you stay on the normal tourist routes and don't eat street food. However, both dengue fever and cholera have

---

Tips **What to Do If You Get Sick**

Any foreign consulate can provide a list of area doctors who speak English. If you get sick, consider asking your hotel concierge to recommend a local doctor—even his or her own. You can also try the emergency room at a local hospital. Many hospitals also have walk-in clinics for emergency cases that are not life-threatening; you may not get immediate attention, but you won't pay the high price of an emergency room visit.

For travel abroad, you may have to pay all medical costs upfront and be reimbursed later. Medicare and Medicaid do not provide coverage for medical costs outside the U.S. Before leaving home, find out what medical services your health insurance covers. To protect yourself, consider buying medical travel insurance (see "Medical Insurance," under "Insurance," above).

Very few health insurance plans pay for medical evacuation back to the U.S. (which can cost $10,000 and up). A number of companies offer medical evacuation services anywhere in the world. If you're ever hospitalized more than 150 miles from home, **MedjetAssist** (*©* **800/ 527-7478**; www.medjetassistance.com) will pick you up and fly you to the hospital of your choice virtually anywhere in the world in a medically equipped and staffed aircraft 24 hours day, 7 days a week. Annual memberships are $225 individual, $350 family; you can also purchase short-term memberships.

appeared in Mexico in recent years. Talk to your doctor or to a medical specialist in tropical diseases about precautions you should take. You can also get medical bulletins from the U.S. State Department and the Centers for Disease Control and Prevention (see "Visitor Information," earlier in this chapter). You can protect yourself by taking some simple precautions: Watch what you eat and drink; don't swim in stagnant water (ponds, slow-moving rivers, or wells); and avoid mosquito bites by covering up, using repellent, and sleeping under netting. The most dangerous areas seem to be on Mexico's west coast, away from the big resorts.

SAFETY
CRIME

Crime in Mexico, especially in Mexico City, in selected cities along the U.S. border, and in some states affected by drug violence, has received attention in the North American press over the past several years. Many feel this unfairly exaggerates the real dangers, but it should be noted that crime rates, including taxi robberies, kidnappings, and highway carjackings, have risen in recent years. The most severe problems have been concentrated in Mexico City, where even longtime foreign residents will attest to the overall lack of security. Violent crime has also continued at high levels in Tijuana, Ciudad Juarez, Nuevo Laredo, Acapulco, and the state of Sinaloa. The U.S. Department of State recommends caution in traveling to the southern states of Oaxaca, Chiapas, and Guerrero due to sporadic incidents of politically motivated violence there. Check the U.S. State Department Consular Information Sheet (and any applicable travel advisories) for Mexico before you travel for any notable "hot spots." See "Visitor Information," earlier in this chapter, for information on the latest **U.S. State Department Consular Information Sheet** for Mexico.

Precautions are necessary, but travelers should be realistic. Common sense is essential. You can generally trust people whom you approach for help or directions—but be wary of anyone who approaches you offering the same. The more insistent the person is, the more cautious you should be. The crime rate is, on the whole, much lower in Mexico than in many parts of the United States, and the nature of crimes in general is less violent.

Travelers should exercise caution in traveling Mexico's highways, avoiding travel at night, and using toll *(cuota)* roads rather than the less secure "free" *(libre)* roads whenever possible. It is also advised that you should not hike alone in backcountry areas, nor walk alone on lightly frequented beaches, ruins, or trails.

All bus travel should be during daylight hours and on first-class conveyances. Although there have been several reports of bus hijackings and robberies on toll roads, buses on toll roads have a markedly lower rate of incidents than buses (second and third class) that travel the less secure "free" highways. The embassy advises caution when traveling by bus from Acapulco toward Ixtapa or Huatulco. Although the police have made some progress in bringing this problem under control, armed robberies of entire busloads of passengers still occur.

BRIBES & SCAMS

As is the case around the world, there are the occasional bribes and scams in Mexico, targeted at people believed to be naive—such as the telltale tourist. For years Mexico was known as a place where bribes—called *mordidas* (bites)—were expected; however, the country is rapidly changing. Frequently, offering a bribe today, especially to a police officer, is considered an insult, and it can land you in deeper trouble.

If you believe a **bribe** is being requested, here are a few tips on dealing with the situation. Even if you speak Spanish, don't utter a word of it to Mexican officials. That way you'll appear innocent, all the while understanding every word.

When you are crossing the border, should the person who inspects your car ask for a tip, you can ignore this request—but understand that the official may suddenly decide that a complete search of your belongings is in order. If faced with a situation where you feel you're being asked for a *propina* (literally, "tip"; colloquially, "bribe"), how much should you offer? Usually $3 to $5 or the equivalent in pesos will do the trick. Many tourists have the impression that everything works better in Mexico if you "tip"; however, in reality, this only perpetuates the *mordida* attitude. If you are pleased with a service, feel free to tip, but you shouldn't tip simply to attempt to get away with something illegal or inappropriate, whether it is crossing the border without having your car inspected or not getting a ticket that's deserved.

Whatever you do, **avoid impoliteness;** under no circumstances should you insult a Latin American official. Extreme politeness, even in the face of adversity, rules Mexico. In Mexico, *gringos* have a reputation for being loud and demanding. By adopting the local custom of excessive courtesy, you'll have greater success in negotiations of any kind. Stand your ground, but do it politely.

As you travel in Mexico, you may encounter several types of **scams,** which are typical throughout the world. One involves some kind of a **distraction** or feigned commotion. While your attention is diverted, a pickpocket makes a grab for your wallet. In another common scam, an **unaccompanied child** pretends to be lost and frightened and takes your hand for safety. Meanwhile the child or an accomplice plunders your pockets. A third involves **confusing currency.** A shoeshine boy, street musician, guide, or other individual might offer you a service for a price that seems reasonable—in pesos. When it comes time to pay, he or she tells you the price is in dollars, not pesos. Be very clear on the price and currency when services are involved.

7 Tips for Travelers with Special Needs
FOR FAMILIES

Children are considered the national treasure of Mexico, and Mexicans will warmly welcome and cater to your children.

Before leaving, you should check with your doctor to get advice on medications to take along. Disposable diapers cost about the same in Mexico but are of poorer quality. You can get Huggies Supreme and Pampers identical to the ones sold in the United States, but at a higher price. Dry cereals, powdered formulas, baby bottles, and purified water are easily available in midsize and large cities or resorts. Gerber's baby foods are sold in many stores. Dry cereals, powdered formulas, baby bottles, and purified water are all easily available in midsize and large cities or resorts.

Cribs, however, may present a problem; only the largest and most luxurious hotels provide them. However, rollaway beds to accommodate children staying in the room with parents are often available. Child seats or highchairs at restaurants are common, and most restaurants will go out of their way to accommodate the comfort of your child. Consider bringing your own car seat, as they are not readily available for rent in Mexico.

Every country's regulations differ, but in general children traveling abroad should have plenty of documentation on hand, particularly if they're traveling with someone other than their own parents (in which case a notarized form letter from a parent is often required). For details on entry requirements for children traveling abroad, go to the U.S. State Department website (www.travel.state.gov); click on "International Travel," "Travel Brochures," and "Foreign Entry Requirements."

Recommended family travel websites include **Family Travel Forum** (www.familytravelforum.com), a comprehensive site that offers customized trip planning; **Family Travel Network** (www.familytravelnetwork.com), an online magazine providing travel tips; and **TravelWithYourKids.com** (www.travelwithyour kids.com), a comprehensive site written by parents for parents offering sound advice for long-distance and international travel with children.

FOR GAY & LESBIAN TRAVELERS

Mexico is a conservative country, with deeply rooted Catholic religious traditions. Public displays of same-sex affection are rare, especially outside of urban or resort areas. Women in Mexico frequently walk hand in hand, but anything more might cross the boundary of acceptability. However, gay and lesbian travelers are generally treated with respect and should not experience any harassment, assuming they give the appropriate regard to local culture and customs.

The **International Gay and Lesbian Travel Association** (**IGLTA;** ✆ **800/448-8550** or 954/776-2626; www.iglta.org) is the trade association for the gay and lesbian travel industry, and offers an online directory of gay- and lesbian-friendly travel businesses; go to their website and click on "Members."

Many agencies offer tours and travel itineraries specifically for gay and lesbian travelers. Among them are **Above and Beyond Tours** (✆ **800/397-2681;** www.abovebeyondtours.com); **Now, Voyager** (✆ **800/255-6951;** www.nowvoyager.com); and **Olivia Cruises & Resorts** (✆ **800/631-6277;** www.olivia.com).

Gay.com Travel (✆ **800/929-2268** or 415/644-8044; www.gay. com/travel or www.outandabout.com) is an excellent online successor to the popular *Out & About* print magazine. It provides regularly updated information about gay-owned, gay-oriented, and gay-friendly lodging, dining, sightseeing, nightlife, and shopping establishments in every important destination worldwide. British travelers should click on the "Travel" link at **www.uk.gay.com** for advice and gay-friendly trip ideas. The Canadian website **Gay Traveler** (**gaytraveler.ca**) offers ideas and advice for gay travel all over the world.

FOR TRAVELERS WITH DISABILITIES

Mexican airports are upgrading their services, but it is not uncommon to board from a remote position, meaning you either descend stairs to a bus that ferries you to the plane, which you board by climbing stairs, or you walk across the tarmac to your plane and ascend the stairs. Deplaning presents the same problem in reverse.

Escalators (and there aren't many in the country) are often out of order. Stairs without handrails abound. Few restrooms are equipped for travelers with disabilities; when one is available, access to it may be through a narrow passage that won't accommodate a wheelchair or a person on crutches. Many deluxe hotels (the most expensive) now have rooms with bathrooms for people with disabilities. Those traveling on a budget should stick with one-story hotels or hotels with elevators. Even so, there will probably still be obstacles somewhere. Generally speaking, no matter where you are, someone will lend a hand, although you may have to ask for it.

Organizations that offer a vast range of resources and assistance to disabled travelers include **MossRehab** (© **800/CALL-MOSS;** www.mossresourcenet.org); the **American Foundation for the Blind (AFB;** © **800/232-5463;** www.afb.org); and **SATH** (Society for Accessible Travel & Hospitality; © **212/447-7284;** www.sath. org). **AirAmbulanceCard.com** is now partnered with SATH and allows you to pre-select top-notch hospitals in case of an emergency.

Access-Able Travel Source (© **303/232-2979;** www.access-able.com) offers a comprehensive database on travel agents from around the world with experience in accessible travel; destination-specific access information; and links to such resources as service animals, equipment rentals, and access guides.

Many travel agencies offer customized tours and itineraries for travelers with disabilities. Among them are **Flying Wheels Travel** (© **507/451-5005;** www.flyingwheelstravel.com); and **Accessible Journeys** (© **800/846-4537** or 610/521-0339; www.disability travel.com).

Flying with Disability (www.flying-with-disability.org) is a comprehensive information source on airplane travel. **Avis Rent a Car** (© **888/879-4273**) has an "Avis Access" program that offers services for customers with special travel needs. These include specially outfitted vehicles with swivel seats, spinner knobs, and hand controls; mobility scooter rentals; and accessible bus service. Be sure to reserve well in advance.

FOR SENIORS

Mexico is a popular country for retirees. For decades, North Americans have been living indefinitely in Mexico by returning to the border and recrossing with a new tourist permit every 6 months. Mexican immigration officials have caught on, and now limit the maximum time in the country to 6 months within any year. This is to encourage even partial residents to comply with the proper documentation.

Some of the most popular places for long-term stays are Guadalajara, Lake Chapala, Ajijic, and Puerto Vallarta, all in the state of Jalisco; San Miguel de Allende and Guanajuato in Guanajuato state; Cuernavaca in Morelos; Alamos in Sinaloa; and increasingly destinations in Baja California.

AIM, Apartado Postal 31–70, 45050 Guadalajara, Jal., is a well-written, informative newsletter for prospective retirees. Subscriptions are $18 to the United States and $25 to Canada. Back issues are three for $5.

Sanborn Tours, 2015 S. 10th St., Post Office Drawer 519, McAllen, TX 78505-0519 (*©* **800/395-8482;** www.sanborns.com), offers a "Retire in Mexico" orientation tour.

Mention the fact that you're a senior when you make your travel reservations. Although all the major U.S. airlines have canceled their senior discount and coupon book programs, many hotels still offer lower rates for seniors. In most cities, people over the age of 60 qualify for reduced admission to theaters, museums, and other attractions, and discounted fares on public transportation.

Members of **AARP,** 601 E St. NW, Washington, DC 20049 (*©* **888/687-2277;** www.aarp.org), get discounts on hotels, airfares, and car rentals. AARP offers members a wide range of benefits, including *AARP: The Magazine* and a monthly newsletter. Anyone over 50 can join.

Many reliable agencies and organizations target the 50-plus market. **Elderhostel** (*©* **800/454-5768;** www.elderhostel.org) arranges study programs for those aged 55 and over. **ElderTreks** (*©* **800/ 741-7956;** www.eldertreks.com) offers small-group tours to off-the-beaten-path or adventure-travel locations, restricted to travelers 50 and older.

FOR WOMEN

Mexicans in general, and men in particular, can be nosy about single travelers, especially women. If a taxi driver or anyone else with whom you don't want to become friendly asks about your marital status, family, and so forth, my advice is to make up a set of answers (regardless of the truth): "I'm married, traveling with friends, and I have three children." Saying you are single and traveling alone may send the wrong message. U.S. television—widely viewed now in Mexico—has given many Mexican men the image of American single women as being sexually promiscuous.

Check out the award-winning website **Journeywoman** (www.journeywoman.com), a "real-life" women's travel information network where you can sign up for a free e-mail newsletter and get advice on everything from etiquette and dress to safety; or the travel guide *Safety and Security for Women Who Travel* by Sheila Swan and Peter Laufer (Travelers' Tales, Inc.), offering common-sense tips on safe travel.

FOR STUDENTS

Because many Mexicans consider higher education more a luxury than a birthright, there is no formal network of student discounts and programs. Most Mexican students travel with their families rather than with other students, so student discount cards are not commonly recognized.

However, more hostels have entered the student travel scene. The **Mexican Youth Hostel Network,** or Red Mexicana de Albergues Juveniles (© **55/5518-1726;** www.hostellingmexico.com), offers a list of hostels that meet international standards in Mexico City, Cuernavaca and surrounding areas, Oaxaca, and Veracruz. The **Mexican Youth Hostel Association (Asociación Mexicana de Albergues Juveniles;** www.hostels.com), offers a list of hostels in Mexico City, Zacatecas, Guanajuato, Puerto Escondido, Uxmal, Palenque, Tulum, Cancún, and Playa del Carmen.

If you're a student planning to travel outside the U.S., you'd be wise to arm yourself with an **International Student Identity Card (ISIC),** which offers substantial savings on rail passes, plane tickets, and entrance fees. It also provides you with basic health and life insurance and a 24-hour help line. The card is available from **STA Travel** (© **800/781-4040** in North America; www.sta.com or www.statravel.com), the biggest student travel agency in the world. If you're no longer a student but are still under 26, you can get an **International Youth Travel Card (IYTC)** from the same people, which entitles you to similar discounts.

8 Getting There

BY PLANE

The airline situation in Mexico is rapidly improving, with many new regional carriers offering scheduled service to areas previously not served. In addition to regularly scheduled service, charter service direct from U.S. cities to resorts is making Mexico more accessible.

THE MAJOR INTERNATIONAL AIRLINES

The main airlines operating direct or nonstop flights from the United States to Mexico include **AeroMexico** (© 800/237-6639; www.aeromexico.com), **Air France** (© 800/237-2747; www.airfrance.com), **Alaska Airlines** (© 800/252-7522; www.alaskaair.com), **American Airlines** (© 800/223-5436; www.aa.com), **Continental** (© 800/537-9222; www.continental.com), **Frontier Airlines** (© 800/432-1359; www.frontierairlines.com), **Mexicana** (© 800/531-7921; www.mexicana.com), **Northwest/KLM** (© 800/225-2525; www.nwa.com), **Taca** (© 800/400-8222; www.taca.com), **United** (© 800/538-2929; www.united.com), and **US Airways** (© 800/428-4322; www.usairways.com). **Southwest Airlines** (© 800/435-9792; www.southwest.com) serves the U.S. border.

The main departure points in North America for international airlines are Atlanta, Chicago, Dallas/Fort Worth, Denver, Houston, Los Angeles, Las Vegas, Miami, New York, Orlando, Philadelphia, Phoenix, Raleigh/Durham, San Antonio, San Francisco, Seattle, Toronto, and Washington, D.C.

GETTING THROUGH THE AIRPORT

With the federalization of airport security, security procedures at U.S. airports are more stable and consistent than ever. Generally, you'll be fine if you arrive at the airport at least **1 hour** before a domestic flight and at least **2 hours** before an international flight; if you show up late, tell an airline employee and she'll probably whisk you to the front of the line. You can check the average wait times at your airport by going to the TSA **Security Checkpoint Wait Times** site (waittime/tsa.dhs.gov).

Know what you can carry on and what you can't. For the latest updates on items you are prohibited to bring in carry-on luggage, go to **www.tsa.gov/travelers/airtravel**.

Beat the ticket-counter lines by using the self-service electronic ticket kiosks at the airport or even printing out your boarding pass at home from the airline website. Using curbside check-in is also a smart way to avoid lines.

Bring a **current, government-issued photo ID** such as a driver's license or passport. Keep your ID at the ready to show at check-in, the security checkpoint, and sometimes even the gate. (Children under 18 do not need government-issued photo IDs for domestic flights, but they do for international flights to most countries.)

BY CAR

Driving is not the cheapest way to get to Mexico, but it is the best way to see the country. Even so, you may think twice about taking your own car south of the border once you've pondered the bureaucracy that affects foreign drivers here. One option is to rent a car for touring around a specific region once you arrive in Mexico. Rental cars in Mexico are now generally modern, clean, and well maintained. Although pricier than in the United States, discounts are often available for rentals of a week or longer, especially when arrangements are made in advance from the United States. (See "Car Rentals," later in this chapter, for more details).

If, after reading the section that follows, you have any additional questions or you want to confirm the current rules, call your nearest Mexican consulate, or the Mexican Government Tourist Office. To check on road conditions or to get help with any travel emergency while in Mexico, call ✆ **01-800/482-9832**, or 55/5089-7500 in Mexico City. English-speaking operators staff both numbers.

In addition, check with the **U.S. State Department** (see "Visitor Information," earlier in this chapter) for warnings about dangerous driving areas.

CAR DOCUMENTS

To drive your car into Mexico, you'll need a **temporary car-importation permit,** which is granted after you provide a required list of documents (see below). The permit can be obtained through Banco del Ejército (Banjercito) officials, who have a desk, booth, or office at the Mexican Customs *(Aduana)* building, after you cross the border into Mexico.

You must carry your temporary car-importation permit, tourist permit and, if you purchased it, your proof of Mexican car insurance (see below) in the car at all times. The temporary car-importation permit papers are valid for 6 months to a year, while the tourist permit is usually issued for 30 days. It's a good idea to overestimate the time you'll spend in Mexico, so that if you have to (or want to) stay longer, you'll avoid the hassle of getting your papers extended.

Whatever you do, don't overstay either permit. Doing so invites heavy fines, confiscation of your vehicle (which will not be returned), or both.

The following strict requirements for border crossing were accurate at press time:

- **A valid driver's license,** issued outside of Mexico.
- **Current, original car registration and a copy of the original car title.** If the registration or title is in more than one name and not all the named people are traveling with you, a notarized letter from the absent person(s) authorizing use of the vehicle for the trip is required; have it ready just in case. The registration and your credit card (see below) must be in the same name.
- **A valid international major credit card.** With a credit card, you are required to pay a $29.70 car-importation fee. The credit card must be in the same name as the car registration. If you do not have a major credit card (American Express, Diners Club, MasterCard, or Visa), you must post a bond or make a deposit equal to the value of the vehicle. Check cards are not accepted.
- **Original immigration documentation.** This is either your tourist permit (FMT) or the original immigration booklet, FM2 or FM3, if you hold more permanent status.
- **A signed declaration promising to return to your country of origin with the vehicle.** Obtain this form *(Carta Promesa de Retorno)* from AAA or Sanborn's before you go, or from Banjercito officials at the border. There's no charge. The form does not stipulate that you must return by the same border entry through which you entered.
- **Temporary Importation Application.** By signing this form, you state that you are only temporarily importing the car for your personal use and will not be selling it. This is to help regulate the entry and restrict the resale of unauthorized cars and trucks. Vehicles in the U.S. are much less expensive and for years were brought into Mexico for resale. Make sure the permit is canceled when you return to the U.S.

If you receive your documentation at the border, Mexican officials will make two copies of everything and charge you for the copies. For up-to-the-minute information, a great source is the Customs office in Nuevo Laredo, or *Módulo de Importación Temporal de Automóviles, Aduana Nuevo Laredo* (© **867/712-2071**).

Important reminder: Someone else may drive, but the person (or relative of the person) whose name appears on the car-importation permit must *always* be in the car. (If stopped by police, a non-registered family member driving without the registered driver must be prepared to prove familial relationship to the registered driver—no joke.) Violation of this rule subjects the car to impoundment and the driver to imprisonment, a fine, or both. You can drive a car with foreign license plates only if you have a foreign (non-Mexican) driver's license. You do not need an international driver's license in Mexico.

MEXICAN AUTO INSURANCE

Liability auto insurance is legally required in Mexico. U.S. insurance is invalid; to be insured in Mexico, you must purchase Mexican insurance. Any party involved in an accident who has no insurance may be sent to jail and have his or her car impounded until all claims are settled. This is true even if you just drive across the border to spend the day. U.S. companies that broker Mexican insurance are commonly found at the border crossing, and several quote daily rates.

You can also buy car insurance through **Sanborn's Mexico Insurance,** P.O. Box 52840, 2009 S. 10th, McAllen, TX (© **800/222-0158;** fax 800/222-0158 or 956/686-0732; www.sanborns insurance.com). The company has offices at all U.S. border crossings. Its policies cost the same as the competition's do, but you get legal coverage (attorney and bail bonds if needed) and a detailed mile-by-mile guide for your proposed route. Most of Sanborn's border offices are open Monday through Friday, and a few are staffed on Saturday and Sunday. **AAA** auto club also sells insurance.

RETURNING TO THE UNITED STATES WITH YOUR CAR

You *must* return the car documents you obtained when you entered Mexico when you cross back with your car, or at some point within 180 days. (You can cross as many times as you wish within the 180 days.) If the documents aren't returned, heavy fines are imposed ($250 for each 15 days late), your car may be impounded and confiscated, or you may be jailed if you return to Mexico. You can return the car documents only to a Banjercito official on duty at the Mexican Customs *(Aduana)* building *before* you cross back into the United States. Some border cities have Banjercito officials on duty 24 hours a day, but others do not; some do not have Sunday hours.

On the U.S. side, Customs agents may or may not inspect your car from top to bottom.

BY SHIP

Numerous cruise lines serve Mexico. Possible trips might cruise from California down to ports of call on the Pacific Coast. Several cruise-tour specialists arrange substantial discounts on unsold cabins if you're willing to take off at the last minute. One such company is **Cruises Only** (© **800/278-4373;** www.cruisesonly.com).

BY BUS

Greyhound-Trailways or its affiliates (© **800/229-9424;** www.greyhound.com) offer service from around the United States to the Mexican border, where passengers disembark, cross the border, and buy a ticket for travel into the interior of Mexico. At many border crossings there are scheduled buses from the U.S. bus station to the Mexican bus station.

9 Package Tours for the Independent Traveler

Package tours are simply a way to buy the airfare, accommodations, and other elements of your trip (such as car rentals, airport transfers, and sometimes even activities) at the same time and often at discounted prices.

One good source of package deals is the airlines themselves. Most major airlines offer air/land packages, including **American Airlines Vacations** (© 800/321-2121; www.aavacations.com), **Delta Vacations** (© 800/654-6559; www.deltavacations.com), **Continental Airlines Vacations** (© 800/301-3800; www.covacations.com), and **United Vacations** (© 888/854-3899; www.unitedvacations.com). Several big **online travel agencies**—Expedia, Travelocity, Orbitz, Site59, and Lastminute.com—also do a brisk business in packages.

Travel packages are also listed in the travel section of your local Sunday newspaper. Or check ads in the national travel magazines such as *Arthur Frommer's Budget Travel Magazine, Travel + Leisure, National Geographic Traveler,* and *Condé Nast Traveler.*

RECOMMENDED PACKAGERS

- **AeroMexico Vacations** (© **800/245-8585;** www.aeromexico.com) offers year-round packages to almost every destination it serves, including Acapulco and Ixtapa/Zihuatanejo. AeroMexico has a large selection (more than 100) of resorts in these destinations and more, in a variety of price ranges.

- **Alaska Airlines Vacations** (© 800/468-2248; www.alaskaair. com) sells packages to Ixtapa/Zihuatanejo, and flies direct from Los Angeles, San Diego, San Jose, San Francisco, Seattle, Vancouver, Anchorage, and Fairbanks.
- **American Airlines Vacations** (© 800/321-2121; www.aa vacations.com) has year-round deals to Acapulco, and other locations in Mexico. You don't have to fly with American if you can get a better deal on another airline; land-only packages include hotel, hotel tax, and airport transfers. American's hubs to Mexico are Dallas/Fort Worth, Chicago, and Miami.
- **US Airways Vacations** (© 800/235-9298; www.usairways vacations.com) has deals to Acapulco and many other locations in Mexico. The website offers discounted featured specials that are not available through the operators. You can also book hotels without air by calling the toll-free number.
- **Apple Vacations** (© 800/365-2775; www.applevacations. com) offers inclusive packages to all the beach resorts, and has the largest choice of hotels in Acapulco. Scheduled carriers for the air portion include American, United, Mexicana, Delta, US Airways, Reno Air, Alaska Airlines, and AeroMexico. Apple perks include baggage handling and the services of a company representative at major hotels.
- **Classic Vacations** (© 800/635-1333; www.classicvacations. com) specializes in package vacations to Mexico's finest luxury resorts. It combines discounted first-class and economy airfare on American, Continental, Mexicana, Alaska, America West, and Delta with stays at the most exclusive hotels in Ixtapa/Zihuatanejo and Acapulco. The prices are not for bargain hunters but for those who seek luxury, nicely packaged.
- **Continental Vacations** (© 800/301-3800; www.covacations. com) has year-round packages to Acapulco, Ixtapa, and other locations throughout Mexico. The best deals are from Houston; Newark, N.J.; and Cleveland. You must fly Continental. The Internet deals offer savings not available elsewhere.
- **Delta Vacations** (© 800/654-6559; www.deltavacations. com) has year-round packages to Acapulco, and, Ixtapa/Zihu-atanejo. Atlanta is the hub, so expect the best prices from there.
- **Funjet Vacations** (© 888/558-6654; www.funjet.com) is one of the largest vacation packagers in the United States. Funjet has packages to Acapulco and Ixtapa. You can choose a charter

Finds **Out-of-the-Ordinary Places to Stay**

Mexico lends itself beautifully to the concept of small, private hotels in idyllic settings. They vary in style from grandiose estate to palm-thatched bungalow. **Mexico Boutique Hotels** (www.mexicoboutiquehotels.com) specializes in smaller places to stay with a high level of personal attention and service. Most options have fewer than 50 rooms, and the accommodations consist of entire villas, *casitas,* bungalows, or a combination.

or fly on American, Continental, Delta, AeroMexico, US Airways, Alaska Air, or United.

- **GOGO Worldwide Vacations** (© 888/636-3942; www.gogo wwv.com) has trips to all the major beach destinations, including Acapulco. It offers several exclusive deals from higher-end hotels. Book through any travel agent.

- **Mexicana Vacations,** or MexSeaSun Vacations (© 800/531-7921; www.mexicana.com) offers getaways to all the resorts. Mexicana operates daily direct flights from Los Angeles to Ixtapa/Zihuatanejo.

- **Mexico Travel Net** (© 800/511-4848 or 619/474-0100; www.mexicotravelnet.com) offers most of the well-known travel packages to Mexico beach resorts, plus offers last-minute specials.

- **Pleasant Mexico Holidays** (© 800/742-9244; www.pleasant holidays.com) is one of the largest vacation packagers in the United States, with hotels in Acapulco, Ixtapa/Zihuatanejo, and other resort locations.

10 Active Vacations in Pacific Coast Mexico

Golf, tennis, water-skiing, surfing, bicycling, and **horseback riding** are all sports visitors can enjoy in Pacific coast Mexico. **Scuba diving** is excellent, as is snorkeling, all along this coast. **Mountain climbing** is a rugged sport where you'll meet like-minded folks from around the world. A popular spot for this is in the mountainous areas surrounding Huatulco.

PARKS

Most of the national parks and nature reserves are understaffed or unstaffed. In addition to the reliable Mexican companies offering adventure trips (such as the AMTAVE members; see below), many U.S.-based companies also offer this kind of travel, with trips led by specialists.

OUTDOORS ORGANIZATIONS & TOUR OPERATORS

AMTAVE (Asociación Mexicana de Turismo de Aventura y Ecoturismo, A.C.) is an active association of ecotour and adventure tour operators. It publishes an annual catalog of participating firms and their offerings, all of which must meet certain criteria for security, quality, and training of the guides, as well as for sustainability of natural and cultural environments. For more information, contact AMTAVE (© **55/5688-3883;** www.amtave.org).

The **Archaeological Conservancy,** 5301 Central Ave. NE, Suite 402, Albuquerque, NM 87108 (© **505/266-1540;** www.american archaeology.org), presents one trip per year led by an expert, usually an archaeologist. The trips change from year to year and space is limited; make reservations early.

Culinary Adventures, 6023 Reid Dr. NW, Gig Harbor, WA 98335 (© **253/851-7676;** fax 253/851-9532; www.marilyn tausend.com), specializes in a short but special list of cooking tours in Mexico, featuring well-known cooks and traveling to particular regions known for excellent cuisine. The owner, Marilyn Tausend, is the coauthor of *Mexico the Beautiful Cookbook* and *Cocinas de la Familia* (Family Kitchens).

Mexico Art Tours (© **888/783-1331,** or 480/730-1764 in the U.S.; fax 480/730-1496; 1233 East Baker Dr., Tempe, AZ 85282; www.mexicanarttours.com). Led by Jean Grimm, a specialist in the arts and cultures of Mexico, these unique tours focusing on the authentic arts and cultures of Mexico are accompanied by compelling speakers who are themselves respected scholars and artists. Itineraries include visits to Oaxaca, Chiapas, Guadalajara and Puerto Vallarta, Mexico City, and other locales. Special tours include a Day of the Dead tour, and one on the Art of Mexican Masks.

Oaxaca Reservations/Zapotec Tours, 4955 North Claremont Ave., Suite B, Chicago, IL 60625 (© **800/446-2922** or 773/506-2444; fax 773/506-2445; www.oaxacainfo.com), offers a variety of tours to Oaxaca City and the Oaxaca coast (including Puerto Escondido and Huatulco). Its specialty trips include Day of the Dead in Oaxaca and the Food of the Gods Tour of Oaxaca. The coastal trips emphasize nature, while the Oaxaca City tours focus on the immediate area, with visits to weavers, potters, markets, and archaeological sites. This is also the U.S. contact for several hotels in Oaxaca City that offer a 10% discount for reserving online.

Trek America, P.O. Box 189, Rockaway, NJ 07866 (© **800/ 221-0596** or 973/983-1144; fax 973/983-8551; www.trekamerica. com), organizes lengthy, active trips that combine trekking, hiking, van transportation, and camping in the Yucatán, Chiapas, Oaxaca, the Copper Canyon, and Mexico's Pacific coast, and a trip that covers Mexico City, Teotihuacán, Taxco, Guadalajara, Puerto Vallarta, and Acapulco.

11 Getting Around

An important note: If your travel schedule depends on an important connection, say a plane trip between points or a ferry or bus connection, use the telephone numbers in this book or other information resources mentioned here to find out if the connection you are depending on is still available. Although we've done our best to provide accurate information, transportation schedules can and do change.

BY PLANE

To fly from point to point within Mexico, you'll rely on Mexican airlines. Mexico has two large private national carriers: **Mexicana** (© **800/531-7921;** www.mexicana.com), and **AeroMexico** (© **800/ 237-6639;** www.aeromexico.com), in addition to several up-and-coming low-cost carriers. Mexicana and AeroMexico offer extensive connections to the United States as well as within Mexico.

Up-and-coming low-cost carriers include **Aviacsa** (www.aviacsa. com), **Click Mexicana** (www.click.com.mx), and **Interjet** (www. interjet.com.mx). Regional carriers include **Aerovega** (www. aerovega.com), **Aero Tucán** (www.aero-tucan.com), and Aero Mexico's **Aerolitoral** (www.aeroliteral.com.mx). The regional carriers can be expensive, but they go to difficult-to-reach places. In each applicable section of this book, we've mentioned regional carriers with all pertinent telephone numbers.

Because major airlines can book some regional carriers, read your ticket carefully to see if your connecting flight is on one of these smaller carriers—they may use a different airport or a different counter.

AIRPORT TAXES

Mexico charges an airport tax on all departures that is included in the price of plane tickets. Passengers leaving the country on international flights pay roughly $24—in dollars or the peso equivalent. Taxes on each domestic departure within Mexico are around $17, unless you're on a connecting flight and have already paid at the start of the flight.

Mexico also charges an $18 "tourism tax," the proceeds of which go into a tourism promotional fund. Your ticket price may not include it, so be sure to have enough money to pay it at the airport upon departure.

RECONFIRMING FLIGHTS

Although Mexican airlines say it's not necessary to reconfirm a flight, it's still a good practice. To avoid getting bumped on popular, possibly overbooked flights, check in for international flights at least 2 hours in advance of travel.

BY CAR

Most Mexican roads are not up to U.S. standards of smoothness, hardness, width of curve, grade of hill, or safety marking. Driving at night is dangerous—the roads aren't good and are rarely lit; trucks, carts, pedestrians, and bicycles usually have no lights; and you can hit potholes, animals, rocks, dead ends, or bridges out with no warning.

The spirited style of Mexican driving sometimes requires super vision and reflexes. Be prepared for new customs, as when a truck driver flips on his left turn signal when there's not a crossroad for miles. He's probably telling you the road's clear ahead for you to pass. Another custom that's very important to respect is turning left. Never turn left by stopping in the middle of a highway with your left signal on. Instead, pull onto the right shoulder, wait for traffic to clear, then proceed across the road.

GASOLINE

There's one government-owned brand of gas and one gasoline station name throughout the country—**Pemex** (Petroleras Mexicanas). There are two types of gas in Mexico: *magna,* 87-octane unleaded gas, and premium 93 octane. In Mexico, fuel and oil are sold by the liter, which is slightly more than a quart (40 liters equals about 10½ gal.). Many franchise Pemex stations have bathroom facilities and convenience stores—a great improvement over the old ones. Gas stations accept both credit and debit cards for gas purchases, although some will only accept cash at night.

TOLL ROADS

Mexico charges some of the highest tolls in the world for its network of toll roads (called *cuotas*); as a result, they are rarely crowded.

Generally speaking though, using the toll roads will cut your travel time and will be safer than using non-toll roads (called *libres*).

BREAKDOWNS

If your car breaks down on the road, help might already be on the way. Radio-equipped green repair trucks operated by uniformed English-speaking officers patrol major highways during daylight hours to aid motorists in trouble. These **"Green Angels"** perform minor repairs and adjustments free, but you pay for parts and materials.

Your best guide to repair shops is the Yellow Pages. For repairs, look under "Automóviles y Camiones: Talleres de Reparación y Servicio"; auto-parts stores are under "Refacciones y Accesorios para Automóviles." To find a mechanic on the road, look for a sign that says TALLER MECANICO.

Places called *vulcanizadora* or *llantera* repair flat tires, and it is common to find them open 24 hours a day on the most traveled highways. Even if the place looks empty, chances are you will find someone who can help you fix a flat.

MINOR ACCIDENTS

When possible, many Mexicans drive away from minor accidents, or try to make an immediate settlement, to avoid involving the police. If the police arrive while the involved persons are still at the scene, everyone may be locked in jail until blame is assessed. In any case, you have to settle up immediately, which may take days. Foreigners who don't speak fluent Spanish are at a distinct disadvantage when trying to explain their version of the event. Three steps may help the foreigner who doesn't wish to do as the Mexicans do: If you were in your own car, notify your Mexican insurance company, whose job it is to intervene on your behalf. If you were in a rental car, notify the rental company immediately and ask how to contact the nearest adjuster. (You did buy insurance with the rental, right?) Finally, if all else fails, ask to contact the nearest Green Angel, who may be able to explain to officials that you are covered by insurance. See also "Mexican Auto Insurance" under "Getting There," earlier in this chapter.

CAR RENTALS

You'll get the best price if you reserve a car at least a week in advance in the United States. U.S. car-rental firms include **Advantage** (© 800/777-5500 in the U.S. and Canada; www.arac.com), **Avis** (© 800/331-1212 in the U.S., 800/879-2847 in Canada; www.avis.com), **Budget** (© 800/527-0700 in the U.S. and Canada; www.budget.com), **Hertz** (© 800/654-3131 in the U.S. and Canada;

www.hertz.com), **National** (© 800/227-7368 in the U.S. and Canada; www.nationalcar.com), and **Thrifty** (© 800/847-4389 in the U.S. and Canada; www.thrifty.com), which often offers discounts for rentals in Mexico. For European travelers, **Kemwel Holiday Auto** (© 800/678-0678; www.kemwel.com) and **Auto Europe** (© 800/223-5555; www.autoeurope.com) can arrange Mexican rentals, sometimes through other agencies. These and some local firms have offices in Mexico City and most other large Mexican cities. You'll find rental desks at airports, all major hotels, and many travel agencies.

Cars are easy to rent if you are 25 or over and have a major credit card, valid driver's license, and passport with you. Without a credit card you must leave a cash deposit, usually a big one. One-way rentals are usually simple to arrange but more costly.

Car-rental costs are high in Mexico because cars are more expensive. The condition of rental cars has improved greatly over the years, and clean new cars are the norm. You will pay the least for a manual car without air-conditioning. Prices may be considerably higher if you rent around a major holiday. Also double-check charges for insurance—some companies will increase the insurance rate after several days. Always ask for detailed information about all charges you will be responsible for.

DEDUCTIBLES   Be careful—these vary greatly; some are as high as $2,500, which comes out of your pocket immediately in case of damage. On the simplest car, Hertz's deductible is about $1,000 and Avis's is $500.

INSURANCE   Insurance is offered in two parts: **Collision and damage** insurance covers your car and others if the accident is your fault, and **personal accident** insurance covers you and anyone in your car. Read the fine print on the back of your rental agreement and note that insurance may be invalid if you have an accident while driving on an unpaved road.

DAMAGE   Always inspect your car carefully and note every damaged or missing item, no matter how minute, on your rental agreement, or you may be charged.

BY TAXI

Taxis are the preferred way to get around in almost all of the resort areas of Mexico, and also around Mexico City. Short trips within towns are generally charged by preset zones, and are quite reasonable compared with U.S. rates. For longer trips, or excursions to nearby cities, taxis can generally be hired for around $10 to $15 per hour, or for a negotiated daily rate. Even drops to different destinations, say between Huatulco and Puerto Escondido, can be arranged. A negotiated one-way price is usually less than the cost of a rental car for a day, and service is much faster than traveling by bus. For anyone who is uncomfortable driving in Mexico, this is a convenient, comfortable alternative. An added bonus is that you have a Spanish-speaking person with you in case you run into any car or road trouble. Many taxi drivers speak at least some English. Your hotel can assist you with the arrangements.

BY BUS

Mexican buses are frequent, readily accessible, and can get you to almost anywhere you want to go. They're often the only way to get from large cities to other nearby cities and small villages. Don't hesitate to ask questions if you're confused about anything.

Dozens of Mexican companies operate large, air-conditioned, Greyhound-type buses between most cities. Travel class is generally labeled second *(segunda)*, first *(primera)*, and deluxe *(ejecutiva)*, which is referred to by a variety of names. The deluxe buses often have fewer seats than regular buses, show video movies en route, are air-conditioned, and have few stops; some have complimentary refreshments. Many run express from origin to the final destination. They are well worth the few dollars more that you'll pay. In rural areas, buses are often of the school-bus variety, with lots of local color.

Whenever possible, it's best to buy your reserved-seat ticket, often via a computerized system, a day in advance on many long-distance routes and especially before holidays. Schedules are fairly dependable, so be at the terminal on time for departure. Current information may be obtained from local bus stations. See the appendix for a list of helpful bus terms in Spanish.

Bus Tip
Little English is spoken at bus stations, so come prepared with your destination written down, then double-check the departure.

FAST FACTS: Mexico

Abbreviations Dept. (apartments); Apdo. (post office box); Av. (*avenida;* avenue); c/: (*calle;* street); Calz. (*calzada;* boulevard). "C" on faucets stands for *caliente* (hot), and "F" stands for *fría* (cold). PB *(planta baja)* means ground floor, and most buildings count the next floor up as the first floor (1).

Business Hours In general, businesses in larger cities are open between 9am and 7pm; in smaller towns many close between 2 and 4pm. Most are closed on Sunday. In resort areas it is common to find more stores open on Sundays, as well as extended business hours for shops, often until 8pm or even 10pm. Bank hours are Monday through Friday from 9 or 9:30am to anywhere between 3 and 7pm. Increasingly, banks open on Saturday for at least a half-day.

Cameras & Film Film costs about the same as in the United States.

Doctors & Dentists Every embassy and consulate is prepared to recommend or refer local doctors and dentists with good training and modern equipment; some of the doctors and dentists even speak English. See the list of embassies and consulates under "Embassies & Consulates," below. Hotels with a large foreign clientele are often prepared to recommend English-speaking doctors. Almost all first-class hotels in Mexico have a doctor on call.

Drug Laws To be blunt, don't use or possess illegal drugs in Mexico. Most Mexican officials have no tolerance for drug users, and jail is their solution, with very little hope of getting out until the sentence (usually a long one) is completed or heavy fines or bribes are paid. Remember, in Mexico the legal system assumes you are guilty until proven innocent. (*Important note:* It isn't uncommon to be befriended by a fellow user, only to be turned in by that "friend," who's collected a bounty.) Bring prescription drugs in their original containers. If possible, pack a copy of the original prescription with the generic name of the drug.

U.S. Customs officials are also on the lookout for diet drugs sold in Mexico but illegal in the United States, possession of which could also land you in a U.S. jail.

Drugstores *Farmacias* (pharmacies) will sell you just about anything, with or without a prescription. Most pharmacies are open Monday to Saturday from 8am to 8pm. The major resort areas generally have one or two 24-hour pharmacies. Pharmacies take turns staying open during off hours, so if you are in a smaller town and need to buy medicine during off hours, ask for the *farmacia de turno*.

Electricity The electrical system in Mexico is 110 volts AC (60 cycles), as in the United States and Canada. However, in reality it may cycle more slowly and overheat your appliances. To compensate, select a medium or low speed for hair dryers. Many older hotels still have electrical outlets for flat two-prong plugs; you'll need an adapter for any modern electrical apparatus that has an enlarged end on one prong or that has three prongs. Many first-class and deluxe hotels have the three-holed outlets (*trifásicos* in Spanish). Those that don't may have loan adapters, but to be sure, it's always better to carry your own.

Embassies & Consulates They provide valuable lists of doctors and lawyers, as well as regulations concerning marriages in Mexico. Contrary to popular belief, your embassy cannot get you out of a Mexican jail, provide postal or banking services, or fly you home when you run out of money. Consular officers can provide you with advice on most matters and problems, however.

The Embassy of the **United States** in Mexico City is at Paseo de la Reforma 305, next to the Hotel María Isabel Sheraton at the corner of Río Danubio (© 55/5080-2000 or 5511-9980); hours are Monday through Friday from 8:30am to 5:30pm. Visit www.usembassy-mexico.gov for addresses of the U.S. consulates inside Mexico. In addition, there are consular agencies in Acapulco (© 744/469-0556), Ixtapa/Zihuatanejo (© 755/553-2100), and in other locations throughout Mexico

The Embassy of **Australia** in Mexico City is at Rubén Darío 55, Col. Polanco (© 55/51101-2200). It's open Monday through Friday from 9am to 1pm.

The Embassy of **Canada** in Mexico City is at Schiller 529, Col. Polanco (© 55/5724-7900); it's open Monday through Friday from 9am to 1pm. At other times, the name of a duty officer is posted on the door. Visit www.dfait-maeci.gc.ca for addresses of consular agencies in Mexico. There is also a Canadian consulate in Acapulco (© 744/484-1305).

The Embassy of **New Zealand** in Mexico City is at Jaime Balmes 8, 4th floor, Col. Los Morales, Polanco (© 55/5283-9460;

kiwimexico@compuserve.com.mx). It's open Monday through Thursday from 8:30am to 2pm and 3 to 5:30pm, and Friday from 8:30am to 2pm.

The Embassy of the **United Kingdom** in Mexico City is at Río Lerma 71, Col. Cuauhtémoc (© **55/5242-8500;** www.embajada britanica.com.mx). It's open Monday through Friday from 8:30am to 3:30pm.

The Embassy of **Ireland** in Mexico City is at Bulevar Cerrada, Avila Camacho 76, 3rd floor, Col. Lomas de Chapultepec (© **55/5520-5803**). It's open Monday through Friday from 9am to 5pm.

The **South African** Embassy in Mexico City is at Andrés Bello 10, 9th floor, Col. Polanco (© **55/5282-9260**). It's open Monday through Friday from 8am to 4pm.

Emergencies In case of emergency, dial © 065 from any phone within Mexico. For police emergency numbers, turn to "Fast Facts" in the chapters that follow. The 24-hour **Tourist Help Line** in Mexico City is © **01-800/987-8224** or 55/5089-7500, or you can now simply dial **078**. The operators don't always speak English, but they are always willing to help. The tourist legal assistance office (Procuraduría del Turista) in Mexico City (© **55/5625-8153** or 55/5625-8154) always has an English speaker available. Though the phones are frequently busy, they operate 24 hours.

Internet Access In large cities and resort areas, a growing number of five-star hotels offer business centers with Internet access. You'll also find cybercafes in destinations that are popular with expats and business travelers.

Language Spanish is the official language in Mexico. English is spoken and understood to some degree in most tourist areas. Furthermore, you will find that Mexicans are very accommodating with foreigners who try to speak Spanish, even in broken sentences.

Legal Aid **International Legal Defense Counsel,** 111 S. 15th St., 24th Floor, Packard Building, Philadelphia, PA 19102 (© **215/977-9982**), is a law firm specializing in legal difficulties of Americans abroad. See also "Embassies & Consulates" and "Emergencies," above.

Liquor Laws The legal drinking age in Mexico is 18; however, it is extremely rare that anyone will be asked for ID or denied purchase (often, children are sent to the stores to buy beer for their parents). Grocery stores sell everything from beer and wine to national and imported liquors. You can buy liquor 24 hours a day; but during major elections, dry laws often are enacted for as much as 72 hours in advance of the election—and those laws apply to foreign tourists as well as local residents. Mexico also does not have any "open container" laws for transporting liquor in cars, but authorities are beginning to target drunk drivers more aggressively. It's a good idea to drive defensively.

Mail Postage for a postcard or letter is 8 pesos; it may arrive anywhere from 1 to 6 weeks later. The price for registered letters and packages depends on the weight, and unreliable delivery time can take 2 to 6 weeks. The recommended way to send a package or important mail is through FedEx, DHL, UPS, or another reputable international mail service.

Passports Allow plenty of time before your trip to apply for a passport; processing normally takes 3 weeks but can take longer during busy periods (especially spring). And keep in mind that if you need a passport in a hurry, you'll pay a higher processing fee.

For Residents of Australia: You can pick up an application from your local post office or any branch of Passports Australia, but you must schedule an interview at the passport office to present your application materials. Call the **Australian Passport Information Service** at © **131-232,** or visit the government website at www.passports.gov.au.

For Residents of Canada: Passport applications are available at travel agencies throughout Canada or from the central **Passport Office,** Department of Foreign Affairs and International Trade, Ottawa, ON K1A 0G3 (© **800/567-6868;** www.ppt.gc.ca).

For Residents of Ireland: You can apply for a 10-year passport at the **Passport Office,** Setanta Centre, Molesworth Street, Dublin 2 (© **01/671-1633;** www.irlgov.ie/iveagh). Those under age 18 and over 65 must apply for a 3-year passport. You can also apply at 1A South Mall, Cork (© **021/ 272-525**) or at most main post offices.

For Residents of New Zealand: You can pick up a passport application at any New Zealand Passports Office or download it from the website. Contact the **Passports Office** at © **0800/ 225-050** in New Zealand or 04/474-8100, or log on to www.passports.govt.nz.

For Residents of the United Kingdom: To pick up an application for a standard 10-year passport (5-year passport for children under 16), visit your nearest passport office, major post office, or travel agency or contact the **United Kingdom Passport Service** at © 0870/521-0410 or search its website at www.ukpa.gov.uk.

For Residents of the United States: Whether you're applying in person or by mail, you can download passport applications from the U.S. State Department website at http://travel.state.gov. To find your regional passport office, either check the U.S. State Department website or call the **National Passport Information Center** toll-free number (© 877/487-2778) for automated information.

Pets Taking a pet into Mexico is easy but requires a little planning. Animals coming from the United States and Canada need to be checked for health within 30 days before arrival in Mexico and require paperwork from your vet. If your stay extends beyond the 30-day time frame of your U.S.-issued certificate, you'll need to get another Certificate of Health issued by a veterinarian in Mexico.

Police In Mexico City, police are to be suspected as frequently as they are to be trusted; however, you'll find many who are quite honest and helpful. In the rest of the country, especially in the tourist areas, the majority are very protective of international visitors. Several cities, including Acapulco, have gone as far as to set up a special corps of English-speaking Tourist Police to assist with directions, guidance, and more.

Restrooms Public toilets are not common in Mexico, but an increasing number are available, especially at fast-food restaurants and Pemex gas stations. These facilities and restaurant and club restrooms commonly have attendants, who expect a small tip (about 50¢).

Smoking Smoking is permitted and generally accepted in most public places, including restaurants, bars, and hotel lobbies. Nonsmoking areas and hotel rooms for nonsmokers are becoming more common in higher-end establishments, but they tend to be the exception rather than the rule.

Taxes There's a 15% IVA (value-added) tax on goods and services in most of Mexico, and it's supposed to be included in the posted price. There is an exit tax of around $18 imposed on every foreigner leaving the country, usually included in the price of airline tickets.

Telephones Mexico's telephone system is slowly but surely catching up with modern times. All telephone numbers have 10 digits. Every city and town that has telephone access has a two-digit (Mexico City, Monterrey, and Guadalajara) or three-digit (everywhere else) area code. In Mexico City, Monterrey, and Guadalajara, local numbers have eight digits; elsewhere, local numbers have seven digits. To place a local call, you do not need to dial the area code. Many fax numbers are also regular telephone numbers; ask whoever answers for the fax tone *("me da tono de fax, por favor")*. Cellular phones are very popular for small businesses in resort areas and smaller communities. To call a cellular number inside the same area code, dial 044 and then the number. To dial the cellular phone from anywhere else in Mexico, first dial 01, and then the three-digit area code and the seven-digit number. To dial it from the U.S., dial 011-52, plus the three-digit area code and the seven-digit number.

The **country code** for Mexico is **52.**

To call Mexico: If you're calling Mexico from the United States:

1. Dial the international access code: 011
2. Dial the country code: 52
3. Dial the two- or three-digit area code, then the eight- or seven-digit number. For example, if you wanted to call the U.S. consulate in Acapulco, the whole number would be 011-52-744-469-0556. If you wanted to dial the U.S. embassy in Mexico City, the whole number would be 011-52-55-5209-9100.

To make international calls: To make international calls from Mexico, first dial 00, then the country code (U.S. or Canada 1, U.K. 44, Ireland 353, Australia 61, New Zealand 64). Next, dial the area code and number. For example, to call the British Embassy in Washington, you would dial 00-1-202-588-7800.

For directory assistance: Dial ✆ 040 if you're looking for a number inside Mexico. *Note:* Listings usually appear under the owner's name, not the name of the business, and your chances to find an English-speaking operator are slim to none.

For operator assistance: If you need operator assistance in making a call, dial 090 to make an international call, and 020 to call a number in Mexico.

Toll-free numbers: Numbers beginning with 800 within Mexico are toll-free, but calling a U.S. toll-free number from Mexico costs the same as an overseas call. To call an 800 number in the U.S., dial 001-880 and the last seven digits of the toll-free number. To call an 888 number in the U.S., dial 001-881 and the last seven digits of the toll-free number.

Time Zone Central Standard Time prevails throughout most of Mexico, and all of the areas covered in this book. Mexico observes **daylight saving time.**

Tipping Most service employees in Mexico count on tips for the majority of their income—this is especially true for bellboys and waiters. Bellboys should receive the equivalent of 50¢ to $1 per bag; waiters generally receive 10% to 20%, depending on the level of service. It is not customary to tip taxi drivers, unless they are hired by the hour or provide touring or other special services.

Useful Phone Numbers **Tourist Help Line,** available 24 hours (© 01-800/987-8224 toll-free inside Mexico; or dial 078). **Mexico Hot Line** (© 800/446-3942). **U.S. Dept. of State Travel Advisory,** staffed 24 hours (© 202/647-5225). **U.S. Passport Agency** (© 877/487-2777). **U.S. Centers for Disease Control and Prevention International Traveler's Hot Line** (© 877/394-8747).

Water Most hotels have decanters or bottles of purified water in the rooms, and the better hotels have either purified water from regular taps or special taps marked *agua purificada.* Virtually any hotel, restaurant, or bar will bring you purified water if you specifically request it, but you'll usually be charged for it. Bottled purified water is sold widely at drugstores and grocery stores. Some popular brands are Santa María, Ciel, and Bonafont. Evian and other imported brands are also widely available.

Acapulco

I like to think of Acapulco as a diva—maybe a little past her prime, perhaps overly made up, but still capable of captivating an audience. It's tempting to dismiss Acapulco as a passé resort, but the town's temptations are hard to resist. Where else do bronzed men dive from cliffs into the sea at sunset, and where else does the sun shine 360 days a year? Though most beach resorts are made for relaxing, Acapulco has nonstop, 24-hours-a-day energy. Its perfectly sculpted bay is an adult playground filled with water-skiers in *tanga* swimsuits and darkly tanned, mirror-shaded studs on jet skis. Visitors play golf and tennis with intensity, but the real sport is the nightlife, which has made this city famous for decades. Back in the days when there was a jet set, they came to Acapulco—filmed it, sang about it, wrote about it, and lived it.

It's not hard to understand why: The view of Acapulco Bay, framed by mountains and beaches, is breathtaking day or night. And I dare anyone to take in the lights of the city and not feel the pull to go out and get lively.

Though a few years ago, tourism to Acapulco was in a state of decline, it's now attempting a renaissance, in a style reminiscent of Miami's South Beach. Classic hotels are slowly being renovated and areas gentrified. Clean-up efforts have put an entirely new face on a place that was once aging less than gracefully.

International travelers began to reject Acapulco when it became clear that the cost of development was the pollution of the bay and surrounding areas. The city government responded, and invested over $1 billion in public and private infrastructure improvements. In addition, a program instituted in the early 1990s has cleaned up the water—whales have even been sighted offshore.

Acapulco tries hard to hold on to its image as the ultimate extravagant party town, and remains a top weekend and vacation destination for affluent residents of Mexico City, in particular. It's still the top choice for those who want to have dinner at midnight, dance until dawn, and sleep all day on a sun-soaked beach.

Acapulco Bay Area

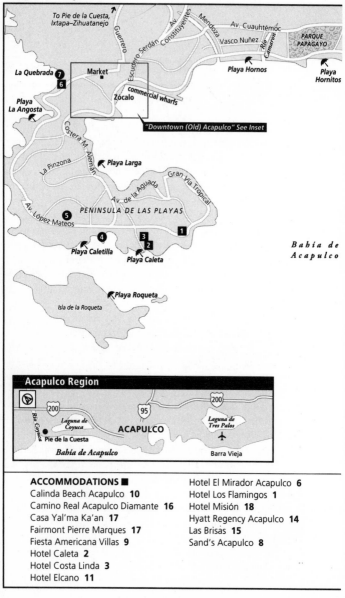

To Pie de la Cuesta, Ixtapa–Zihuatanejo

Av. Cuauhtémoc

Mendoza

Vasco Nuñez

PARQUE PAPAGAYO

Guerrero

Escudér Serdán

Constituyentes

Av.

Río Camarón

Playa Hornos

Playa Hornitos

La Quebrada **7**
6
Market

Playa La Angosta

Commercial wharfs

Zócalo

"Downtown (Old) Acapulco" See Inset

Costera M. Alemán

La Pinzona

Playa Larga

Av. de la Aguada

Gran Vía Tropical

Av. López Mateos

5

PENINSULA DE LAS PLAYAS

1

4

3
2

Playa Caletilla

Playa Caleta

Bahía de Acapulco

Playa Roqueta

Isla de la Roqueta

Acapulco Region

200

95

200

Río Coyuca

Laguna de Coyuca

ACAPULCO

Laguna de Tres Palos

Pie de la Cuesta

Bahía de Acapulco

Barra Vieja

ACCOMMODATIONS ■
Calinda Beach Acapulco **10**
Camino Real Acapulco Diamante **16**
Casa Yal'ma Ka'an **17**
Fairmont Pierre Marques **17**
Fiesta Americana Villas **9**
Hotel Caleta **2**
Hotel Costa Linda **3**
Hotel Elcano **11**

Hotel El Mirador Acapulco **6**
Hotel Los Flamingos **1**
Hotel Misión **18**
Hyatt Regency Acapulco **14**
Las Brisas **15**
Sand's Acapulco **8**

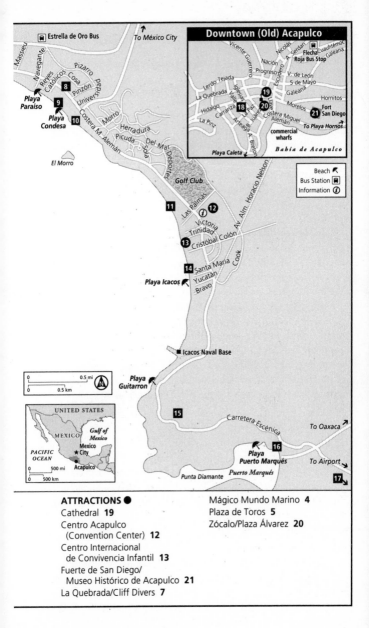

Downtown (Old) Acapulco

To México City

Estrella de Oro Bus

Playa Paraíso

Playa Condesa

El Morro

Golf Club

Playa Icacos

Icacos Naval Base

Playa Guitarrón

Carretera Escénica

To Oaxaca

Playa Puerto Marqués

Punta Diamante   Puerto Marqués

To Airport

Bahía de Acapulco

Flecha Roja Bus Stop

Fort San Diego

To Playa Hornos

commercial wharfs

Playa Caleta

Beach
Bus Station
Information

UNITED STATES

Gulf of Mexico

MEXICO

Mexico City

PACIFIC OCEAN

Acapulco

0   500 mi
0   500 km

0   0.5 mi
0   0.5 km

ATTRACTIONS ●

Cathedral **19**

Centro Acapulco (Convention Center) **12**

Centro Internacional de Convivencia Infantil **13**

Fuerte de San Diego/ Museo Histórico de Acapulco **21**

La Quebrada/Cliff Divers **7**

Mágico Mundo Marino **4**

Plaza de Toros **5**

Zócalo/Plaza Álvarez **20**

1 Essentials

366km (227 miles) S of Mexico City; 272km (169 miles) SW of Taxco; 979km (607 miles) SE of Guadalajara; 253km (157 miles) SE of Ixtapa/Zihuatanejo; 752km (466 miles) NW of Huatulco

GETTING THERE & DEPARTING

BY PLANE See chapter 1 for information on flying from the United States or Canada to Acapulco. Local numbers for major airlines with nonstop or direct service to Acapulco are **AeroMexico** (© **744/485-1625,** or 01-800/021-4010 and -4000 inside Mexico), **American** (© **744/466-9232,** or 01-800/904-6000 inside Mexico for reservations), **Continental** (© **744/466-9063**), **Mexicana** (© **744/466-9121** or 486-7586), and **US Airways** (© **744/ 466-9257**).

AeroMexico flies from Guadalajara, Mexico City, Tijuana, and Monterrey; **Aviacsa** (© **01-800/711-6733**) flies from Mexico City; **Interjet** (© **01-800/011-2345**) is a new low-cost carrier that flies from Toluca, near Mexico City; **Mexicana** flies from Mexico City. Check with a travel agent about **charter** flights.

The airport (airport code: ACA) is 22km (14 miles) southeast of town, over the hills east of the bay. Private **taxis** are the fastest way to get downtown; they cost $30 to $50 (£17–£28). The major **rental-car** agencies all have booths at the airport. **Transportes Terrestres** has desks at the front of the airport where you can buy tickets for minivan *colectivo* transportation into town ($20/£11). You must reserve return service to the airport through your hotel.

BY CAR From Mexico City, take either the curvy toll-free **Highway 95D** south (6 hr.) or scenic **Highway 95,** the four- to six-lane toll highway (3½ hr.), which costs around $50 (£28) one-way. The free "libre" road from Taxco is in good condition; you'll save around $40 (£22) in tolls from there through Chilpancingo to Acapulco. From points north or south along the coast, the only choice is **Highway 200,** where you should (as on all Mexican highways) always try to travel by day.

BY BUS The **Estrella de Oro** terminal is at Av. Cuauhtémoc 1490, and the **Estrella Blanca** terminal is at Av. Cuauhtémoc 1605. **Turistar, Estrella de Oro,** and **Estrella Blanca** have almost hourly service for the 5- to 7-hour trip to Mexico City ($30–$50/£17–£28), and daily service to Zihuatanejo ($14/£7.70). Buses also serve other points in Mexico, including Chilpancingo, Cuernavaca, Iguala, Manzanillo, Puerto Vallarta, and Taxco.

> **Tips Car & Bus Travel Warning Eases**
>
> Car robberies and bus hijackings on Highway 200 south of Acapulco on the way to Puerto Escondido and Huatulco used to be common, and you may have heard warnings about the road. The trouble has all but disappeared, thanks to military patrols and greater police protection. However, as in most of Mexico, it's advisable to travel the highways during daylight hours only—not so much because of carjackings, but because highways are unlit, and animals can wander onto them.

VISITOR INFORMATION

The **State of Guerrero Tourism Office** operates the **Procuraduría del Turista** (©/fax **744/484-4416**), on street level in front of the **International Center,** a convention center set back from the main Costera Alemán, down a lengthy walkway with fountains. The office offers maps and information about the city and state, as well as police assistance for tourists; it's open Monday to Saturday from 8am to 11pm, Sunday from 8am to 8pm.

CITY LAYOUT

Acapulco stretches more than 6km (4 miles) around the huge bay, so trying to take it all in by foot is impractical. The tourist areas are roughly divided into three sections. On the western end of the bay is **Acapulco Viejo (Old Acapulco),** the original town that attracted the jet-setters of the 1950s and 1960s—and today it looks as if it's still locked in that era, though a renaissance is slowly getting underway.

The second section, in the center of the bay, is the **Zona Hotelera (Hotel Zone);** it follows the main boulevard, **Costera Miguel Alemán** (or just "the Costera"), as it runs east along the bay from downtown. Towering hotels, restaurants, shopping centers, and strips of open-air beach bars line the street. At the far eastern end of the Costera lie the golf course and the International Center (a convention center). **Avenida Cuauhtémoc** is the major artery inland, running roughly parallel to the Costera.

The third major area begins just beyond the Hyatt Regency Hotel, where the name of the Costera changes to **Carretera Escénica (Scenic Hwy.),** which continues all the way to the airport. The hotels along this section of the road are lavish, and extravagant private villas, gourmet restaurants, and flashy nightclubs built into the hillside offer dazzling views. The area fronting the beach here is **Acapulco Diamante,** Acapulco's most desirable address.

Street names and numbers in Acapulco can be confusing and hard to find—many streets are not well marked or change names unexpectedly. Street numbers on the Costera do not follow logic, so don't assume that similar numbers will be close together.

GETTING AROUND

BY TAXI   Taxis are more plentiful than tacos in Acapulco—and practically as inexpensive, if you're traveling in the downtown area only. Just remember that you should always establish the price with the driver before starting out. Hotel taxis may charge three times the rate of a taxi hailed on the street, and nighttime taxi rides cost extra, too. Taxis are also more expensive if you're staying in the Diamante section or south. The minimum fare is $2 (£1.10) per ride for a roving VW Bug–style taxi in town; the fare from Puerto Marqués to the hotel zone is $8 (£4.40), or $10 (£5.50) into downtown. *Sitio* taxis are nicer cars, but more expensive, with a minimum fare of $4 (£2.20).

The fashion among Acapulco taxis is flashy, with Las Vegas–style lights—the more colorful and pulsating, the better.

BY BUS   Even though the city has a confusing street layout, using city buses is amazingly easy and inexpensive. Two kinds of buses run along the Costera: pastel color-coded buses and regular "school buses." The difference is the price: New, air-conditioned tourist buses (Aca Tur Bus) are 50¢ (30p); old buses are 45¢ (25p). Covered bus stops are all along the Costera, with handy maps on the walls showing routes to major sights and hotels.

The best place near the *zócalo* to catch a bus is next to Sanborn's, 2 blocks east. CALETA DIRECTO or BASE-CALETA buses will take you to the Hornos, Caleta, and Caletilla beaches along the Costera. Some buses return along the same route; others go around the peninsula and return to the Costera.

For expeditions to more distant destinations, there are buses to **Puerto Marqués** to the east (marked PUERTO MARQUES–BASE) and **Pie de la Cuesta** to the west (marked ZOCALO–PIE DE LA CUESTA). Be sure to verify the time and place of the last bus back if you hop on one of these.

BY CAR   Rental cars are available at the airport and at hotel desks along the Costera. Unless you plan on exploring outlying areas, trust me, you're better off taking taxis or using the easy and inexpensive public buses.

FAST FACTS: Acapulco

American Express The main office is in the Gran Plaza shopping center, Costera Alemán 1628 (© **744/435-2200**). It's open Monday through Friday from 9am to 6pm and Saturday 9am to 1pm.

Area Code The telephone area code is **744**.

Climate Acapulco boasts sunshine 360 days a year, with average daytime temperatures of 80°F (27°C). Humidity varies, with approximately 59 inches of rain per year. June through October is the rainy season, though July and August are relatively dry. Tropical showers are brief and usually occur at night.

Consular Agents The **United States** has an agent at the Hotel Acapulco Continental, Costera Alemán 121, Loc. 14 (© **744/469-0556**); the office is open Monday through Friday from 10am to 2pm. The **Canadian** office is at the Centro Comercial Marbella, Loc. 23 (© **744/484-1305**). The toll-free emergency number inside Mexico is © **01-800/706-2900**. The office is open Monday through Friday from 9am to 5pm. The **United Kingdom** office is at the Las Brisas Hotel on Carretera Escénica near the airport (© **744/481-2533**). Most other countries in the European Union also have consulate offices in Acapulco.

Currency Exchange Numerous banks along the Costera are open Monday through Friday from 9am to 6pm, Saturday from 10am to 2pm. Banks and their ATMs generally have the best rates. *Casas de cambio* (currency-exchange booths) along the street may have better rates than hotels.

Drugstores One of the largest drugstores in town is **Farmacía Daisy**, Francia 49, across the traffic circle from the convention center (© **744/48126350**). Sam's Club and Wal-Mart, both on the Costera, have pharmacy services and lower prices on medicine.

Hospital **Hospital Magallanes,** Av. Wilfrido Massieu 2, Fracc. Magallanes (© **744/485-6194** or -6197), has an English-speaking staff and doctors. For local emergencies, call the **Cruz Roja (Red Cross),** Av. Ruiz Cortines s/n (© **065** or 744/445-5912).

Internet Access **@canet,** Costera Alemán 1632 Int., La Gran Plaza, Loc. D-1, lower floor (©/fax **744/486-9186** or -8182), is open weekdays from 10am to 9pm and weekends from noon to 9pm. Internet access costs $2.50 (£1.40) per hour. This is a computer shop that also offers Internet access and has a very helpful staff. Also along the Costera strip is the **Santa Clara Cafe,** Costera Alemán 136, serving coffee, pastries, and ice cream, along with Internet service for $1 (55p) for 20 minutes. It's open 9am to 11pm. Internet access kiosks are also available inside **Wal-Mart,** Costera Miguel Alemán 500 (© **744-469-0203**), with varying rates depending on usage.

Parking It is illegal to park on the Costera at any time. Try parking along side streets or in one of the few covered parking lots, such as in Plaza Bahía and in Plaza Mirabella.

Post Office The *correo* is next door to Sears, close to the Fideicomiso office. It's open Monday through Friday from 9am to 5pm, Saturday from 9am to 2pm. Other branches are in the Estrella de Oro bus station on Cuauhtémoc, inland from the Acapulco Qualton Hotel, and on the Costera near Caleta Beach.

Safety Riptides claim a few lives every year, so pay close attention to warning flags posted on Acapulco beaches. Red or black flags mean stay out of the water, yellow flags signify caution, and white or green flags mean it's safe to swim.

As is the case anywhere, tourists are vulnerable to thieves. This is especially true when shopping in a market, lying on the beach, wearing jewelry, or visibly carrying a camera, purse, or bulging wallet.

Telephone Acapulco phone numbers seem to change frequently. The most reliable source for telephone numbers is the **Procuraduría del Turista,** on the Costera in front of the convention center (© **744/484-4416**), which has an exceptionally friendly staff.

Tourist Police Policemen in white and light-blue uniforms belong to the Tourist Police (© **065** for emergencies, or 744/485-0490), a special corps of English-speaking police established to assist tourists.

2 Where to Stay

The listings below begin with the very expensive resorts south of town (nearest the airport) and continue along Costera Alemán to the less expensive, more traditional hotels north of town, in the downtown or "Old Acapulco" part of the city. Especially in the Very

---

Fun Fact Acapulco, Queen of the Silver Screen

Along with hosting some of the legendary stars of the silver
screen, Acapulco has also played a few starring roles. Over
250 films have been shot here, including 1985's *Rambo II*,
which used the Pie de la Cuesta lagoon as its backdrop.

Expensive and Expensive categories, inquire about promotional
rates or check with the airlines for air-hotel packages. During
Christmas and Easter weeks, some hotels double their normal rates.
The rates below do not include the 17% tax.

Private **villas** are available for rent all over the hills south of town;
staying in one of these palatial homes is an unforgettable experience.
Se Renta (www.acapulcoluxuryvillas.com) handles some of the
most exclusive villas.

SOUTH OF TOWN
Acapulco's most exclusive and renowned hotels, restaurants, and villas nestle in the steep forested hillsides here, between the naval base
and Puerto Marqués. This area is several kilometers from the heart
of Acapulco; you'll pay about $20 (£11) round-trip taxi fare every
time you venture off the property into town.

VERY EXPENSIVE
Camino Real Acapulco Diamante ★★ *Kids*   Tucked in a
secluded location on 32 hectares (79 acres), this relaxing, self-con-
tained resort is an ideal choice for families, or for those who already
know Acapulco and don't care to explore much. I consider it one of
Acapulco's finest places in terms of contemporary decor, services,
and amenities. I like its location on the Playa Puerto Marqués,
which is safe for swimming, but you do miss out on compelling
views of Acapulco Bay. From Carretera Escénica, a handsome brick
road winds down to the hotel, overlooking Puerto Marqués Bay.
The lobby has an inviting terrace facing the water. The spacious
rooms have balconies or terraces, small sitting areas, marble floors,
ceiling fans (in addition to air-conditioning), and contemporary
Mexican furnishings.

Carretera Escénica Km 14, Baja Catita s/n, Pichilingue, 39867 Acapulco, Gro.
© **744/435-1010.** Fax 744/435-1020. www.caminoreal.com/acapulco. 157 units.
High season $429 (£236) double; $611 (£336) master suite. Rates include buffet
breakfast. Ask about low-season and midweek discounts. AE, MC, V. Parking $6
(£3). **Amenities:** 2 restaurants; lobby bar; 3 outdoor pools (1 for children); tennis

court; health club w/aerobics, spa treatments, massage, and complete workout equipment (extra charge); watersports equipment rentals; children's activities; concierge; tour desk; car-rental desk; salon; room service; babysitting; laundry service. *In room:* A/C, TV, minibar, hair dryer, iron, safe.

Casa Yal'ma Ka'an ￼ ￼ *(Finds)*

A romantic hideaway 20 minutes south of Diamante, Casa Yal'ma Ka'an is a small ecological retreat with its own ocean beach. Stone paths with little bridges meander past several lookout towers and over lily ponds with palms and flowers, and the beautiful pool lies just steps from the Pacific. In addition to featuring its own beach club, Casa Yal'ma Ka'an offers a *temazcal,* a Mayan rustic steam bath that will be prepared for you with candles and aromatherapy amenities. Seven individual thatched-roof cottages have king-size beds, rustic wood furnishings, stone bathrooms, and private sitting decks. Gourmet breakfasts are served under a giant *palapa* overlooking the pool and beach. Service throughout this exclusive hotel is outstanding; children younger than 17 are not allowed.

Carretera hacia Barra Vieja Km 29 L189, 39867 Acapulco, Gro. ✆ **744/444-6389** or -6390. www.casayalmakaan.com. 7 units. High season $280 (£154) double; low season $250 (£138) double. Rates include American breakfast. MC, V. Free parking. **Amenities:** Restaurant; pool bar; outdoor pool; beach club; spa treatments. *In room:* A/C, TV, safe.

Fairmont Pierre Marqués ￼ ￼ ￼

The refined Fairmont Pierre Marqués is both more exclusive and relaxed than the famous Fairmont Princess next door, to which guests also have access. It once served as a private home for J. Paul Getty and is today one of Acapulco's most prestigious hotels. Together, the Pierre Marqués and the Princess offer more activities than you are likely to have time for, with three pools alone at the Pierre Marqués, a beautiful Pacific beach with watersports activities, championship golf, tennis, and a state-of-the-art fitness center. Luxurious guest rooms include villas, bungalows, and low-rise pavilions overlooking the pools, tropical gardens, or beach. Fine dining is available here or at the Princess, with a shuttle regularly connecting the two hotels. Service throughout the hotel is outstanding. The Fairmont is in Diamante, about a 20-minute drive from the center of Acapulco.

Playa Revolcadero s/n, Colonia Granjas del Marques, 39907 Acapulco, Gro. ✆ **800/441-1414** in the U.S., or 744/435-2600. Fax 744/466-1046. www.fairmont.com/pierremarques. 335 units. $259 (£142) and up double. AE, MC, V. Free parking. **Amenities:** Restaurant; cafe; 2 bars; 3 outdoor pools; health club and spa; championship golf course; 5 outdoor lighted tennis courts (10 additional courts at Fairmont Princess, including 2 indoor courts); concierge; room service; laundry service. *In room:* A/C, TV, safe.

Las Brisas ✿✿✿ *(Moments)* This is a local landmark, often considered Acapulco's signature hotel, and my personal favorite. Perched on a hillside overlooking the bay, Las Brisas is known for its tiered pink stucco facade, private pools, and 50 pink jeeps rented exclusively to guests. If you stay here, you ought to like pink, because the color scheme extends to practically everything. Las Brisas is also known for inspiring romance and is best enjoyed by couples indulging in time together—alone.

The hotel is a community unto itself: The simple, marble-floored rooms are like separate villas sculpted from a terraced hillside, with panoramic views of Acapulco Bay from a balcony or terrace. Each room has a private or semiprivate swimming pool. Las Brisas has a total of 150 pools. The spacious Regency Club rooms, at the apex of the property, offer the best views. You stay at Las Brisas more for the panache and setting than for luxury amenities, though rooms have been upgraded, with new bedding and a freshening up of the decor, although it still retains the beloved "Las Brisas" style. Early each morning, continental breakfast arrives in a cubbyhole. If you tire of your own pool, Las Brisas has a beach club less than a kilometer (a half-mile) away, on Acapulco Bay; continuous shuttle service departs from the lobby. The club offers casual dining, a large swimming pool, and a natural saltwater pool—actually a rocky inlet. Mandatory service charges cover shuttle service from the hillside rooms to the lobby and from the lobby to the beach club, plus tips. The hotel is on the southern edge of the bay, overlooking the road to the airport and close to the hottest area nightclubs.

Apdo. Carretera Escénica 5255, Las Brisas, 39868 Acapulco, Gro. ✆ 888/559-4329 in the U.S., or 744/469-6900. Fax 744/446-5332. www.brisas.com.mx. 263 units. High season $330 (£182) shared pool, $435 (£239) private pool, $540 (£297) Royal Beach Club; low season $230 (£127) shared pool, $345 (£190) private pool, $432 (£238) Royal Beach Club. $20 (£11) per day service charge plus 17% tax. Rates include continental breakfast. AE, MC, V. Free parking. **Amenities:** 2 restaurants; deli; private beach club w/fresh- and saltwater pools; 5 tennis courts; gym; concierge; guest-only tours and activity program; tour desk; jeeps rental; shopping arcade; salon; room service; in-room massage; babysitting; laundry service; dry cleaning. *In room:* A/C, TV, minibar, hair dryer, safe.

COSTERA HOTEL ZONE
EXPENSIVE
Fiesta Americana Villas Acapulco ✿ The Fiesta Americana is a long-standing favorite deluxe hotel in the heart of the beach-bar action. The 18-story structure towers above Condesa Beach, just east and up the hill from the Glorieta Diana traffic circle. The

recently renovated studios, suites, and villas have marble floors, and can be loud if you're overlooking the pool area. Each has a private terrace or balcony with ocean view. The more expensive rooms have the best bay views, and all have purified tap water. The hilltop swimming pool affords one of the city's finest views. The location is great for enjoying the numerous beach activities, shopping, and more casual nightlife of Acapulco.

Costera Alemán 97, 39690 Acapulco, Gro. © **800/343-7821** in the U.S., or 744/484-2355. Fax 744/484-1828. www.fiestamericana.com. 324 units. High season $230 (£127) double, $290 (£160) suite; low season $100–$130 (£55–£72) double, $200 (£110) suite. AE, DC, MC, V. Free parking. **Amenities:** 3 restaurants; coffee shop; lobby bar; theme nights w/buffet dinner; 3 outdoor pools; travel agency; shopping arcade; salon; room service; laundry service. *In room:* A/C, TV, minibar, safe.

Hotel Elcano ✿✿✿ *(Finds)*   An Acapulco classic, the Elcano is another personal favorite. It offers exceptional service and a prime location—on a broad stretch of beach in the heart of the hotel zone. The retro-style, turquoise-and-white lobby, and beachside pool area are the closest you can get to a South Beach, Miami, atmosphere in Acapulco, and its popular open-air restaurant adds to the lively waterfront scene. On the whole, the Elcano reminds me of a set from a classic Elvis-in-Acapulco movie. Rooms are continually upgraded, bright, and very comfortable. They feature classic navy-and-white tile accents, ample oceanfront balconies, and tub/shower combinations. The very large junior suites, all on corners, have two queen-size beds and huge closets. Studios are small but adequate, with king-size beds and small sinks outside the bathroom area. In the studios, a small portion of the TV armoire serves as a closet, and there are no balconies, only large sliding windows. All rooms have purified tap water. This is an ideal place if you're attending a convention or simply want the best of all possible locations, between hillside nightlife and the Costera beach zone. It's an excellent value.

Costera Alemán 75, 39690 Acapulco, Gro. © **744/435-1500.** Fax 744/484-2230. http://hotel-elcano.com. 180 units. High season $145 (£80) studio, $185 (£102) standard double, $195 (£107) junior suite, $250 (£138) master suite; low season about $50 (£28) less for each room type. Ask about promotional discounts. AE, MC, V. Free parking. **Amenities:** 2 restaurants; beachside pool; small workout room; video-game room; travel agency; shopping arcade; salon; room service; massage; babysitting; laundry service. *In room:* A/C, TV, minibar, hair dryer, safe.

Hyatt Regency Acapulco ✿   A sprawling oasis, the Hyatt is one of the largest of Acapulco's hotels, although no longer as modern as many other resorts. The buzzing lobby encloses a sitting area and bar where there's live music every evening. A free-form pool fronts a broad stretch of beach with calm waters, one of the most inviting in Acapulco. The guest rooms are beginning to show their age, but they also have balconies with spectacular views of Acapulco Bay. Some contain kitchenettes. Regency Club guests receive continental breakfast, afternoon canapés, and other upgraded amenities. This hotel caters to a large Jewish clientele and has a full-service kosher restaurant, synagogue, and Sabbath elevator. Cruise passengers docking in Acapulco often stay here as well. The Alory Spa offers a broad menu of spa services and massage treatments.

Costera Alemán 1, 39869 Acapulco, Gro. ⓒ **800/233-1234** in the U.S. and Canada, 01-800/005-0000 in Mexico, or 744/469-1234. Fax 744/484-3087. www. acapulco.regency.hyatt.com. 640 units. High season $300–$360 (£165–£198) double, $390 (£215) Regency Club, $460 (£253) suite; low season $220 (£121) double, $290 (£160) Regency Club, $360 (£200) suite. AE, DC, MC, V. Valet parking $5 (£3). **Amenities:** 3 restaurants; cantina; lobby bar; 2 large, shaded free-form outdoor pools; small gym; spa; children's programs; concierge; tour desk; car-rental desk; business center; shopping arcade; salon; room service; in-room massage; babysitting; laundry service; dry cleaning; safe. *In room:* A/C, TV, minibar, hair dryer, iron, safe.

MODERATE

Calinda Beach   You'll see this tall cylindrical tower rising at the eastern edge of Condesa Beach. Each room has a view, usually of the bay. Though not exceptionally well furnished, guest rooms are large and comfortable; most have two double beds. It's the most modern of the reasonably priced lodgings along the strip of hotels facing popular Condesa Beach. Package prices are available, and the hotel frequently offers promotions, such as rates that include breakfast.

Costera Alemán 1260, 39300 Acapulco, Gro. ⓒ **744/435-0600.** Fax 744/484-4676. www.hotelescalinda.com.mx. 357 units. High season $180 (£99) double; low season $140 (£77) double. Ask about promotional specials. AE, DC, MC, V. Limited free parking. **Amenities:** 2 restaurants; poolside snacks; lobby bar w/live music; 2 outdoor pools; small gym; travel agency; salon; room service; babysitting; laundry service; pharmacy. *In room:* A/C, TV, safe.

Sand's Acapulco *(Kids* *(Value*   A great option for budget-minded families, this unpretentious, comfortable hotel nestles on the inland side, opposite the giant resort hotels and away from the din of Costera traffic. A stand of umbrella palms and a pretty garden restaurant—with terrific, authentic Mexican food at reasonable prices—lead into the lobby. The rooms are light and airy, in the style of a good modern motel, with basic furnishings and wall-to-wall carpeting. Some units have kitchenettes, and all have a terrace or balcony. The family-friendly hotel includes a kids' pool and a special play area for youngsters. The rates are reasonable, the accommodations satisfactory, and the location excellent.

Costera Alemán 178, 39670 Acapulco, Gro. © 744/484-2260. Fax 744/484-1053. www.sands.com.mx. 94 units. High season $150 (£83) standard double, $100 (£55) bungalow; low season $70 (£39) standard double, $50 (£28) bungalow. Rates include coffee in the lobby and are higher during Christmas, Easter, and other major holidays. AE, MC, V. Limited free parking. **Amenities:** Restaurant; 2 outdoor pools (1 for children); squash court; volleyball; Ping-Pong; children's playground; concierge; babysitting; laundry service; dry cleaning. *In room:* A/C, TV, minibar.

DOWNTOWN (ON LA QUEBRADA) & OLD ACAPULCO BEACHES

Numerous budget hotels dot the streets fanning out from the *zócalo*. They're among the best values in town, but be sure to check your room first to see that it meets your needs. Several hotels in this area are close to Caleta and Caletilla beaches, or on the back of the hilly peninsula, at Playa la Angosta.

MODERATE

Hotel Caleta ⟨⟩ The all-inclusive Hotel Caleta is more familiar to Mexican travelers than to their U.S. counterparts. This high-quality, nine-floor resort, adjacent to one of the liveliest beaches in Old Acapulco, offers excellent value. Stay here if you seek the authentic feel of a Mexican holiday, with all its boisterous, family-friendly charms. The hotel is built into a cliff on the Caleta peninsula, overlooking the beach. Rooms surround a plant-filled courtyard, topped by a glass ceiling. All have large terraces with ocean views, although some connect to the neighboring terrace. The simply decorated rooms are very clean and comfortable, with a large closet and desk. Each room has two queen-size beds with firm mattresses, and cable TV.

A succession of terraces holds tropical gardens, restaurants, and pools. A private beach and boat dock are down a brief flight of stairs. The resort has a changing agenda of theme nights and evening entertainment.

Cerro San Martín 325, Fracc. Las Playas, 39390 Acapulco, Gro. © 744/483-9140. Fax 744/483-9125. meigaca@prodigy.net.mx. 245 units. High season $140 (£77) double; low season $90 (£50) double. Rates are all-inclusive. Room-only prices sometimes available. AE, DC, MC, V. Free private parking. **Amenities:** Restaurant; snack bar; large fresh- and saltwater outdoor pools; tour desk; car-rental desk; shopping arcade. *In room:* A/C, TV, fan.

Hotel Mirador Acapulco ⚔ One of the landmarks of Old Acapulco, the El Mirador Hotel overlooks the famous cove where the cliff divers perform. Renovated with tropical landscaping and lots of Mexican tile, this hotel offers attractively furnished rooms. Each holds double or queen-size beds, a small kitchenette area with minifridge and coffeemaker, and a large bathroom with marble counters. Most have a separate living room, some have a whirlpool tub, and all are accented with colorful Saltillo tile and other Mexican decorative touches. Ask for a room with a balcony or ocean view.

A set-price dinner ($39/£21) offers great views of the cliff-diving show. The large, breezy lobby bar is a favorite spot to relax as day fades into night on the beautiful cove and bay. Nearby is a protected cove with good snorkeling.

Quebrada 74, 39300 Acapulco, Gro. © **744/483-1221** for reservations. Fax 744/482-4564. www.hotelelmiradoracapulco.com.mx. 132 units, including 9 junior suites with whirlpools. High season $185 (£102) double, $231 (£127) junior suite; low season $85 (£47) double, $110 (£61) junior suite. Add $13 (£7.15) for kitchenette. AE, MC, V. Street parking. **Amenities:** Restaurant; coffee shop; lobby bar; 3 outdoor pools, including 1 rather run-down saltwater pool; travel agency; room service; laundry service. *In room:* A/C, TV.

INEXPENSIVE

Hotel Costa Linda *(Value)* Budget-minded American and Mexican couples are drawn to the sunny, well-kept rooms of the Costa Linda, one of the best values in the area. All rooms have individually controlled air-conditioning and a minifridge, and some have a small kitchenette (during low season there is a $5/£2.75 charge for using the kitchenette). Closets and bathrooms are ample in size, and mattresses are firm. Cozy as the Costa Linda is, it is adjacent to one of the busier streets in Old Acapulco, so traffic noise can be bothersome. It's just a 1-block walk down to lively Caleta beach.

Costera Alemán 1008, 39390 Acapulco, Gro. © **744/482-5277** or -2549. Fax 744/483-4017. 44 units. High season $100 (£55) double; low season $45 (£25) double. Children younger than 8 stay free in parent's room. MC, V. Free parking. **Amenities:** Restaurant; bar; small outdoor pool; tennis court; tour desk. *In room:* A/C, TV, minibar.

Hotel Los Flamingos ⚔⚔ *(Finds)* An Acapulco landmark, Los Flamingos, perched on a cliff 150m (492 ft.) above Acapulco Bay, once entertained John Wayne, Cary Grant, Johnny Weissmuller, Fred McMurray, Errol Flynn, Red Skelton, Roy Rogers, and others. In fact, the stars liked it so much that at one point they bought it and converted it into a private club. The place is a real find in a kitschy campy sort of way—although the aged rooms are simple and lack modern luxuries, much of the hotel maintains the charm of a grand era. Photographs of the old movie stars line the hotel walls, and outdoor passages wind their way along the cliff overlooking the ocean. Most rooms have dramatic sea views and a large balcony or terrace, although few have air-conditioning and bathrooms are bare-bones. Thursdays at Los Flamingos are especially popular, with a *pozole* party and live music by a Mexican band that was probably around in the era of Wayne and Weissmuller—note the seashell-pink bass. Even if you don't stay here, plan to at least come for a margarita at sunset and a walk along the dramatic lookout point.

López Mateos s/n, Fracc. Las Playas, 39300 Acapulco, Gro. ℂ **744/482-0690.** Fax 744/483-9806. 40 units. High season $76 (£42) double, $95 (£52) superior double with A/C, $112 (£62) junior suite; low season $65 (£36) double, $78 (£43) superior double, $91 (£50) junior suite. AE, MC, V. **Amenities:** Restaurant; bar; outdoor pool; tour desk; car rental; room service; laundry service. *In room:* TV (in some), no phone.

Hotel Misión   Enter this hotel's plant-filled brick courtyard, shaded by two enormous mango trees, and you'll retreat into an earlier, more peaceful Acapulco. This tranquil 19th-century hotel lies 2 blocks inland from the Costera and the *zócalo*. The original L-shaped building is at least a century old. The rooms have colonial touches, such as colorful tile and wrought iron, and come simply furnished, with a fan and one or two beds with good mattresses. Breakfast is served on the patio.

Felipe Valle 12, 39300 Acapulco, Gro. ℂ **744/482-3643.** Fax 744/482-2076. 27 units. High season $50 (£28) double; low season $30 (£17) double. No credit cards. Limited free parking.

3 Where to Dine

Diners in Acapulco enjoy stunning views and fresh seafood. The quintessential setting is a candlelit table with the glittering bay spread out before you. If you're looking for a romantic spot, Acapulco brims with such inviting places; most sit along the southern coast, with views of the bay. If you're looking for simple food or an authentic local dining experience, you're best off in Old Acapulco.

A deluxe establishment in Acapulco may not be much more expensive than a mass-market restaurant. The proliferation of U.S. franchise restaurants has increased competition, and even the more expensive places have reduced prices. Trust me—the locally owned restaurants offer the best food and the best value.

SOUTH OF TOWN: LAS BRISAS AREA
VERY EXPENSIVE

Baikal 🐟🐟 FUSION/FRENCH/ASIAN The exquisite and ultrahot Baikal is the best place in Acapulco for an over-the-top dining experience. You enter from the street, then descend a spiral staircase into the stunning bar and restaurant, awash in muted tan and cream colors of luxurious fabrics and natural accents of stone, wood, and water. The restaurant itself is constructed into the cliff, providing sweeping views of Acapulco Bay's glittering lights. The large dining room, with a two-story ceiling, has comfortable seating, including sofas that border the room. The creative menu combines fusion fare, and then adds a dash of Mexican flare. Start with the scallops in chipotle vinaigrette or the Asian-style salad. Notable entrees include steamed red snapper with lobster butter sauce, chicken breast rolled and stuffed with asparagus in a white-wine reduction, or medallions of New Zealand lamb in a sweet garlic sauce. The service is as impeccable as the presentation. There's also an extensive selection of wines, as well as live jazz and bossa nova music nightly. Periodically during the evening, large projector screens descend over the floor-to-ceiling glass windows and show short films of Old Acapulco or cavorting whales and dolphins, providing a brief reprise from conversation and dining. A fashionably late dining spot (expect a crowd at midnight), the attire is chic resort wear, as most patrons are headed to the clubs following dinner. Baikal also has wheelchair access, a private VIP dining room, a wine cellar, and an ample bar, ideal for enjoying a sunset cocktail or after-dinner drink. It's east of town on the scenic highway just before the entrance to the Las Brisas hotel.

Carretera Escénica 16 and 22. 🕐 **744/446-6845** or -6867. www.baikal.com.mx. Reservations required (reservaciones@baikal.com.mx). Main courses: $21–$74 (£12–£41). AE, MC, V. Sun–Thurs 7pm–1am; Fri–Sat 7pm–2am. Closed Mon during summer.

🎬 Moments **Dining with a View**

Restaurants with unparalleled views of Acapulco include **Baikal, Mezzanotte, Zibu,** and **Casa Nova** in the Las Brisas area; **El Olvido** along the Costera; **Su Casa** on a hill above the convention center; and the appropriately named **Bella Vista Restaurant** at the Las Brisas hotel.

Casa Nova ✿ GOURMET ITALIAN   Enjoy an elegant though expensive meal and a fabulous view of glittering Acapulco Bay at this spot east of town. The cliff-side restaurant offers several refined dining rooms, awash in marble and stone accents, and outdoor terrace dining with a stunning view. If you arrive before your table is ready, have a drink in the comfortable lounge. This is a long-standing favorite of Mexico City's elite; dress tends toward fashionable, tropical attire. The best dishes include veal scaloppine and homemade pastas, such as linguine with fresh clams. A changing tourist menu offers a sampling of the best selections for a fixed price. There's also an ample selection of reasonably priced national and imported wines. And there's live piano music nightly.

Carretera Escénica 5256. ✆ **744/446-6237**. Reservations required. Main courses $28–$50 (£15–£28); fixed-price 4-course meal $39 (£21). AE, MC, V. Mon–Sat 7–11:30pm.

Mezzanotte Acapulco ✿ ITALIAN   Mezzanotte offers a contemporary blending of classic Italian cuisines, but its strongest asset is the spectacular floor-to-ceiling view of the bay. This location has changed hands several times; it currently offers a mix of trendy international dishes served in an atmosphere that tries a bit too hard to be upscale and fashionable. Music is loud and hip, so if you're looking for a romantic evening, this is probably not the place. It's a better choice if you want a taste of Mexican urban chic. The view of the bay remains outstanding, though the food still strives for consistency. Dress up a bit for dining here. Mezzanotte is in the La Vista complex near the Las Brisas hotel.

Plaza La Vista, Carretera Escénica a Puerto Márquez 28-2. ✆ **744/446-5727** or -5728. Reservations recommended. Main courses $20–$35 (£11–£19). AE, MC, V. Daily 6:30pm–midnight. Closed Mon during low season.

Zibu ✿✿✿ SEAFOOD/THAI   With a gorgeous view over the sea, Zibu blends Mexican and Thai architectural and culinary styles to create a breathtaking dining experience. The open-air venue is furnished with rattan tables and chairs surrounded by warm lighting of candles, Tiki torches, and lamps; a semi-circular pool serves as a moat between the ultrachic restaurant and *palapa*-topped lounge. Consider starting with the sea scallop carpaccio or seabass tartar, and continue with the shrimp medallions with ginger and mango or grilled fish filet with almonds and soy (there are also meat dishes). The beautiful glass-enclosed wine cellar houses a well-balanced though expensive collection, including a thoughtful selection of French wines. Service is gracious and attentive, and Asian lounge and Thai music plays in the background.

Av. Escénica s/n, Fracc. Glomar. ⓒ 744/433-3058 or -3069. Reservations recommended. Main courses $14–$50 (£7.70–£28). AE, MC, V. Sun–Thurs 7pm–midnight; Fri–Sat 7pm–1am.

COSTERA HOTEL ZONE
VERY EXPENSIVE

El Olvido ⓡⓡ FRENCH/MEXICAN   El Olvido gives you all the glittering bayview ambience of the posh Las Brisas restaurants, without the taxi ride. The menu is one of the most sophisticated in the city. It's expensive, but each dish is delightful in presentation and taste. Start with 1 of the 12 house specialty drinks, such as Olvido, made with tequila, rum, Cointreau, tomato juice, and lime juice. Soups include delicious cold avocado, and thick black bean and chorizo. Among the innovative entrees are quail with honey and *pasilla* chiles, thick sea bass with a mild sauce of cilantro and avocado, and lamb chops with chipotle. For dessert, try chocolate fondue or *guanábana* (a tropical fruit) mousse in a rich *zapote negro* (black tropical fruit) sauce. El Olvido sits at the back of the Plaza Marbella shopping center fronting Diana Circle. Although the bay view is lovely, a drawback is that the dance clubs down the shoreline can often be heard after 10pm.

Glorieta Diana traffic circle, Plaza Marbella. ⓒ **744/481-0203**, -0256, or -0214. www.elolvido.com.mx. Reservations recommended. Main courses $15–$40 (£8.25–£22). AE, MC, V. Daily 6pm–midnight.

Su Casa/La Margarita ⓡⓡ INTERNATIONAL   Relaxed elegance and terrific food at reasonable prices are what you get at Su Casa. Owners Shelly and Angel Herrera created this pleasant, breezy, open-air restaurant on the patio of their hillside home overlooking the city (La Margarita is the indoor restaurant below Su Casa that's open during the rainy season). Both Shelly and Angel are experts in the kitchen and are on hand nightly to greet guests on the patio. The menu changes often. Some items are standard, such as shrimp *a la patrona* in garlic; grilled fish, steak, and chicken; and flaming *filet al Madrazo,* a delightful brochette marinated in tropical juices. Many entrees come with garnishes of cooked banana or pineapple. The margaritas are big and delicious. Su Casa is the hotpink building on the hillside above the convention center.

V. Anahuac 110. ⓒ **744/484-4350** or -1261. Fax 744/484-0803. www.sucasaacapulco.com. Reservations recommended. Main courses $17–$35 (£9.35–£19). MC, V. Daily 6pm–midnight.

MODERATE

El Cabrito &&& NORTHERN MEXICAN   With its hacienda-inspired entrance, waitresses in white dresses and *charro*-style neckties, and location in the heart of the Costera, this typical Mexican restaurant targets tourists. But its authentic and delicious food attracts Mexicans in the know—a comforting stamp of approval. Among its specialties are *cabrito al pastor* (roasted goat), *charro* beans, Oaxaca-style mole, and *burritos de machaca* (made with shredded beef). Bottles of beer are brought to your table in buckets of ice and then poured in frosty cold mugs. El Cabrito lies on the ocean side of the Costera, south of the convention center.

Costera Alemán 1480. ℂ **744/484-7711.** Main courses $6.50–$18 (£3.60–£9.90). AE, MC, V. Daily 2pm–midnight.

INEXPENSIVE

Ika Tako &&& *(Finds* SEAFOOD/TACOS   These fresh fish, shrimp, and seafood tacos (served in combinations that include grilled pineapple, fresh spinach, grated cheese, garlic, and bacon) are so tasty that they're addicting. A spicy array of eight salsas accompanies them, and there are also excellent burritos, meat and chicken dishes, and vegetarian selections. Unlike most inexpensive places to eat, the setting is also lovely, with a handful of tables overlooking tropical trees and the bay below. The lighting may be bright, the atmosphere occasionally hectic, and the service dependably slow, but the tacos are delectable. You can also order beer, wine, soft drinks, and dessert. This restaurant is along the Costera, next to Beto's lobster restaurant. There's another branch across from the Hyatt Regency hotel that lacks the atmosphere of this one.

Costera Alemán 99. ℂ **744/484-9521.** Main courses $5–$16 (£2.75–£8.80). AE, MC, V. Daily 5pm–3am.

100% Natural *(Kids* MEXICAN/HEALTH FOOD   Healthful versions of Mexican standards are the specialty at this clean, breezy, plant-filled restaurant, on the second level of the shopping center across from the Acapulco Plaza Hotel. (This chain has five other branches in Acapulco, including another one farther east on the Costera.) Especially notable are the fruit *licuados,* blended fresh fruit with your choice of yogurt or milk. Yogurt shakes, steamed vegetables, and cheese enchiladas are alternatives to their yummy sandwiches served on whole-grain breads. If you've over-indulged the night before, get yourself back on track here. It's wide selection of sandwiches and smoothies make this a great place for families.

Costera Miguel Alemán 200, across from the Costa Club Hotel. ⓒ **744/485-3982.**
Sandwiches $5–$6 (£2.75–£3.30); other food items $5–$10 (£2.75–£5.50). AE, MC,
V. Daily 7am–11pm.

DOWNTOWN: THE *ZOCALO* AREA

The old downtown area abounds with simple, inexpensive restaurants serving tasty eats. It's easy to pay more elsewhere and not get
food as consistently good as you'll find in this part of town. To
explore this area, start at the *zócalo* and stroll west along Juárez.
After about 3 blocks, you'll come to Azueta, lined with small
seafood cafes and street-side stands.

MODERATE

El Amigo Miguel ⓕ *(Finds)* MEXICAN/SEAFOOD   Locals know
that El Amigo Miguel is a standout among downtown seafood
restaurants—you can easily pay more elsewhere but not eat better.
Impeccably fresh seafood reigns; the large, open-air dining room, 3
blocks west of the *zócalo*, is usually brimming with seafood lovers.
When it overflows, head to a branch across the street, with the same
menu. Try delicious *camarones borrachos* (drunken shrimp), in a
sauce made with beer, ketchup, and bits of fresh bacon—it tastes
nothing like the individual ingredients. *Filete Miguel* is a fresh fish
filet (often red snapper or sea bass) stuffed with seafood and covered
in a wonderful chipotle pepper sauce. Grilled shrimp with garlic and
mojo de ajo (whole red snapper) are served at their classic best. Meat
dishes are available, as well.

Juárez 31, at Azueta. ⓒ **744/483-6981.** Main courses $6.50–$15 (£3.60–£8.25).
AE, MC, V. Daily 10am–9pm.

Moments **If There's *Pozole*, It Must Be Thursday**

If you're visiting Acapulco on a Thursday, indulge in the local
custom of eating *pozole,* a bowl of white hominy and meat
in broth, garnished with sliced radishes, shredded lettuce,
onions, oregano, and lime, served with crispy tostadas. The
traditional version includes pork, but a newer chicken version
has also become a standard. You can also find green *pozole,*
which is made by adding a paste of roasted pumpkin seeds to
the traditional *pozole* base. Green *pozole* is also traditionally
served with a side of sardines. For a singular Acapulco experience, enjoy your Thursday *pozole* at the cliff-side restaurant
of Hotel Los Flamingos (see earlier in this chapter).

Mariscos Pipo ✿ SEAFOOD Check out the photographs of Old Acapulco on the walls while relaxing in this airy dining room decorated with hanging nets, fish, glass buoys, and shell lanterns. The English-language menu lists a wide array of seafood, including *ceviche*, lobster, octopus, crayfish, clams, baby-shark quesadillas, and fish prepared anyway you want. This local favorite is 2 blocks west of the *zócalo* on Breton, just off the Costera. Another bustling branch, open daily from 1 to 9:30pm, is at Costera Alemán and Canadá (© **744/484-0165**).

Almirante Breton 3. © **744/482-2237**. Main courses $8–$25 (£4.40–£14). AE, MC, V. Daily 11am–8pm.

4 Activities On & Off the Beach

Acapulco is known for its great beaches and watersports, and few visitors bother to explore its traditional downtown area. But the shaded *zócalo* (also called Plaza Alvarez) is worth a trip, to experience a glimpse of local life and color. Inexpensive cafes and shops border the plaza. At its far north end is the **cathedral Nuestra Señora de la Soledad,** with blue, onion-shaped domes and Byzantine towers. Though reminiscent of a Russian Orthodox church, it was originally (and perhaps appropriately) built as a movie set, then later adapted into a house of worship. From the church, turn east along the side street going off at a right angle (Calle Carranza, which doesn't have a marker) to find an arcade with newsstands and more shops. The hill behind the cathedral provides an unparalleled view of Acapulco. Take a taxi to the top of the hill from the main plaza, and follow signs to **El Mirador (lookout point).**

Local travel agencies book city tours, day trips to Taxco, cruises, and other excursions and activities. Taxco is about a 3-hour drive inland from Acapulco (see chapter 5 for more information).

THE BEACHES

Here's a rundown on the beaches, going from west to east around the bay. **Playa la Angosta** is a small, sheltered, often-deserted cove just around the bend from **La Quebrada** (where the cliff divers perform).

South of downtown on the Peninsula de las Playas lie the beaches **Caleta** and **Caletilla.** Separating them is a small outcropping of land that contains the aquarium and water park **Mágico Mundo Marino,** which is open daily from 9am to 6pm (© **744/483-1215**) and costs $4 (£2.25) to enter. You'll find thatched-roofed restaurants, watersports equipment for rent, and brightly painted boats that ferry passengers to **Roqueta Island.** You can rent beach chairs and umbrellas for the day. Mexican families favor these beaches because they're close to several inexpensive hotels. In the late afternoon, fishermen pull their colorful boats up on the sand; you can buy the fresh catch of the day and, occasionally, oysters on the half shell.

Pleasure boats dock at **Playa Manzanillo,** south of the *zócalo.* Charter fishing trips sail from here. In the old days, the downtown beaches—Manzanillo, Honda, Caleta, and Caletilla—were the focal point of Acapulco. Today, beaches and resort developments stretch along the 6.5km (4-mile) length of the shore.

East of the *zócalo,* the major beaches are **Hornos** (near Papagayo Park), **Hornitos, Paraíso, Condesa,** and **Icacos,** followed by the naval base (La Base) and **Punta del Guitarrón.** After Punta del Guitarrón, the road climbs to the legendary Las Brisas hotel. Past Las Brisas, the road continues to the small, clean bay of **Puerto Marqués,** followed by **Punta Diamante,** about 20km (12 miles) from the *zócalo.* The fabulous Acapulco Princess, the Quinta Real, and the Pierre Marqués hotels dominate the landscape, which fronts the open Pacific.

Playa Puerto Marqués, in the bay of Puerto Marqués, is an attractive area for swimming. The water is calm and the bay sheltered. Water-skiing can also be arranged. Past the bay lies **Revolcadero Beach,** a magnificent wide stretch of beach on the open ocean, where many of Acapulco's grandest resorts are found.

Other beaches lie farther north and are best reached by car, though buses also make the trip. **Pie de la Cuesta** is 13km (8 miles) west of town. Buses along the Costera leave every 5 or 10 minutes; a taxi costs about $20 (£11). The water is too rough for swimming,

---

Tips To Swim or Not to Swim in the Bay?

In the past decade, the city has gone to great lengths (and great expense) to clean up the waters off Acapulco. Nevertheless, this is an industrial port that was once heavily polluted, so many choose to stick to the hotel pool. You may notice the fleet of power-sweeper boats that skim the top of the bay each morning to remove debris and oil.

Among the bay beaches that remain popular with visitors and locals are **Caleta** and **Caletilla beaches,** as well as **Playa Puerto Marqués.**

⟨ Tips Tide Warning

Each year, at least one or two unwary swimmers drown in Acapulco because of deadly riptides and undertow (see "Safety" in "Fast Facts," earlier in this chapter). Swim only in Acapulco Bay or Puerto Marqués Bay—and be careful of the undertow no matter where you go. If you find yourself caught in the undertow, head back to shore at an angle instead of trying to swim straight back.

---

but it's a great spot for checking out big waves and the spectacular sunset, especially over *coco locos* (drinks served in fresh coconuts with the tops whacked off) at a rustic beachside restaurant. The area is known for excellent birding and surrounding coconut plantations.

If you're driving, continue west along the peninsula, passing **Coyuca Lagoon** on your right, until almost to the small air base at the tip. Along the way, various private entrepreneurs, mostly young boys, will invite you to park near different sections of beach. You'll also find *colectivo* boat tours of the lagoon offered for about $10 (£5.50).

BAY CRUISES & ROQUETA ISLAND

Acapulco has virtually every kind of boat to choose from—yachts, catamarans, and trimarans (single- and double-deckers). Cruises run morning, afternoon, and evening. Some offer buffets, open bars, and live music; others just snacks, drinks, and taped music. Prices range from $24 to $40 (£13–£22). Cruise operators come and go, and their phone numbers change so frequently from year to year that it's pointless to list them here; to find out what cruises are currently operating, contact any Acapulco travel agency or your hotel's tour desk, and ask for brochures or recommendations.

Boats from Caletilla Beach to **Roqueta Island**—a good place to snorkel, sunbathe, hike to a lighthouse, visit a small zoo, or have lunch—leave every 15 minutes from 7am until the last one returns at 7pm. There are also primitive-style glass-bottom boats that circle the bay as you look down at a few fish and watch a diver swim down to the underwater sanctuary of the Virgin of Guadalupe, patron saint of Mexico. The statue of the Virgin—created by sculptor Armando Quesado—was placed there in 1958, in memory of a group of divers who lost their lives at the spot. You can purchase tickets ($5/£2.75) directly from any boat that's loading.

WATERSPORTS & BOAT RENTALS

An hour of **water-skiing** at Coyuca Lagoon can cost as little as $35 (£19) or as much as $65 (£36).

Scuba diving costs $50 (£28) for 1½ hours of instruction if you book directly with the instructor on Caleta Beach. It costs about $70 (£39) if you book through a hotel or travel agency. Dive trips start at around $70 (£39) per person for one dive. One reputable shop, near Club de Esquís, is **Divers de México** (© 744/482-1398). Another recommended company, both PADI and NAUI certified, is the **Acapulco Scuba Center,** Paseo del Pescador 13–14, downtown Acapulco (© 744/482-9474; www.acapulco scuba.com). They offer a variety of dives from half-day (9am–2pm) shallow dives for beginners to instructor training. Prices for two-tank dives are $90 (£50), and include transportation from your hotel, onboard lunch, boat, and gear. **Boat rentals** are cheapest on Caletilla Beach, where an information booth (© 744/482-2389) rents inner tubes, small boats, canoes, paddleboats, and chairs. It also arranges water-skiing and scuba diving.

For **deep-sea fishing** excursions, go to the boat cooperative's pink building opposite the *zócalo,* or book a day in advance (© 744/482-1099). Charter trips run $250 to $450 (£138–£248) for 6 hours, tackle and bait included, with an extra charge for ice, drinks, and lunch. Credit cards are accepted, but you're likely to get a better deal by paying cash. Boats leave at 7am and return at 2pm. If you book through a travel agent or hotel, prices start at around $250 (£138) for four people. Also recommendable is **Fish-R-Us,** Costera Alemán 100 (© 877/347-4787 in the U.S., or 744/482-8282). In addition to traditional fishing charters, they also offer private yacht charters, scuba diving, and a 3-hour Night of Delight cruise, complete with dinner served on board. Prices vary with the service requested and number of people, so call for details.

Parasailing, though not free from risk (the occasional thrill-seeker has collided with a palm tree or even a building), can be brilliant. Floating high over the bay hanging from a parachute towed by a motorboat costs about $25 (£14). Most of these rides operate on Condesa Beach, but they also can be found independently operating on the beach in front of most hotels along the Costera.

GOLF & TENNIS

Both the **Acapulco Princess** (© **744/469-1000**) and **Pierre Marqués** (© **744/466-1000**) hotels have top-notch courses. The Princess's course is a rather narrow, level, Ted Robinson design. The Marqués course, redesigned by Robert Trent Jones, Sr., in 1972 for the World Cup Golf Tournament, is longer and more challenging. A morning round of 18 holes at either course costs $135 (£74) for guests and $150 (£83) for nonguests (discounted rates for afternoon rounds); American Express, Visa, and MasterCard are accepted, and the cart is included in the fee. Tee times begin at 7:30am, and reservations should be made a day in advance. Club rental is available for an extra $40 (£22). The **Mayan Palace Golf Club,** Geranios 22 (© **744/469-6043** or 466-2260), designed by Latin American golf great Pedro Guericia, lies farther east. Greens fees are $135 (£74) for visitors, and caddies are available for an additional $18 (£9.90). At the **Club de Golf Acapulco,** off the Costera next to the convention center (© **744/484-0781**), you can play 9 holes for $50 (£28) and 18 holes for $80 (£44), with equipment renting for $16 (£8.80).

The newest addition to Acapulco's golf scene is the spectacular Robert von Hagge–designed course at the exclusive **Tres Vidas Golf Club,** Carretera a Barra Vieja Km 7 (© **744/444-5138** or -5126). The par-72, 18-hole course, right on the edge of the ocean, is landscaped with nine lakes, dotted with palms, and home to a flock of ducks and other birds. The club is open only to members, guests of members, and guests at Tres Vidas. Greens fees are $195 (£107), including cart; a caddy costs $15 (£8.25). Also here is a clubhouse with a restaurant (daily 7:30am–7:30pm), as well as a pool and beach club. American Express, Visa, and MasterCard are accepted.

The **Club de Tenis Hyatt,** Costera Alemán 1 (© **744/484-1225**), is open daily from 7am to 11pm. Outdoor and indoor courts cost $10 (£5.50) per hour during the day, $15 (£8.25) per hour at night; Rackets rent for $3 (£1.65) and a set of balls costs $5.50 (£3). Many of the hotels along the Costera have tennis facilities for guests; the best are at the Acapulco Princess, Pierre Marqués, Mayan Palace, and Las Brisas hotels.

RIDING & BULLFIGHTS

You can go **horseback riding** along the beach. Independent operators stroll the Hotel Zone beachfront offering rides for about $25 to $45 (£14–£25) for 1 to 2 hours. Horses are also commonly found on the beach in front of the Acapulco Princess Hotel. There is no phone; you go directly to the beach to make arrangements.

Traditionally called Fiesta Brava, **bullfights** are held during Acapulco's winter season at a ring up the hill from Caletilla Beach. Tickets purchased through travel agencies cost around $17 to $40 (£9.35–£22) and usually include transportation to and from your hotel. You can also buy a general admission ticket at the stadium for $4.50 (£2.50). Be forewarned that this is a true bullfight—meaning things generally do not fare well for the bull. The festivities begin at 5:30pm each Sunday from January to March.

A MUSEUM & A WATER PARK

The original **Fuerte de San Diego,** Costera Alemán, east of the *zócalo* (② **744/482-3828**), was built in 1616 to protect the town from pirate attacks. At that time, the port reaped considerable income from trade with the Philippine Islands (which, like Mexico, were part of the Spanish Empire). The fort you see today was rebuilt after considerable earthquake damage in 1776, and most recently underwent renovation in 2000. The structure houses the **Museo Histórico de Acapulco (Acapulco Historical Museum)** ⊛⊛, with

---

Moments Death-Defying Divers

High divers perform at La Quebrada each day at 12:30, 7:15, 8:15, 9:15, and 10:30pm. Admission is $3.50 (£1.90). From a spotlit ledge on the cliffs, divers (holding torches for the final performance) plunge into the roaring surf of an inlet that's just 7m (23 ft.) wide, 4m (13 ft.) deep, and 40m (131 ft.) below—after wisely praying at a small shrine nearby. To the applause of the crowd, divers climb up the rocks and accept congratulations and gifts of money from onlookers. This is the quintessential Acapulco experience. No visit is complete without watching the cliff divers—and that goes for jaded travelers as well. To get there from downtown, take the street called La Quebrada from behind the cathedral for 4 blocks.

The public areas have great views, but arrive early, because performances quickly fill up. Another option is to watch from the lobby bar and restaurant terraces of the **Hotel Plaza Las Glorias/El Mirador.** The bar imposes a $19 (£10) cover charge, which includes two drinks. You can get around the cover by having dinner at the hotel's **La Perla restaurant.** Reservations (② **744/483-1155,** ext. 802) are recommended during high season.

---

exhibits that tell the story of Acapulco from its role as a port in the conquest of the Americas to a center for local Catholic conversion campaigns and for exotic trade with the Orient. Other exhibits chronicle Acapulco's pre-Hispanic past, the coming of the conquistadors (complete with Spanish armor), and Spanish imperial activity. Temporary exhibits are also on display. Admission to the museum is $3.50 (£1.90), free on Sunday. It's open Tuesday through Sunday from 9:30am to 6:30pm. To reach the fort, follow Costera Alemán past Old Acapulco and the *zócalo;* the fort is on a hill on the right.

The **Parque Acuático el CICI** ⌘, Costera Alemán at Colón (Ⓒ 744/484-8033), is a sea-life and water park east of the convention center. It offers guests swimming pools with waves, water slides, and water toboggans, and has a cafeteria and restrooms. The park, which underwent a $3-million renovation, is open daily from 10am to 6pm. General admission is $10 (£5.50) and free for children younger than 2. There are **dolphin shows** (in Spanish) weekdays at 2pm and weekends at 2 and 4pm. There's also a dolphin swim program, which includes 30 minutes of introduction and 30 minutes to

---

A House of Art

Of all the exclusive villas and homes in Acapulco, one stands far apart from the others. Though not as elegantly impressive as the villas of Las Brisas, the **home of Dolores Olmedo** in Acapulco's traditional downtown area is a veritable work of art. In 1956, the renowned Mexican artist Diego Rivera covered its outside wall with a mural of colorful mosaic tiles, shells, and stones. The work is unique and one of the last he created. Rivera, considered one of Mexico's greatest artists, has been credited with being one of the founders of the 20th-century Mexican-muralist movement. The Olmedo mural, which took him 18 months to complete, features Aztec deities such as Quetzalcoatl and Tepezcuincle, the Aztec dog. Rivera and Olmedo were lifelong friends, and Rivera lived in this house for the last 2 years of his life, during which time he also covered the interior with murals. However, because this home isn't a museum, you have to settle for enjoying the exterior masterpiece. The house is a few blocks behind the Casablanca Hotel, a short cab ride from the central plaza, at Calle Cerro de la Pinzona 6. Have the driver wait while you look around.

---

1 hour of swim time. The cost for this option is $90 (£50) for a half-hour swim, $130 (£72) for an hour, and they are by prior reservation only. Shows are at 10am, 12:30, and 4pm. Reservations are required; there is a 10-person maximum per show for the dolphin swim option. The minimum age is 4 years.

5 Shopping

Acapulco is not among the best places to buy Mexican crafts, but it does have a few interesting shops, and the Costera is lined with places to buy tourist souvenirs, including silver jewelry, Mexico knickknacks, and the ubiquitous T-shirt.

The shopkeepers aren't pushy, but they'll test your bargaining mettle. The starting price will be steep, and dragging it down may take some time. Before buying silver, examine it carefully and look for ".925" stamped on the back. This supposedly signifies that the silver is 92.5% pure, but the less expensive silver metal called "alpaca" may also bear this stamp. (Alpaca is generally stamped MEXICO or MEX, often in letters so tiny that they are hard to read and look similar to the three-digit ".925.") The market is open daily from 9am to 6pm.

Sanborn's, a good department store and drugstore chain, offers an array of staples, including cosmetics, music, clothing, books, and magazines. It has a number of locations in Acapulco, including downtown at Costera Miguel Alemán 209, across from the boat docks (📞 **744/482-6167**); Costera Miguel Alemán 1226 at the Condo Estrella Tower, close to the convention center (📞 **744/484-2025**); and on Costera Miguel Alemán 163, at the Hotel Calinda (📞 **744/481-2426** or 484-4465).

Acapulco also has a Sam's Club and a Wal-Mart on the inland side of the main highway just prior to its ascent to Las Brisas.

Boutiques selling resort wear crowd the Costera Alemán. These stores carry attractive summer clothing at prices lower than you generally pay in the United States. If there's a sale, you can find incredible bargains. One of the nicest air-conditioned shopping centers on the Costera is **Plaza Bahía,** Costera Alemán 125 (📞 **744/485-6939** or -6992), which has four stories of shops, movie theaters, a bowling alley, and small fast-food restaurants. The center is just west of the Costa Club Hotel. The bowling alley, **Aca Bol in Plaza Bahía** (📞 **744/485-0970** or -7464), is open daily from noon to 1am. Another popular shopping strip is the **Plaza Condesa,** adjacent to the Fiesta Americana Condesa, with shops that include Guess, Izod, and Bronce Swimwear. **Olvido Plaza,** near the restaurant of the same name, has Tommy Hilfiger and Aca Joe.

Acapulco has a few notable fine-art galleries. My favorite, **Galería Espacio Pal Kepenyes** *★★*, Costera Guitarrón 140, on the road to the Radisson (© **744/484-3738**), carries the work of Pal Kepenyes, whose stunning bronzes are among Acapulco's most notable public sculptures. The gallery shows smaller versions, as well as signature pieces of jewelry in brass, copper, and silver, by appointment only.

Works by another notable Mexican artist, **Sergio Bustamante,** are available inside the gallery of the Hotel Mayan Palace, Costera de las Palmas (© **744/469-6003**). You can see his capricious suns, moons, and fantasy figures in a variety of materials.

6 Acapulco After Dark

SPECIAL ATTRACTIONS

The **"Gran Noche Mexicana"** combines a performance by the Acapulco Ballet Folklórico with one by Los Voladores from Papantla. It takes place in the plaza of the convention center Monday, Wednesday, and Friday at 7pm. With dinner and open bar, the show costs about $62 (£34); general admission (including three drinks) is $42 (£23). Call for reservations (© **744/435-0105**), or consult a local travel agency. Many major hotels also schedule Mexican fiestas and other theme nights that include dinner and entertainment. Local travel agencies will have information.

NIGHTCLUBS & DANCE CLUBS

Acapulco is even more famous for its nightclubs than for its beaches. Because clubs frequently change ownership—and often, names—it's difficult to give specific and accurate recommendations. But some general tips will help. Clubs have varying cover charges that are almost always higher for men. Drinks can cost anywhere from $5 to $15 (£2.75–£8.25). Don't even think about going out to one of the hillside dance clubs before 11pm, and don't expect much action until after midnight. But it will keep going until 4 or 5am, and possibly later.

Many dance clubs periodically waive their cover charge or offer some other promotion to attract customers. Look for promotional materials in hotel reception areas, at travel desks or concierge booths, in local publications, and on the beach.

The high-rise hotels have their own bars and sometimes dance clubs. Informal lobby or poolside cocktail bars often offer free live entertainment.

THE BEACH BAR ZONE

Prefer a little fresh air with your nightlife? The young, hip crowd favors the growing number of open-air oceanfront dance clubs along Costera Alemán, most of which feature techno or alternative rock. There's a concentration of them between the Fiesta Americana and Continental Plaza hotels. An earlier and more casual option to the glitzy dance clubs, these places include the jamming **Disco Beach** ⭑⭑ (① 744/484-8230), **El Sombrero** (you'll know it when you see it), **Tabú,** and the pirate-themed **Barbaroja.** These mainly charge a cover (around $10/£5.50) and offer an open bar. Women frequently drink free or with a lesser charge (men may pay more, but then, this is where the beach babes are). Disco Beach is the most popular of the bunch and occasionally—such as during spring break—has live bands on the beachfront stage. Their Friday night foam parties are especially popular. Most of the smaller establishments do not accept credit cards; when they do, MasterCard and Visa are more widely accepted than American Express.

If you are brave enough—or inebriated enough—there's a **bungee jump** in the midst of the beach bar zone at Costera Alemán 101 (① **744/484-7529**). For $60 (£33) you get one jump, plus a T-shirt, diploma, and membership. Additional jumps are $20 (£11), and your fourth jump is free. For $90 (£50), you can jump as many times as you like from 4 to 11pm.

Alebrijes   Stadium seating, booths, and round tables surround the vast dance floor—the club (capacity 1,200) doubles as a venue for concerts and live performances by some of Mexico's most notable singers. Music includes pop, hip-hop, rock, and electronic music. The dress code forbids shorts, T-shirts, tennis shoes, flip-flops, and jeans. Average age here is late teens to early 20s. Open daily from 11pm to 5am. Costera Alemán 3308, across from the Hyatt Regency Acapulco. ① **744/484-5902.** Cover (including open bar with national drinks) $30 (£17) for women, $40 (£22) for men.

Baby-O ⭑⭑⭑   This longtime Acapulco hot spot is a throwback to the town's heady disco days, although the music is exceptionally contemporary. The mid- to late-20s crowd dances to everything from house to hip-hop and techno to dance. Across from the Days Inn and Hooters, Baby-O has a dance floor surrounded by several tiers of tables and sculpted, cavelike walls, serviced by three bars. Drinks cost $5 to $7 (£2.75–£3.85). Three-dimensional laser shows and vapor effects keep the dancing going strong. Service is excellent.

This is a high-class dance club attracting a beautiful clientele. It opens at 10:30pm, and you'd be wise to make a reservation. Costera Alemán 22. ⓒ 744/484-7474 or 481-1035. www.babyo.com.mx. Cover $20 (£11) for women, $60 (£33) for men.

Carlos 'n' Charlie's For fun, danceable music, and good food, you can't go wrong with this branch of the Carlos Anderson chain. It's always packed. Come early and get a seat on the terrace overlooking the Costera. This is a great place to go for late dinner and a few drinks before moving on to a club. It's east of the Glorieta Diana traffic circle, across the street from the Fiesta Americana Condesa. It's open daily from 1pm to 1am. Costera Alemán 999. ⓒ 744/484-1285 or -0039. www.carlosandcharlies.com/acapulco/index.htm.

Mambo Café ⚑⚑ Part of a national chain, the vibrant Mambo Café hosts groups from the Dominican Republic, Cuba, Mexico, Venezuela, and Colombia. Sexy dancers swing their hips to salsa, merengue, cumbia, and pop. The tropical club attracts locals as well as tourists, and is considered the best Latin dance spot in town. Tables surround the dance floor, and patrons can order drinks by the glass or the bottle. Open Wednesday to Saturday from 10pm to 5am. Costera Alemán 1632. ⓒ 744/485-9688. www.gpofreedom.com.mx. Cover $8 (£4.40).

Mandara ⚑⚑ *Moments* Venture into this stylish chrome-and-neon extravaganza (formerly Enigma) perched on the side of the mountain for a true Acapulco nightlife experience. The plush, dim club has a sunken dance floor and panoramic view of the lights of Acapulco Bay. The club also has an intimate piano bar, Siboney, upstairs overlooking the dance floor; it has a special champagne menu and draws a more mature and moneyed crowd. The after-hours lounge Privado, also in the same building, opens its doors at 4:30am. Downstairs, there's pumped-in mood smoke, alternating with fresh oxygen to keep you dancing. Tight and slinky is the norm for women; no shorts for men. The club opens nightly at 10:30pm; fireworks rock the usually full house at 3am, which is when a stylized dance performance takes place on weekends, in the style of Euro clubs. Call to find out if you need reservations; this club tends to be busiest on Friday nights. Carretera Escénica, between Los Rancheros Restaurant and La Vista Shopping Center. ⓒ 744/446-5711 or -5712. www.acapulco nightclubs.com (reservations: rsvpmandara@hotmail.com). Cover $30 (£17) for women, $40 (£22) for men, includes open bar; or pay $10 (£5.50) for entrance to Siboney, and purchase drinks separately.

Palladium ✿✿   This cliff-side club currently reigns as the top spot in town, and is found just down the road from Mandara. Generally, it welcomes a younger, rowdier crowd that enjoys the fabulous views and the dancing platforms set in the 50m-wide (164-ft.) glass windows overlooking the bay. Around 3:30am, Silver Man—complete with an Aztec headdress—performs, followed by a spray of fireworks outside the windows. Palladium has welcomed the world's finest DJs as special guests. The layout of the club is more open, which makes it easier than most places for meeting people. Carretera Escénica. ✆ **744/481-0330** or **446-5483.** www.palladium.com.mx. Cover $30 (£17) for women, $40 (£22) for men, includes open bar.

Pepe's Piano Bar   Pepe's has surely been one of the most famous piano bars in the hemisphere, although it appears those days may be numbered. It has inspired patrons of all ages to sing their hearts out for decades, and it still draws a crowd, though it now caters to karaoke instead of piano—a big mistake, in my opinion. I keep hoping the owners will come to their senses and return to their roots. It's open Wednesday to Sunday from 10pm to 4am. Carretera Escénica, Comercial La Vista, Loc. 10. ✆ **744/446-5736.**

Salon Q   This place bills itself as "the cathedral of salsa," and it's a fairly accurate claim—Salon Q is *the* place to get down and enjoy the Latin·rhythms. Frequently, management raises the cover and features impersonators of top Latin American musical acts. Open daily from 10pm to 4am. Costera Alemán 3117. ✆ **744/481-0114.** Cover $13–$25 (£7.15–£14).

3

Northward to Zihuatanejo & Ixtapa

Side-by-side beach resorts, Ixtapa and Zihuatanejo share geography, but they couldn't be more different in character. Ixtapa is a model of modern infrastructure, services, and luxury hotels, while Zihuatanejo—"Zihua" to the locals—is the quintessential Mexican beach village. For travelers, this offers the intriguing possibility of visiting two distinct destinations in one vacation. Those looking for luxury should opt for Ixtapa (eex-*tah*-pah). You can easily and quickly make the 6.5km (4-mile) trip into Zihuatanejo for a sampling of the simple life in a *pueblo* by the sea. Those who prefer a more rustic retreat with real personality should settle in Zihuatanejo (see-wah-tah-*neh*-hoh). It's known for its long-standing community of Swiss and Italian immigrants, and its legendary beach playboys.

The area, with a backdrop of the Sierra Madre and a foreground of Pacific Ocean waters, provides a full range of activities and diversions. Scuba diving, deep-sea fishing, bay cruises to remote beaches, and golf are among the favorites. Nightlife in both towns borders on subdued; Ixtapa is the livelier.

This dual destination is the choice for the traveler looking for a little of everything, from resort-style indulgence to unpretentious simplicity. These two resorts are more welcoming to couples and adults than families, with a number of places that are off-limits to children younger than 16—something of a rarity in Mexico.

1 Essentials

576km (357 miles) SW of Mexico City; 565km (350 miles) SE of Manzanillo; 253km (157 miles) NW of Acapulco

GETTING THERE & DEPARTING

BY PLANE These destinations tend to be even more seasonal than most resorts in Mexico. Flights are available year-round from U.S. gateways, but they operate less frequently in the summer. **AeroMexico, Click Mexicana,** and **Interjet** fly daily from Mexico

Zihuatanejo & Ixtapa Area

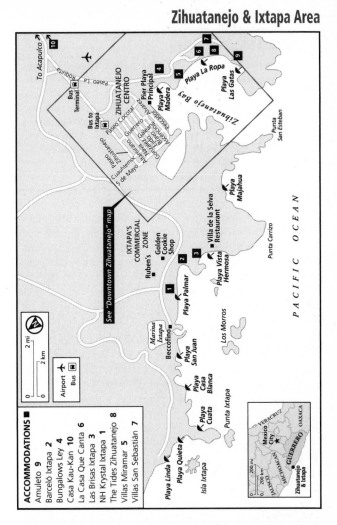

ACCOMMODATIONS ■

Amuleto **9**
Barceló Ixtapa **2**
Bungalows Ley **4**
Casa Kau-Kan **10**
La Casa Que Canta **6**
Las Brisas Ixtapa **3**
NH Krystal Ixtapa **1**
The Tides Zihuatanejo **8**
Villas Miramar **5**
Villas San Sebastián **7**

City. Here are the local numbers of some carriers: **AeroMexico** (© 755/554-2018 or -2019), **Alaska Airlines** (© 755/554-8457), **Continental** (© 755/554-4219), **Click Mexicana** (© 01-800/112-5425 toll-free in Mexico), **Interjet** (© 01-800/011-2345 toll-free in Mexico), and **US Airways** (© 755/554-8634). Ask your travel agent about **charter flights** and packages.

The **Ixtapa/Zihuatanejo airport** (© **755/554-2070**) is about 11km (7 miles) and 15 minutes south of Zihuatanejo. Taxi fares are

---

Tips **Motorist Advisory**

Motorists planning to follow Highway 200 northwest up the coast from Íxtapa or Zihuatanejo toward Lázaro Cárdenas and Manzanillo should be aware of reports of car and bus hijackings on that route, especially around Playa Azul, with bus holdups more common than car holdups. Before heading in that direction, ask locals and the tourism office about the status of the route. Don't drive at night. According to tourism officials, police and military patrols of the highway have increased, and the number of incidents has dropped dramatically.

---

about $28 (£15). **Transportes Terrestres** *colectivos* (minivans) transport travelers to hotels in Zihuatanejo and Íxtapa and to Club Med; tickets cost $8 to $10 (£4.40–£5.50) and can be purchased just outside the baggage-claim area. Car-rental agencies with booths in the airport include **Hertz** (© 800/654-3131 in the U.S., or 755/554-2952), and **Budget** (© 800/527-0700 in the U.S., or 755/553-0397).

BY CAR   From Mexico City (about 8–9 hr.), you can take **Highway 15** to Toluca, then **Highway 130/134** the rest of the way. On the latter road, highway gas stations are few. Another route is the four-lane **Highway 95D** to Iguala, then **Highway 51** west to **Highway 134.** A new toll road, **Highway 37** from Morelia to Íxtapa, cuts about an hour off the total trip time.

From Acapulco (2½–3 hr.) or Manzanillo (11 hr.), the only choice is the coastal **Highway 200.** The ocean views along the winding, mountain-edged drive from Manzanillo can be spectacular.

BY BUS   Zihuatanejo has two bus terminals: the **Central de Autobuses Estrella Blanca** (© 755/554-3477), Paseo Zihuatanejo at Paseo la Boquita, opposite the Pemex station and IMSS Hospital, from which most lines operate, and the **Estrella de Oro** station (© 755/554-2175), a block away. At the Central de Autobuses, several companies offer daily service to and from Acapulco, Puerto Escondido, Huatulco, Manzanillo, Puerto Vallarta, and other cities. At the other station, first-class Estrella de Oro buses run daily to Acapulco.

The trip from Mexico City to Zihuatanejo (bypassing Acapulco) takes 9 hours; from Acapulco, it's 4 to 5 hours. From Zihuatanejo, it's 6 or 7 hours to Manzanillo, and it's an additional 6 hours to Puerto Vallarta.

VISITOR INFORMATION

The **State Tourism Office** (©/fax **755/544-8361**) is in the center of Zihuatanejo on Galo 1, next to Plaza Kyoto; it's open Monday through Friday from 8am to 6pm and Saturday from 9am to 2pm. The **Zihuatanejo Tourism Office** (© **755/554-2001;** www.ixtapa-zihuatanejo.com) is on the main square by the basketball court at Alvarez; it's open Monday through Friday from 9am to 4pm and serves basic tourist-information purposes. The **Convention and Visitor's Bureau** is another source of information; it's in Ixtapa at Paseo de Las Gaviotas 12 (© **755/553-1270;** www.ixtapa-zihuatanejo.org).

CITY LAYOUT

The fishing village and resort of **Zihuatanejo** spreads out around the beautiful Bay of Zihuatanejo, framed by downtown to the north and a beautiful long beach and the Sierra foothills to the east. The heart of Zihuatanejo is the waterfront walkway **Paseo del Pescador** (also called the *malecón*), bordering the Municipal Beach. Rather than a plaza, as in most Mexican villages, the town centerpiece is a **basketball court,** which fronts the beach. It's a point of reference for directions. The main thoroughfare for cars is **Juan Alvarez,** a block behind the *malecón.* Sections of several of the main streets are designated *zona peatonal* (pedestrian zone).

A cement-and-sand walkway runs from the *malecón* in downtown Zihuatanejo along the water to **Playa Madera.** The walkway is lit at night. Access to Playa La Ropa (Clothing Beach) is by the main road, **Camino a Playa La Ropa.** Playa La Ropa and Playa Las Gatas (Cats Beach) are connected only by boat.

A good highway connects Zihua to **Ixtapa,** 6km (4 miles) north-west. The 18-hole **Ixtapa Golf Club** marks the beginning of the inland side of Ixtapa. Tall hotels line Ixtapa's wide beach, **Playa Palmar,** against a backdrop of lush palm groves and mountains. Access is by the main street, **Bulevar Ixtapa.** On the opposite side of the main boulevard lies a large expanse of small shopping plazas (many with air-conditioned shops) and restaurants. At the far end of Bulevar Ixtapa, **Marina Ixtapa** has excellent restaurants, private yacht slips, and an 18-hole golf course. Condominiums and private homes surround the marina and golf course, and additional exclusive residential areas are rising in the hillsides past the marina on the road to Playa Quieta and Playa Linda. Ixtapa also has a paved bicycle track that begins at the marina and continues around the golf course and on toward Playa Linda.

GETTING AROUND

Taxi fares are reasonable, but from midnight to 5am, rates increase by 50%. The average fare between Ixtapa and Zihuatanejo is $5.50 (£3). Within Zihua, the fare runs about $3 (£1.65); within Ixtapa it averages $3 to $5 (£1.65–£2.75). Radio cabs are available by calling © **755/554-3680** or -3311; however, taxis are available from most hotels. A **shuttle bus** (35¢/20p) runs between Zihuatanejo and Ixtapa every 15 or 20 minutes from 5am to 11pm daily, but it is almost always very crowded with commuting workers. In Zihuatanejo, it stops near the corner of Morelos/Paseo Zihuatanejo and Juárez, about 3 blocks north of the market. In Ixtapa, it makes numerous stops along Bulevar Ixtapa.

Note: The road from Zihuatanejo to Ixtapa is a broad, four-lane highway, which makes driving between the towns easier and faster than ever. Street signs are becoming more common in Zihuatanejo, and good signs lead in and out of both towns. However, both locations have an area called the Zona Hotelera (Hotel Zone), so if you're trying to reach Ixtapa's Hotel Zone, signs in Zihuatanejo pointing to that village's Hotel Zone may be confusing.

FAST FACTS: Zihuatanejo & Ixtapa

American Express The main office is in Av. Colegio Heróico Militar 38 in Plaza San Rafael, Loc. 7, Centro (© **755/544-6242;** fax 755/544-6242). It's open Monday through Friday from 9am to 6pm.

Area Code The telephone area code is **755.**

Banks Ixtapa's banks include **Bancomer,** in the La Puerta Centro shopping center. The most centrally located of Zihuatanejo's banks is **Banamex,** Cuauhtémoc 4. Banks change money during normal business hours, which are generally Monday through Friday from 9am to 3 or 5pm, Saturday from 10am to 1pm. ATMs and currency exchange are available during these and other hours.

Climate Summer is hot and humid, though tempered by sea breezes and brief showers; September is the peak of the tropical rainy season, with showers concentrated in the late afternoons.

Drugstore There's a branch of **Farmacías Coyuca** in Zihu-atanejo, open from 8am to 11pm—hours that will also deliver; call (✆ **755/554-5390**.

Hospital **Hospital de la Marina Ixtapa** is at Bulevar Ixtapa s/n, in back of the artisans' market (✆ **755/553-0499**). In Zihuatanejo, there's the **Clínica Maciel** (✆ **755/554-2380**; La Palmas 12), or **Hospital Hernández Montejano,** Juan Alvarez s/n (✆ **755/554-5404**). Dial (✆ **065** from any phone for emergencies.

Internet Access Ixtapa has many Internet cafes. **Comunicación Mundial** is in Local 105 (✆ **755/553-1177**). Go to the back of the shopping center and take the stairs to the second level; Comunicación Mundial is to your right. The cost of Internet access is $3 (£1.65) per hour. Access is cheaper in Zihuatanejo; the most popular Internet cafe is **Zihuatanejo Bar Net,** Agustín Ramírez 9, on the ground floor of the Hotel Zihuatanejo Centro (✆ **755/554-3661**). Offering high-speed access for $2 (£1.10) per hour, it's open from 9am to 11pm daily.

Post Office The *correo* is in the SCT building, Edificio SCT, behind El Cacahuate in Zihuatanejo (✆ **755/554-2192**). It's open Monday through Friday from 8am to 6pm, Saturday from 9am to 1pm.

2 Where to Stay

Larger high-rise hotels, including many all-inclusive resorts, dominate accommodations in Ixtapa and on Playa Madera. There are only a few choices in the budget range. If you're looking for lower-priced rooms, Zihuatanejo offers more selection and better values. Many long-term guests in Ixtapa and Zihuatanejo rent apartments and condos. **Lilia Valle** (✆ **755/554-2084** or -4649) is an excellent source for apartment and villa rentals. All lodgings in both towns offer free parking. The rates quoted below do not include the 17% tax.

ZIHUATANEJO

Some of the hotels in Zihuatanejo and its nearby beach communities are more economical than those in Ixtapa, while others are far more expensive and exclusive. The term "bungalow" is used loosely—it may mean an individual unit with a kitchen and bedroom, or just a bedroom. It may also be like a hotel, in a two-story building with multiple units, some of which have kitchens. It may be cozy or rustic, with or without a patio or balcony. Accommodations in town are generally very basic, though clean and comfortable.

Playa Madera and Playa La Ropa, separated by a craggy shoreline, are both accessible by road. Prices tend to be higher here than in town, but the value is much better, and people tend to find that the beautiful, tranquil setting is worth the extra cost. The town is 5 minutes away by taxi and 20 minutes by foot.

IN TOWN

Apartamentos Amueblados Valle   These well-furnished apartments cost only as much as an inexpensive hotel room. Five one-bedroom units accommodate up to three people; the three two-bedroom apartments fit four comfortably. Units that do not face the street are less noisy than those that do. Each airy apartment is different; all have ceiling fans, private balconies, and kitchenettes. There's daily maid service, and a paperback-book exchange in the office. Owner Guadalupe Rodríguez and her son Luis Valle are good sources of information about cheaper apartments elsewhere, for long-term visitors. Reserve well in advance during high season. It's about 2 blocks from the waterfront.

Vicente Guerrero 33 (between Ejido and N. Bravo), 40880 Zihuatanejo, Gro. Ⓒ **755/554-2084.** Fax 755/554-3220. 8 units. High season $60 (£33) 1-bedroom apt, $90 (£50) 2-bedroom apt; low season $45 (£25) 1-bedroom apt, $80 (£44) 2-bedroom apt. Ask about low-season and long-term discounts. No credit cards. *In room:* Kitchenette, fan.

Posada Citlali   In this cheerful, three-story hotel, small rooms with fans surround a shaded, plant-filled courtyard that holds comfortable rockers and chairs. It's a good value for the price. Bottled water is in help-yourself containers on the patio. The stairway to the top two floors is narrow and steep.

Vicente Guerrero 3 (near Alvarez), 40880 Zihuatanejo, Gro. Ⓒ **755/554-2043.** 19 units. $50 (£28) double. No credit cards. *In room:* No phone.

PLAYA MADERA

Madera Beach is a 15-minute walk along the street, a 10-minute walk along the beach pathway, or a cheap taxi ride from Zihuatanejo. Most of the accommodations are on Calle Eva S. de López Mateos, the road overlooking the beach. Most hotels are set against the hill and have steep stairways.

Bungalows Ley   No two suites are the same at this small complex, one of the nicest on Playa Madera. If you're traveling with a group, you may want to book the most expensive suite (Club

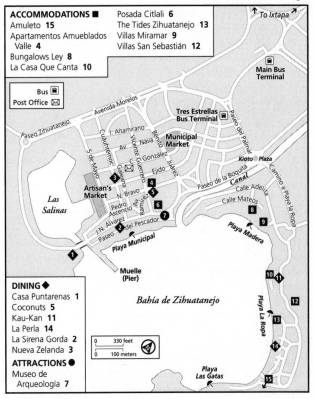

ACCOMMODATIONS ■
Amuleto **15**
Apartamentos Amueblados
Valle **4**
Bungalows Ley **8**
La Casa Que Canta **10**

Posada Citlali **6**
The Tides Zihuatanejo **13**
Villas Miramar **9**
Villas San Sebastián **12**

↑ To Ixtapa ↗

Bus 🚌
Post Office ✉

Main Bus
Terminal

Avenida Morelos

Paseo Zihuatanejo

5 de Mayo

Cuauhtémoc

I. Altamirano

Av. Vicente Nava

Benito Juárez

C. González

Ejido

Galeana

N. Bravo

Pedro
Ascencio

Álvarez

J.N. Álvarez

Paseo del Pescador

Tres Estrellas
Bus Terminal

Paseo del Palmar

Municipal
Market

Kioto Plaza

Paseo de la Boquita

Camino a Playa la Ropa

Canal

Calle Adelia

Calle Mateos

Artisan's
Market

Las
Salinas

Playa Municipal

Playa Madera

Playa La Ropa

Muelle
(Pier)

Bahía de Zihuatanejo

0   330 feet
0   100 meters

DINING ◆
Casa Puntarenas **1**
Coconuts **5**
Kau-Kan **11**
La Perla **14**
La Sirena Gorda **2**
Nueva Zelanda **3**
ATTRACTIONS ●
Museo de
Arqueología **7**

*Playa
Las Gatas*

Madera); it has a rooftop terrace with a tiled hot tub, outdoor bar and grill, and spectacular view. All the units are immaculate; the simplest are studios with one bed and a kitchen in the same room. Rooms have terraces or balconies just above the beach, and all are decorated in Miami Beach colors. Bathrooms, however, tend to be small and dark. Guests praise the management and the service.

Calle Eva S. de López Mateos s/n, Playa Madera (Apdo. Postal 466), 40880 Zihuatanejo, Gro. ✆ **755/554-4087.** Fax 755/554-1365. www.zihua.net/bungalosley. 8 units. $90 (£50) double with A/C; $170 (£94) 2-bedroom suite with kitchen (up to 4 persons). Low-season discounts available after 6 nights stay. No credit cards. Follow Mateos to the right up a slight hill; it's on your left. *In room:* A/C, TV.

Villas Miramar ✿   This charming hotel with beautiful gardens offers a welcoming atmosphere, attention to detail, and superb cleanliness. Some of the elegant suites surround a shady patio that doubles as a restaurant. Those across the street center on a lovely pool and have private balconies and sea views. A terrace with a bay view has a bar that features a daily happy hour (5–7pm). TVs get cable channels, and the restaurant serves a basic menu for breakfast, lunch, and dinner.

Calle Adelita, Lote 78, Playa Madera (Apdo. Postal 211), 40880 Zihuatanejo, Gro. ⓒ **755/554-2106** or -3350. Fax 755/554-2149. www.prodigyweb.net.mx/villas miramar. 18 units. High season $95 (£52) suite, $100 (£55) oceanview suite, $190 (£105) 2-bedroom suite; low season $65 (£36) suite, $75 (£41) oceanview suite, $150 (£83) 2-bedroom suite. AE, MC, V. Free enclosed parking. Follow the road leading south out of town toward Playa La Ropa; take the 1st right after the traffic circle, and go left on Adelita. **Amenities:** Restaurant; bar; outdoor pool. *In room:* A/C, TV.

PLAYA LA ROPA

Playa La Ropa is a 20- to 25-minute walk south of town on the east side of the bay, or it's a $3 (£1.65) taxi ride.

Amuleto 𝕲𝕲   Perched on a hill high above the beach, this intimate boutique hotel was designed for people who want to relax in luxury and exclusivity. Amuleto, which has only six units, boasts stunning panoramic views of Zihuatanejo Bay that make it seem like you're on top of the world. The *palapa*-covered restaurant serves innovative international food and overlooks a small infinity pool framed by the bay. Each of the bungalowlike units is individually decorated with Mexican and Asian designs using organic textures and earth colors. The *palapa* suite, for example, features meticulous stone, tile, and woodwork, a bed with 1,000-thread-count Egyptian cotton sheets, a separate sitting area with onyx lamps and bamboo chairs, a rooftop terrace with its own hammock surrounded by bougainvillea, and a private plunge pool. The eco-friendly hotel offers gourmet breakfasts and will customize dishes upon request.

Calle Escénica 9, Playa La Ropa, 40880 Zihuatanejo, Gro. ⓒ **213/280-1037** in the U.S., or 755/544-6222. Fax 310/496-0286 in the U.S. www.amuleto.net. 6 units. High season $400–$700 (£220–£385) double; low season $250–$550 (£138–£303) double. $100 (£55) extra person. AE, MC, V. **Amenities:** Restaurant; outdoor pool, gym, massage. *In room:* A/C, Wi-Fi, minibar.

La Casa Que Canta 𝕲𝕲𝕲   "The House that Sings" opened in 1992, an exclusive boutique hotel that sits on a mountainside overlooking Zihuatanejo Bay. Its striking molded-adobe architecture typifies the rustic-chic style known as Mexican Pacific, with gentle music that plays across the different walkways. Individually decorated rooms have handsome natural-tile floors, unusual painted

Michoacán furniture, antiques, and stretched-leather *equipale*-style chairs and tables with hand-loomed fabrics throughout. All of the romantic accommodations offer large, beautifully furnished terraces with bay views. Hammocks hang under the thatched-roof terraces. Most of the spacious units are suites, and 10 of them have private pools. Rooms meander up and down the hillside, and while no staircase is terribly long, there are no elevators. An adjacent private villa, El Murmello, holds four suites, all with private plunge pools. A "well-being" center has been added, offering massage, spa services, and yoga. La Casa Que Canta sits off the road leading to Playa La Ropa, but not on any beach (Playa La Ropa is down a steep hill). The hotel's service is remarkably gracious, and you'll find La Casa Que Canta pretty close to heaven.

Camino Escénico a Playa La Ropa, 40880 Zihuatanejo, Gro. © **888/523-5050** in the U.S., or 755/555-7000, -7030, or 554-6529. Fax 755/554-7900. www.lacasaque canta.com. 21 units. $435–$785 (£239–£432) double; 5-night minimum stay required Jan–Apr. AE, MC, V. Children younger than 16 not accepted. **Amenities:** Small restaurant; bar; freshwater outdoor pool on main terrace; saltwater outdoor pool on bottom level; room service; laundry service. *In room:* A/C, minibar.

The Tides Zihuatanejo 🐟🐟🐟

A magnificent and timeless resort that caters to guests looking for exclusivity, The Tides Zihuatanejo sits on one of Mexico's most beautiful beaches. Suites feature one or two bedrooms, living areas, large terraces, and private plunge pools. Rooms are decorated with modern Mexican touches and include comfy lounges, excellent reading lights, CD players, and hammocks that beckon at siesta time. There are 11 beachside suites and one presidential suite. Those units that don't overlook the beach surround a fountain-filled lagoon and tropical gardens with enchanted lighting at night. Service is refined and gracious; fresh flower petals are artistically arranged on guest beds in the evenings. A member of the Small Luxury Hotels of the World, The Tides Zihuatanejo allows children only in two-bedroom suites and generally has a quiet feel. The meal plan (breakfast and dinner) is mandatory during the winter high season and includes an excellent variety of cuisine. In addition to the exquisite beach area, pools, restaurants, and bars, The Tides Zihuatanejo offers a full-service spa, tennis courts, and beach club. You can even request a massage on the sand.

Playa la Ropa (Apdo. Postal 84), 40880 Zihuatanejo, Gro. © **888/389-2645** in the U.S., or 755/555-5500. Fax 755/554-2758. www.hotelvilladelsol.com. 70 units. High season $365–$1,400 (£201–£770) double; low season $300–$1,100 (£165–£605) double. Meal plan $60 (£33) per person during high season (mandatory), or $45

(£25) during summer (optional). AE, MC, V. **Amenities:** 2 open-air beachside restaurants; 3 bars; 3 outdoor pools (including 18m/59-ft. lap pool); 2 tennis courts; full-service spa; tour desk; car rental; salon; room service. *In room:* A/C, TV, Wi-Fi, minibar, hair dryer, safe.

Villas San Sebastián   On the mountainside above Playa La Ropa, this nine-villa complex offers great views of Zihuatanejo's bay. The villas surround tropical vegetation and a central swimming pool. Each has a kitchenette and a spacious private terrace, and some have air-conditioning. The personalized service is one reason these villas come so highly recommended; owner Luis Valle, whose family has lived in this community for decades, is always available to help guests with any questions or needs.

Bulevar Escénico Playa La Ropa (across from the Dolphins Fountain). ✆ **755/554-4154.** Fax 755/554-3220. 11 units. High season $155 (£85) 1-bedroom villa; $275 (£151) 2-bedroom villa; low season $115 (£63) 1-bedroom villa, $165 (£91) 2-bedroom villa. No credit cards. **Amenities:** Outdoor pool. *In room:* A/C (some units); kitchenette.

PLAYA ZIHUATANEJO
Casa Kau-Kan 🐟🐟   Casa Kau-Kan is an upscale bohemian oasis on the long, secluded beach of Playa Larga. It's located about 20-minutes south of Zihuatanejo on the open Pacific Ocean. The spacious bungalow-like accommodations surrounded by palm trees feature private sitting areas, canopied beds, and bamboo furnishings; four have private terrace pools. Owned by Ricardo Rodriguez who also runs Kau-Kan restaurant (p. 94), the hotel serves delicious fresh seafood. There's not much to do in the immediate surroundings except tan, swim, eat, read, and enjoy the quiet lazy days, although horseback riding is also offered on the beach immediately in front. You should be an experienced swimmer to go in the ocean here, which typically has waves perfect for bodysurfing. Hotel service is friendly and extremely attentive(whether it's a coconut or a cocktail you desire, it'll be right up.

Playa Larga s/n, 40880 Zihuatanejo, Gro. ✆ **755/113-1379.** Fax 755/553-8168. www.casakaukan.com. 9 units. High season $120–$235 (£66–£129) double; low season $90–$200 (£50–£110) double. AE, MC, V. Children younger than 15 not accepted. **Amenities:** Restaurant; pool. *In room:* A/C.

IXTAPA
EXPENSIVE
Barceló Ixtapa 🐟 *Kids*   This grand 12-story all-inclusive resort hotel (formerly the Sheraton) has large, handsomely furnished public areas facing the beach; it's an inviting place to sip a drink and

people-watch. Most rooms have balconies with views of the ocean or the mountains. Nonsmoking rooms are available. Gardens surround the large pool, which has a swim-up bar and a separate section for children. It's an excellent value and a great choice for families.

Bulevar Ixtapa, 40880 Ixtapa, Gro. ⓒ **755/555-2000.** Fax 755/553-2438. www. barcelo.com. 341 units. High season $380 (£209) double all-inclusive; low season $275 (£151) double all-inclusive. AE, DC, MC, V. **Amenities:** 4 restaurants; lobby bar; nightclub; beachside pool; 3 tennis courts; fitness room; concierge; travel agency; car rental; salon; room service; laundry service; rooms for those w/limited mobility. *In room:* A/C, TV, minibar.

Las Brisas Ixtapa 𝕽𝕽 Set above the high-rise hotels of Ixtapa on a rocky promontory, Las Brisas is the best of Ixtapa's resorts. Notable for its striking stepped architecture, beautiful beach cove, and gracious service, Las Brisas features large stone and stucco public areas, minimalist guest rooms with Mexican-tile floors and plant-decked patios with hammocks, and multitier swimming pools with waterfalls. All rooms face the hotel's gorgeous private beach, which can be accessed by an elevator; although enticing, the water is often rough and can be dangerous for swimming. The six master suites come with private pools, and the 16th floor is reserved for nonsmokers. The hotel could use an upgrade but remains the best option in Ixtapa. Internet specials are usually available.

Bulevar Ixtapa s/n, 40880 Ixtapa, Gro. ⓒ **888/559-4329** in the U.S., or 755/553-2121. Fax 755/553-1091. www.brisas.com.mx. 423 units. High season $285 (£157) deluxe double, $490 (£270) Royal Beach Club; low season $196 (£108) deluxe double, $230 (£127) Royal Beach Club. AE, MC, V. **Amenities:** 4 restaurants; 3 bars (including lobby bar w/live music at sunset); 4 outdoor pools (1 for children); 4 lighted tennis courts w/pro on request; fitness center; travel agency; car rental; shopping arcade; salon; room service; massage; babysitting; laundry service; elevator to secluded beach; rooms for those w/limited mobility. *In room:* A/C, TV, minibar, hair dryer, safe.

NH Krystal Ixtapa 𝕽 (Kids) Krystal hotels are known in Mexico for quality rooms and service, and this was the original hotel in the chain. It upholds its reputation for attentive service and is particularly welcoming toward families. Many staff members have been with the NH Krystal for its 20-some years of operation and are on hand to greet return guests. This large, V-shaped hotel has ample grounds and a terrific pool area. Most of the spacious guest rooms feature oceanview balconies and tile bathrooms, while master suites have larger balconies that double as living areas. Some rates include breakfast buffet. The center of Ixtapa nightlife is here, at Krystal's famed **Christine** dance club.

Bulevar Ixtapa s/n, 40880 Ixtapa, Gro. (C) **888/726-0528** in the U.S., or 755/553-0333. Fax 755/553-0216. www.nh-hotels.com. 255 units. High season $224 (£123) double, $280 (£154) suite; low season $150 (£83) double, $230 (£127) suite. 2 children younger than 12 stay free in parent's room. Ask about special packages. AE, DC, MC, V. **Amenities:** 4 restaurants; lobby bar; nightclub; outdoor pool; gym; kids' club; travel agency; car rental; salon; room service; massage; laundry service. *In room:* A/C, TV, minibar.

3 Where to Dine

ZIHUATANEJO

Zihuatanejo's **central market,** on Avenida Benito Juárez about 5 blocks inland from the waterfront, will whet your appetite for cheap and tasty food. It's best at breakfast and lunch, before the market activity winds down in the afternoon. Look for what's hot and fresh. The market area is one of the best on this coast for shopping and people-watching.

EXPENSIVE

Coconuts ★★ *Finds* INTERNATIONAL/SEAFOOD What a find! Not only is the food innovative and delicious, but the restaurant is also in a historic building—the oldest in Zihuatanejo. This popular restaurant in a tropical garden was the weigh-in station for Zihua's coconut industry in the late 1800s. "Fresh" is the operative word on this creative, seafood-heavy menu. Chef David Dawson checks what's fresh at the market, then uses only top-quality ingredients in dishes like seafood pâté and grilled filet of snapper Coconuts. The bananas flambé (for two) has earned a loyal following, with good reason. Expect friendly, efficient service here.

Augustín Ramírez 1 (at Vicente Guerrero). (C) **755/554-2518** or -7980. Reservations recommended. Main courses $12–$28 (£6.60–£15). AE, MC, V. High season daily 6–11pm. Closed July–Sept (rainy season).

Kau-Kan ★★★ NUEVA COCINA/SEAFOOD A stunning view of the bay is one of the many attractions of this beautiful restaurant. Stucco and whitewashed walls frame the simple, understated furniture. Head chef Ricardo Rodriguez supervises every detail, from the ultrasmooth background music that invites after-dinner conversation to the spectacular presentation of all the dishes. Baked potato with baby lobster and mahimahi carpaccio are two of my favorites, but I recommend you consider the daily specials—

Ricardo always uses the freshest seafood and prepares it with great care. For dessert, pecan and chocolate cake served with dark-chocolate sauce is simply delicious. If you're looking for a romantic dinner outside your hotel, reserve a candlelit table at Kau-Kan and try to arrive in time for the sunset.

Camino a Playa La Ropa. ☎ **755/554-8446.** Reservations recommended. Main courses $10–$34 (£5.50–£19). AE, MC, V. Daily 5–10:30pm. From downtown on the road to La Ropa, Kau-Kan is on the right side of the road past the 1st curve.

INEXPENSIVE

Casa Puntarenas MEXICAN/SEAFOOD   A modest spot with a tin roof and nine wooden tables, Puntarenas is one of the best places in town for fried whole fish served with toasted *bolillos* (crusty white-bread miniloaves), sliced tomatoes, onions, and avocado. The place is renowned for *chiles rellenos,* mild and stuffed with plenty of cheese; the meat dishes are less flavorful. Although it may appear a little too rustic for less-experienced travelers, it is very clean, and the food is known for its freshness.

Calle Noria, Col. Lázaro Cárdenas. No phone. Main courses $5–$10 (£2.75–£5.50). No credit cards. Daily 6:30–9pm. From the pier, turn left on Alvarez and cross the footbridge on your left; turn right after you cross the bridge; the restaurant is on your left.

La Sirena Gorda MEXICAN   For one of the most popular breakfasts in town, head to La Sirena Gorda. "The Fat Mermaid," as it translates to in English, serves a variety of eggs and omelets, hotcakes with bacon, and fruit with granola and yogurt. The house specialty is seafood tacos—fish in a variety of sauces, plus lobster—but I consider them overpriced, at $6 (£3.30) and $23 (£13), respectively. A taco is a taco is a . . . you know. I'd recommend something from the short list of daily specials, such as blackened red snapper, steak, or fish kabobs. The food is excellent, and patrons enjoy the casual sidewalk-cafe atmosphere. Illustrations of colorful fat mermaids decorate the walls.

Paseo del Pescador. ☎ **755/554-2687.** Breakfast $2–$5.50 (£1.10–£3); main courses $6–$15 (£3.30–£8.25). MC, V. Thurs–Tues 8am–10:30pm. From the basketball court, face the water and walk to the right; La Sirena Gorda is on your right just before the town pier.

Nueva Zelanda MEXICAN   This open-air snack shop serves rich cappuccino sprinkled with cinnamon, fresh-fruit *licuados* (milkshakes), and pancakes with real maple syrup. The mainstays of the menu are *tortas* and enchiladas, and service is friendly and efficient.

There's a second location in Ixtapa, in the back section of the Los Patios shopping center (© **755/553-0838**).

Cuauhtémoc 23 (at Ejido). © **755/554-2340**. *Tortas* $3.50 (£1.90); enchiladas $6 (£3.30); *licuados* $2.50 (£1.40); cappuccino $2.50 (£1.40). No credit cards. Daily 8am–10pm. From the waterfront, walk 3 blocks inland on Cuauhtémoc; the restaurant is on your right.

PLAYA MADERA & PLAYA LA ROPA

La Perla SEAFOOD   There are many *palapa*-style restaurants on Playa La Ropa, but La Perla, with tables under the trees and thatched roof, is the most popular. Somehow, the long stretch of pale sand and the group of wooden chairs under *palapas* combine with mediocre food and slow service to make La Perla a local tradition. Rumor has it that it is so hard to get the waiters' attention that you can get takeout food from a competitor and bring it here to eat, and they'll never notice. Still, it's considered the best spot for tanning and socializing.

Playa La Ropa. © **755/554-2700**. Breakfast $4–$6.50 (£2.20–£3.60); main courses $7.50–$24 (£4.15–£13). AE, MC, V. Daily 10am–10pm; breakfast served 10am–noon. Near the southern end of La Ropa Beach, take the right fork in the road; there's a sign in the parking lot.

IXTAPA
VERY EXPENSIVE

Villa de la Selva ✿ MEXICAN/MEDITERRANEAN   Clinging to the edge of a cliff overlooking the sea, this elegant, romantic restaurant enjoys the most spectacular sea and sunset view in Ixtapa. The candlelit tables occupy three terraces; try to come early to get one of the best vistas, especially on the lower terrace. The cuisine is delicious, artfully presented, and classically rich. Filet Villa de la Selva is red snapper topped with shrimp and hollandaise sauce. Tortilla soup or hot lobster bisque makes a good beginning; finish with chocolate mousse or bananas Singapore.

Paseo de la Roca. © **755/553-0362**. www.villadelaselva.com. Reservations recommended during high season. Main courses $19–$40 (£10–£22). AE, MC, V. Daily 6–11pm. Closed Sept.

EXPENSIVE

Beccofino ✿✿✿ NORTHERN ITALIAN   This restaurant is a standout in Mexico. Owner Angelo Rolly Pavia serves the flavorful northern Italian specialties he grew up knowing and loving. The menu is strong on pasta. Ravioli, a house specialty, comes stuffed with seafood (in season). The garlic bread is terrific, and there's an extensive wine list. A popular place in a breezy marina location, the restaurant tends to be loud when it's crowded, which is often. It's also an increasingly popular breakfast spot.

Marina Ixtapa. ⓒ **755/553-1770.** Breakfast $4.50–$10 (£2.50–£5.50); main courses $16–$48 (£8.80–£26). AE, MC, V. Daily 9:30am–midnight.

INEXPENSIVE

Golden Cookie Shop ⓕ PASTRIES/INTERNATIONAL Golden Cookie's freshly baked goods beg for a detour, and the coffee menu is the most extensive in town. Although prices are high for the area, the breakfasts are noteworthy, as are the deli sandwiches. Nutritional cookies, breads, pastries, and cakes are available, as well as vegetarian and low-carb selections. Large sandwiches on fresh soft bread come with a choice of sliced meats. An air-conditioned area is reserved for nonsmokers.

Los Patios Center. ⓒ **755/553-0310.** www.goldencookieshop.com.mx. Breakfast $4–$6 (£2.20–£3.30); sandwiches $4–$6 (£2.20–£3.30); main courses $6–$8.50 (£3.30–£4.70). MC, V. Daily 8am–2:30pm. Go to the second floor of "Los Patios" commercial center, turn left, and you'll see the restaurant on your right.

Ruben's ⓕⓕ *Finds* BURGERS/VEGETABLES The choices are easy here—you can order either a big, juicy burger made from top sirloin grilled over mesquite, or a foil-wrapped packet of baked potatoes, chayote, zucchini, or sweet corn. Ice cream, beer, and soda round out the menu, which is posted on the wall by the kitchen. It's kind of a do-it-yourself place: Patrons snare a waitress and order, grab their own drinks from the cooler, and tally their own tabs. Still, because of the ever-present crowds, it can be a slow process.

Centro Comercial Flamboyant. ⓒ **755/553-0027** or -0358. Burgers $4–$5 (£2.20–£2.75); vegetables $2 (£1.10); ice cream $1.50 (85p). No credit cards. Daily 11am–midnight.

4 Activities On & Off the Beach

The **Museo de Arqueología de la Costa Grande** (ⓒ **755/554-7552**) traces the history of the area from Acapulco to Ixtapa/Zihuatanejo (the Costa Grande) from pre-Hispanic times, when it was known as Cihuatlán, through the colonial era. Most of the museum's pottery and stone artifacts give evidence of extensive trade with far-off cultures and regions, including the Toltec and Teotihuacán near Mexico City, the Olmec on the Pacific and Gulf coasts, and areas known today as the states of Nayarit, Michoacán, and San Luis Potosí. Local indigenous groups gave the Aztec tribute items, including cotton *tilmas* (capes) and *cacao* (chocolate), representations of which can be seen here. This museum, in Zihuatanejo near Guerrero at the east end of Paseo del Pescador, easily merits the half-hour or less it takes to stroll through; signs are in Spanish, but an accompanying brochure is available in English. Admission is $1 (55p), and it's open Tuesday through Sunday from 10am to 6pm.

THE BEACHES

IN ZIHUATANEJO At Zihuatanejo's town beach, **Playa Municipal,** the local fishermen pull their colorful boats up onto the sand, making for a fine photo op. The small shops and restaurants lining the waterfront are great for people-watching and absorbing the flavor of daily village life. **Playa Madera (Wood Beach),** just east of Playa Municipal, is open to the surf but generally peaceful. A number of attractive budget lodgings overlook this area.

All beaches in Zihuatanejo are safe for swimming. Undertow is rarely a problem, and the municipal beach is protected from the main surge of the Pacific. Beaches in Ixtapa are more dangerous for swimming, with frequent undertow problems.

South of Playa Madera is Zihuatanejo's largest and most beautiful beach, **Playa La Ropa** ✿✿, a long sweep of sand with a great view of the sunset. Some lovely small hotels and restaurants nestle in the hills; palm groves edge the shoreline. Although it's also open to the Pacific, waves are usually gentle. A taxi from town costs $3.50 (£1.90). The name Playa La Ropa (Clothing Beach) comes from an old tale of the sinking of a *galeón* during a storm. The silk clothing that it was carrying back from the Philippines washed ashore on this beach—hence the name.

The nicest beach for swimming, and the best for children, is the secluded **Playa Las Gatas (Cats Beach),** across the bay from Playa La Ropa and Zihuatanejo. The small coral reef just offshore is a nice spot for snorkeling and diving, and a little dive shop on the beach rents gear. Shop owner Jean Claude is a local institution—and the only full-time resident of Las Gatas. He claims to offer special rates for female divers and has a collection of bikini tops on display. The waters at Las Gatas are exceptionally clear, without undertow or big waves. Open-air seafood restaurants on the beach make it an appealing lunch spot. Small *pangas* (boats) with shade run to Las Gatas from the Zihuatanejo town pier, a 10-minute trip; the captains will take you across whenever you wish between 9am and 5pm for $3 (£1.65) round-trip. Usually the last boat back leaves Las Gatas at 6:30pm, but check to be sure.

Playa Larga is a beautiful, uncrowded beach between Zihuatanejo and the airport, with several small *palapa* restaurants, hammocks, and wading pools.

IN IXTAPA   Ixtapa's main beach, **Playa Palmar,** is a lovely white-sand arc on the edge of the Hotel Zone, with dramatic rock formations silhouetted in the sea. The surf can be rough; use caution, and don't swim when a red flag is posted. Several of the nicest beaches in the area are essentially closed to the public. Although by law all Mexican beaches are open to the public, it is common practice for hotels to create artificial barriers (such as rocks or dunes).

Club Med and Qualton Club have largely claimed **Playa Quieta,** on the mainland across from Isla Ixtapa. The remaining piece of beach was once the launching point for boats to Isla Ixtapa, but it is gradually being taken over by a private development. Isla Ixtapa–bound boats now leave from the jetty on **Playa Linda,** about 13km (8 miles) north of Ixtapa. Inexpensive water taxis ferry passengers to Isla Ixtapa. Playa Linda is the primary out-of-town beach, with watersports equipment and horse rentals available. **Playa las Cuatas,** a pretty beach and cove a few miles north of Ixtapa, and **Playa Majahua,** an isolated beach just west of Zihuatanejo, are both being transformed into resort complexes. Lovely **Playa Vista Hermosa** is framed by striking rock formations and bordered by the Las Brisas hotel high on the hill. All of these are very attractive beaches for sunbathing or a stroll but have heavy surf and strong undertow. Use caution if you swim here.

WATERSPORTS & BOAT TRIPS

Probably the most popular boat trip is to **Isla Ixtapa** for snorkeling and lunch at the El Marlin restaurant, one of several on the island. You can book this outing as a tour through local travel agencies, or go on your own from Zihuatanejo by following the directions to Playa Linda above and taking a boat from there. Boats leave for Isla Ixtapa every 10 minutes between 9am and 5pm, so you can depart and return as you like. The round-trip boat ride is $3 (£1.65). Along the way, you'll pass dramatic rock formations and see in the distance **Los Morros de Los Pericos islands,** where a great variety of birds nest on the rocky points jutting out into the blue Pacific. On Isla Ixtapa, you'll find good snorkeling, diving, and other watersports. Gear is available for rent on the island. Be sure to catch the last water taxi back at 5pm, and double-check that time upon arrival on the island.

Local travel agencies can usually arrange day trips to Los Morros de Los Pericos islands for **birding,** though it's less expensive to rent a boat with a guide at Playa Linda. The islands are offshore from Ixtapa's main beach.

Sunset cruises on the sailboat *Picante,* arranged through **Yates del Sol** (© 755/554-2694 or -8270; www.picantecruises.com), depart from the Zihuatanejo town marina at Puerto Mío. The evening cruises cost $54 (£30) per person and include an open bar and hors d'oeuvres. There's also a "Sail and snorkel" day trip to **Playa Manzanillo** on the very comfortable, rarely crowded sailboat. It begins at 10am, costs $69 (£38) per person, and includes an open bar and lunch (snorkeling gear extra). Schedules and special trips vary, so call for current information.

You can arrange **fishing trips** with the **boat cooperative** (© 755/554-2056) at the Zihuatanejo town pier. They cost $150 to $450 (£83–£248), depending on boat size, trip length, and so on. Most trips last about 7 hours. The cooperative accepts Visa and Master-Card; paying cash saves you 20% tax, but don't expect a receipt. The price includes soft drinks, beer, bait, and fishing gear, but not lunch. You'll pay more for a trip arranged through a local travel agency. The least expensive trips are on small launches called *pangas;* most have shade. Both small-game and deep-sea fishing are offered. The fishing is adequate, though not on par with that of Mazatlán or Baja. Other trips combine fishing with a visit to the near-deserted ocean beaches that extend for miles along the coast. Sam Lushinsky at **Ixtapa Sportfishing Charters,** 19 Depue Lane, Stroudsburg, PA 18360 (© 570/688-9466; fax 570/688-9554; www.ixtapasportfishing.com), is a noted outfitter. Prices range from $295 to $445 (£162–£245) per day, for 8 to 13m (26–42 ft.) custom cruisers, fully equipped. They accept MasterCard and Visa.

Boating and fishing expeditions from the new **Marina Ixtapa,** a bit north of the Ixtapa Hotel Zone, can also be arranged. As a rule, everything available in or through the marina is more expensive and more Americanized.

Sailboats, sailboards, and other **watersports equipment** rentals are usually available at stands on Playa La Ropa, Playa Las Gatas, Isla Ixtapa, and at the main beach, Playa Palmar, in Ixtapa. There's **parasailing** at La Ropa and Palmar. **Kayaks** are available for rent at hotels in Ixtapa and some watersports operations on Playa La Ropa. **Villa del Sol** has a beach club in front of the hotel on La Ropa with sailboat, sailboard, and kayak rentals open to the public.

The PADI-certified **Carlo Scuba,** on Playa Las Gatas (© 755/554-6003; www.carloscuba.com), arranges **scuba-diving trips.** Fees start at $60 (£33) for a one-tank dive, or $80 (£44) for two dives, including all equipment and lunch. This shop has been around since 1962, and is very knowledgeable about the area, which has nearly 30 different dive sites, including walls and caves. Diving takes place year-round, though the water is clearest July to August and November to February, when visibility is 30m (100 ft.) or better. The nearest decompression chamber is in Acapulco. Advance reservations for dives are advised during Christmas and Easter.

Surfing is particularly good at **Petacalco Beach** north of Ixtapa.

GOLF, TENNIS & HORSEBACK RIDING

In **Ixtapa,** the **Club de Golf Ixtapa Palma Real** (© 755/553-1062 or -1163), in front of the Barceló Hotel, has an 18-hole course designed by Robert Trent Jones, Jr. The greens fee is $80 (£44); caddies cost $20 (£11) for 18 holes, $15 (£8.25) for 9 holes; electric carts are $25 (£14); and clubs are $30 (£17). Tee times begin at 6:30am. The **Marina Ixtapa Golf Course** (© 755/553-1410; fax 755/553-0825), designed by Robert von Hagge, has 18 challenging holes. The greens fee is $80 (£44); carts cost $35 (£19); caddies cost $20 (£11); club rental is $35 (£19). The first tee time is 7am. Call for reservations 24 hours in advance. Both courses accept American Express, MasterCard, and Visa.

In Ixtapa, the **Club de Golf Ixtapa** (© 755/553-1062 or -1163) has lighted **public tennis courts.** Fees are $8 (£4.40) an hour during the day, $13 (£7.15) at night. Call for reservations. In Zihuatanejo, the hotel **Villa del Sol** (© 755/555-5500) has lit tennis courts open to the public for $20 (£11) an hour; private lessons cost $70 (£39) an hour.

For **horseback riding,** the largest local stable is on **Playa Linda** (no phone), offering guided trail rides from the Playa Linda beach (about 13km/8 miles north of Ixtapa). It's just next to the pier where the water taxis debark to Isla Ixtapa. Groups of three or more riders can arrange their own tour, which is especially nice around sunset (though you'll need mosquito repellent). Riders can choose to trace the beach to the mouth of the river and back through coconut plantations, or hug the beach for the entire ride (which usually lasts 1–1½ hr.). The fee is around $40 (£22), cash only. Travel agencies in either town can arrange your trip but will charge a bit more for transportation. Reservations are suggested in high season. Another good place to ride is in Playa Larga. There is a ranch on the first exit coming from Zihuatanejo (no phone, but you can't miss it—it is the first corral to the right as you drive toward the beach). The horses are in excellent shape. The fee is $40 (£22) for 1½ hours. To arrange riding in advance, call co-owner Ignacio Mendiola on his cellphone at *C* **755/559-8884.**

5 Shopping

ZIHUATANEJO

Zihuatanejo has its quota of T-shirt and souvenir shops, but it's becoming a better place to buy crafts, folk art, and jewelry. Shops are generally open Monday through Saturday from 10am to 2pm and 4 to 8pm. Many better shops close Sunday, but some smaller souvenir stands stay open, and hours vary.

The **artisans' market** on Calle Cinco de Mayo is a good place to start shopping before moving on to specialty shops. There's also a **municipal market** on Avenida Benito Juárez (about 5 blocks inland from the waterfront), but most vendors offer the same things—*huaraches,* hammocks, and baskets. The market sprawls over several blocks. Spreading inland from the waterfront some 3 or 4 blocks are numerous small shops well worth exploring.

Besides the places listed below, check out **Alberto's,** Cuauhtémoc 12 and 15 (no phone), for jewelry. Also on Cuauhtémoc, 2 blocks down from the Nueva Zelanda Coffee Shop, is a small shop that looks like a market stand and sells beautiful tablecloths, napkins, and other linens; all are handmade in Aguascalientes.

Casa Marina   This small complex extends from the waterfront to Alvarez near Cinco de Mayo and houses five shops, each specializing in handcrafted wares from all over Mexico. Items include handsome rugs, textiles, masks, colorful woodcarvings, and silver jewelry. Café Marina, the small coffee shop in the complex, sells shelves and shelves of used paperback books in several languages. Open daily from 9am to 9pm during the high season, 9am to 2pm and 5 to 9pm the rest of the year.

Coco Cabaña Collectibles   Next to Coconuts restaurant (p. 94), this impressive shop carries carefully selected crafts and folk art from across the country, including fine Oaxacan woodcarvings. Owner Pat Cummings once ran a gallery in New York, and the inventory reveals her discriminating eye. If you make a purchase, she'll cash your dollars at the going rate. Open Monday through Saturday from 10am to 2pm and 5 to 9pm, closed August and September.

Viva Zapatos   This shop carries bathing suits for every taste and shape, great casual and not-so-casual resort wear, sunglasses, and everything else for looking good in and out of the water. The store is 3 doors down from Apartamentos Amueblados Valle (p. 88). It's open Monday through Saturday from 10am to 2pm and 5 to 9pm.

IXTAPA

Shopping in Ixtapa is not especially memorable, with T-shirts and Mexican crafts the usual wares. **Ferrioni, Bye-Bye, Aca Joe,** and **Navale** sell brand-name sportswear. All of these shops are in the same area on Bulevar Ixtapa, across from the beachside hotels, and most are open daily from 9am to 2pm and 4 to 9pm.

La Fuente   This terrific shop carries gorgeous Talavera pottery, jaguar-shaped wicker tables, hand-blown glassware, masks, tin mirrors and frames, hand-embroidered clothing from Chiapas, and wood furniture. Open daily from 9am to 10pm during high season, daily from 10am to 9pm in low season.

6 Zihuatanejo & Ixtapa After Dark

With an exception or two, Zihuatanejo nightlife dies down around 11pm or midnight. For a good selection of clubs, dance spots, hotel fiestas, special events, and fun watering holes with live music and dancing, head for Ixtapa. Just keep in mind that the shuttle bus stops at 11pm, and a taxi to Zihuatanejo after midnight costs 50% more than the regular price. During the off season (after Easter and before Christmas), hours vary: Some places open only on weekends, while others close completely. In Zihuatanejo, a lively bar showing satellite TV sports is **Bandido's,** at the intersection of Cinco de Mayo and Pedro Ascencio in Zihuatanejo Centro, across from the Artisans' Market (© **755/553-8072**). It features live music Wednesday through Saturday, and is open nightly until 2am, but is closed on Sunday from May to October. A popular hangout for local residents and expats is **Rick's Bar,** Av. Cuauhtémoc 5, in Zihuatanejo Centro (© **755/554-2535**). On Friday's, it's known for its live music jam sessions, open to anyone wanting to share their unique talents. It's open Monday through Saturday from 7pm to midnight.

THE CLUB & MUSIC SCENE

Many dance clubs stay open until the last customers leave, so closing hours depend upon revelers. Most dance clubs have a ladies' night at least once a week—admission and drinks are free for women.

Carlos 'n' Charlie's Knee-deep in nostalgia, bric-a-brac, silly sayings, and photos from the Mexican Revolution, this restaurant/nightclub offers party ambience and good food. The eclectic menu includes iguana in season (with Alka-Seltzer and aspirin on the house). Out back by the beach is a partly shaded open-air section with a raised wooden platform for "pier" dancing at night. The recorded rock 'n' roll mixes with sounds of the ocean surf. The restaurant is open daily from 10am to midnight; pier dancing is nightly from 9pm to 3am.

Christine This glitzy street-side dance club is famous for its midnight light show, which features classical music played on a mega sound system. A semicircle of tables in tiers overlooks the dance floor. No sneakers, flip-flops, or shorts are allowed, and reservations are recommended during high season. Open Wednesday to Saturday at 10pm. Off-season hours vary.

Señor Frog's A companion restaurant to Carlos 'n' Charlie's, Señor Frog's has several dining sections and a warehouselike bar with raised dance floors. Large speakers play electronic, rock, and Latin music, sometimes even prompting dinner patrons to shimmy by their tables between courses. The restaurant is open daily from 6 to 11:30pm; the bar stays open until 3am.

Zen This is Ixtapa's most progressive nocturnal option. Music includes acid jazz, Drum & Bass, and ambient, in a sleek setting. It draws a young, hip crowd.

HOTEL FIESTAS & THEME NIGHTS
A number of hotels hold Mexican fiestas and other special events that include dinner, drinks, live music, and entertainment for a fixed price (generally $44/£24). The **Barceló Ixtapa** (© **755/555-2000**) stages a popular Wednesday night fiesta; the **Dorado Pacífico** (© **755/553-2025**) in Ixtapa hosts a Tuesday night fiesta. Only the Barceló Ixtapa offers them in the off season. Call for reservations or visit a travel agency for tickets, and be sure you understand what the price covers, as drinks, tax, and tip are not always included.

The Oaxaca Coast: From Puerto Escondido to Huatulco

Puerto Escondido, noted for its celebrated surf break, laid-back village ambience, attractive and inexpensive inns, and nearby nature excursions, is a worthy destination and an exceptional value. It's 6 hours south of Acapulco on coastal Highway 200. Most people fly from Mexico City or drive up from Huatulco.

The **Bahías de Huatulco** encompass a total of nine bays—each lovelier than the last—on a pristine portion of Oaxaca's coast. Development of the area has been gradual and well planned, with great ecological sensitivity. The town of **Huatulco,** 130km (80 miles) south of Puerto Escondido, is emerging as Mexico's most authentic adventure tourism haven. In addition to an 18-hole golf course, cruise-ship pier, and a handful of resort hotels, it offers a growing array of soft adventures that range from bay tours to diving, river rafting, and rappelling. Dining and nightlife remain limited, but the setting is beautiful and relaxing.

1 Puerto Escondido ✷✷✷

368km (228 miles) SE of Acapulco; 240km (149 miles) NW of Salina Cruz; 80km (50 miles) NW of Puerto Angel

I consider Puerto Escondido (*pwer*-toh es-cohn-*dee*-doh) the best overall beach value in Mexico, and it retains the same casual beach feel that's drawn people here for decades. Although it has long been known as one of the world's top surf sites, today it's broadening its appeal. Think alternative therapies, great vegetarian restaurants, hip nightlife, awesome hotel and dining values, and some of the best coffee shops in Mexico. It's a place for those whose priorities include the dimensions of the surf break (big), the temperature of the beer (cold), the strength of the coffee (espresso), and the optimal tanning angle. The young and very aware crowd that comes here measures time by the tides, and the pace is relaxed.

The location of "Puerto," as the locals call it, makes it an ideal jumping-off point for ecological explorations of neighboring jungle and estuary sanctuaries, as well as indigenous mountain settlements. Increasingly, it attracts those seeking both spiritual and physical renewal, with abundant massage and bodywork services, yoga classes, and exceptional and varied healthful dining options.

People come from the United States, Canada, and Europe to stay for weeks and even months—easily and inexpensively. Expats have migrated here from Los Cabos, Acapulco, and Puerto Vallarta seeking what originally attracted them to their former homes—stellar beaches, friendly locals, and low prices. Added pleasures include an absence of beach vendors and timeshare sales, an abundance of English speakers, and terrific, inexpensive dining and nightlife.

This is a real place, not a produced resort. A significant number of visitors are European travelers, and it's common to hear a variety of languages on the beach and in the bars. Puerto Escondido is also a favorite among Mexican college students. Solo travelers will probably make new friends within an hour of arriving. There are still surfers here, lured by the best break in Mexico, but espresso cafes and live music are becoming just as ubiquitous.

The city has been dismissed as a colony of former hippies and settled backpackers, but it's so much more. I have a theory that those who favor Puerto are just trying to keep the place true to its name (*escondido* means "hidden") and undiscovered by tourists. Don't let them trick you—visit, and soon, before it, too, changes.

ESSENTIALS
GETTING THERE & DEPARTING
BY PLANE   **Aero Tucán** (© 954/582-3461), and **Aerovega** (© 954/582-0151) operate daily morning flights to and from Puerto Escondido on small planes; the fare is about $150 (£83) each way to Oaxaca. **Click Mexicana** (© 01-800/112-5425 toll-free in Mexico; www.click.com.mx) flies jets to and from Mexico City daily. The price is about $200 (£110) each way.

If flights to Puerto Escondido are booked, you have the (possibly less expensive) option of flying into **Huatulco** on a scheduled or charter flight. This is especially viable if your destination is Puerto Angel, which lies between Puerto Escondido and Huatulco. An airport taxi costs about $80 (£66) to Puerto Angel, and approximately $130 (£72) to Puerto Escondido. If you can find a local taxi, rather than a government-chartered cab, you can reduce these fares by about 50%,

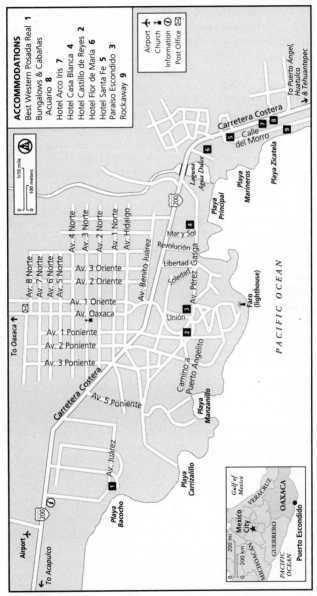

ACCOMMODATIONS

Best Western Posada Real **1**
Bungalows & Cabañas
Acuario **8**
Hotel Arco Iris **7**
Hotel Casa Blanca **4**
Hotel Castillo de Reyes **2**
Hotel Flor de María **6**
Hotel Santa Fe **5**
Paraíso Escondido **3**
Rockaway **9**

Airport ✈
Church ✝▪
Information ⓘ
Post Office ⊠

including the payment of a $5 (£2.75) mandatory airport exit tax. There is frequent bus service between the three destinations. **Budget** (© 958/581-9000 or 800/527-0700 in U.S), at the Huatulco airport, has cars available for one-way travel to Puerto Escondido, with an added drop charge of about $50 (£28). In Puerto Escondido, Budget is at the entrance to Bacocho (© 954/582-0312).

Arriving: The Puerto Escondido **airport** (airport code: PXM) is about 4km (2½ miles) north of the center of town, near Playa Bacocho. The *colectivo* **(minibus)** to hotels costs $3.50 (£1.90) per person. **Aerotransportes de Pasajeros Turistas de Oaxaca** sells *colectivo* tickets to the airport through **Turismo Dimar Travel Agency** (©/fax **954/582-0737** or -2305) on Avenida Pérez Gasga (the pedestrian-only zone) next to Hotel Casa Blanca. The minibus will pick you up at your hotel.

BY CAR From Oaxaca, **Highway 175** via Pochutla is the least bumpy road. The 240km (149-mile) trip takes 5 to 6 hours. **Highway 200** from Acapulco is also a good road and should take about 6 hours to travel. However, this stretch of road has been the site of numerous car and bus hijackings and robberies at night in recent years—travel only during the day.

From Salina Cruz to Puerto Escondido is a 5-hour drive, past the Bahías de Huatulco and the turnoff for Puerto Angel. The road is paved but can be rutty during the rainy season. The trip from Huatulco to Puerto Escondido takes just under 2 hours; you can easily hire a taxi for a fixed rate of about $50 (£28) an hour.

BY BUS Buses run frequently to and from Acapulco and Oaxaca, and south along the coast to and from Huatulco and Pochutla, the transit hub for Puerto Angel. The main bus station for **Estrella Blanca, Oaxaca Pacífico,** and **Estrella del Valle** is the **Central Camionera,** just north of the city center. First-class buses go from here to Huatulco, Oaxaca, and Mexico City. Several buses also leave daily for Pochutla, Salina Cruz (5 hr.), and Oaxaca (7 hr. via second-class bus). **Cristóbal Colón** buses (© **954/582-1073**) serve Salina Cruz, Tuxtla Gutiérrez, San Cristóbal de las Casas, and Oaxaca.

Arriving: Minibuses from Pochutla or Huatulco will let you off anywhere, including the spot where Pérez Gasga leads down to the pedestrians-only zone.

VISITOR INFORMATION
The **State Tourist Office, SEDETUR** (© **954/582-0175**), which has a very helpful staff, is less than 1km (a half-mile) from the

airport at the corner of Carretera Costera and Bulevar Benito Juárez. It's open Monday through Friday from 9am to 7pm, Saturday from 10am to 2pm. A tourist kiosk at the west end of the Adoquín (in town center) is open Monday through Saturday from 9am to 1pm.

CITY LAYOUT

Looking out on the Bahía Principal and its beach, to your left you'll see the eastern end of the bay, consisting of a small beach, **Playa Marineros,** followed by rocks jutting into the sea. Beyond this is **Playa Zicatela,** unmistakably the main surfing beach. Zicatela Beach has come into its own as the most popular area for visitors, with restaurants, bungalows, surf shops, and hotels, well back from the shoreline. The west side of the bay, to your right, is about 1.5km long (1 mile), with a lighthouse and a long stretch of fine sand. Beaches on this end are not quite as accessible by land, but hotels are overcoming this difficulty by constructing beach clubs reached by steep private roads and jeep shuttles.

The town of Puerto Escondido has roughly an east-west orientation, with the long Zicatela Beach turning sharply southeast. Residential areas behind Zicatela Beach tend to have unpaved streets; the older town, with paved streets, is north of the Carretera Costera (Hwy. 200). The streets are numbered; Avenida Oaxaca divides east *(oriente)* from west *(poniente),* and Avenida Hidalgo divides north *(norte)* from south *(sur).*

South of this is the original **tourist zone,** through which Avenida Pérez Gasga makes a loop. Part of this loop is a paved pedestrians-only zone, known locally as the Adoquín, after the hexagonal bricks used in its paving. Hotels, shops, restaurants, bars, travel agencies, and other services are all here. In the morning, taxis, delivery trucks, and private vehicles may drive here, but at noon it closes to all but foot traffic.

Avenida Pérez Gasga angles down from the highway at the east end; on the west, where the Adoquín terminates, it climbs in a wide northward curve to cross the highway, after which it becomes Avenida Oaxaca.

The beaches—Playa Principal in the center of town and Marineros and Zicatela, southeast of the town center—are connected. It's easy to walk from one to the other, crossing behind the separating rocks. Puerto Angelito, Carrizalillo, and Bacocho beaches are west of town and accessible by road or water. Playa Bacocho is where you'll find the few more expensive hotels.

GETTING AROUND

Almost everything is within walking distance of the Adoquín. **Taxis** around town are inexpensive; call ✆ **954/582-0990** or -0955 for service.

It's easy to hire a boat and possible to walk beside the sea from the Playa Principal to the tiny beach of Puerto Angelito, though it's a bit of a hike.

FAST FACTS: Puerto Escondido

Area Code The telephone area code is **954**.

Currency Exchange Banamex, Bancomer, Banorte, and HSBC all have branches in town, and all will change money during business hours; hours vary, but you can generally find one of the above open Monday through Saturday from 9am to 3pm. ATMs are also available, as are currency-exchange offices.

Drugstore **Farmacía de Más Ahorro,** Avenida 1 Norte at Avenida 2 Poniente (✆ **954/582-1911**), is open until 2am.

Hospital **Unidad Médico–Quirúrgica del Sur,** Av. Oaxaca 113 (✆ **954/582-1288**), offers 24-hour emergency services and has English-speaking staff and doctors. The number for the **Tourist Emergency Response Team (IFOPE)** is (✆ **954/540-3816**).

Internet Access On Zicatela Beach, **Internet Acuario** is a small, extremely busy Internet service at the entrance to the Bungalows & Cabañas Acuario, Calle de Morro s/n (✆ **954/582-1026**). It's open daily from 8am to 10pm and charges just $1.50 (85p) per hour.

Post Office The *correo,* on Avenida Oaxaca at the corner of Avenida 7 Norte (✆ **954/582-0959**), is open Monday through Friday from 8am to 3pm.

Safety Depending on whom you talk to, you need to be wary of potential beach muggings, primarily at night. Lighting at Playa Principal and Playa Zicatela has caused the crime rate to drop considerably. Local residents say most incidents happen after tourists overindulge and then go for a midnight stroll along the beach. Puerto is so casual that it's an easy place to let your guard down. Don't carry valuables, and use common sense and normal precautions.

Also, respect the power of the magnificent waves here. Drownings occur all too frequently.

Seasons Season designations are somewhat arbitrary, but most consider high season to be from mid-December to January, around and during Easter week, July and August, and other school and business vacations.

Telephones Numerous businesses offer long-distance telephone service. Many are along the Adoquín; several accept credit cards. The best bet remains a prepaid Ladatel phone card.

WHERE TO STAY

The rates posted below do not include the 17% tax.

MODERATE

Best Western Posada Real *(Kids*   On a cliff top overlooking the beach, the expanse of manicured lawn that backs this all-inclusive hotel is one of the most popular places in town for a sunset cocktail. The smallish standard rooms are less enticing than the hotel grounds. A big plus here is Coco's Beach Club, with a 1km (half-mile) stretch of soft-sand beach, large swimming pool, playground, and bar with occasional live music. A shuttle ride (or a lengthy walk down a set of stairs) will take you there. This is a great place for families, and it's open to the public (nonguests pay $2.50/£1.40 to enter). The hotel lies 5 minutes from the airport and about the same from Puerto Escondido's tourist zone, but you'll need a taxi to get to town. Rates include breakfast, lunch, dinner, and unlimited domestic drinks, tips, and taxes.

Av. Benito Juárez 1, Fracc. Bacocho, 71980 Puerto Escondido, Oax. © 800/582-1234 in the U.S., or 954/582-0237. Fax 954/582-0192. www.posadareal.com.mx. 100 units. High season $130 (£72) double; low season $105 (£58) double. AE, MC, V. Free parking. **Amenities:** 2 restaurants; lobby bar; beach club w/food service; 2 outdoor pools; wading pool; putting green; tennis court; travel agency; car rental; laundry service. *In room:* A/C, TV, hair dryer, safe.

Hotel Santa Fe *(Kids* *(Finds*   If Puerto Escondido is the best beach value in Mexico, then the Santa Fe is without a doubt one of the best hotel values in Mexico. It boasts a winning combination of unique Spanish-colonial style, a welcoming staff, and comfortable if basic rooms. The hotel has grown up with the surfers who came to Puerto in the 1960s and 1970s and nostalgically return today. It's about 1km (a half-mile) southeast of the town center, off Highway 200, at the curve in the road where Marineros and Zicatela beaches join—a prime sunset-watching spot. The three-story hacienda-style buildings have clay-tiled stairs, archways, and blooming bougainvillea. They surround two courtyard swimming pools. The ample but simply styled rooms feature large tile bathrooms, colonial furnishings, hand-woven fabrics, and both air-conditioning and ceiling fans. Most have a balcony or terrace, and the master and presidential suites enjoy ocean views. Bungalows are next to the hotel; each has a living room, kitchen, and bedroom with two double beds. The restaurant (see "Where to Dine," below) is one of the best on the southern Pacific coast.

Calle del Morro (Apdo. Postal 96), 71980 Puerto Escondido, Oax. ⓒ 954/582-0170 or -0266. Fax 954/582-0260. www.hotelsantafe.com.mx. 61 units, 8 bungalows. High season $165 (£91) double, $180 (£99) junior suite, $260 (£143) suite, $175 (£96) bungalow; low season $120 (£66) double, $155 (£85) junior suite, $260 (£143) suite, $130 (£72) bungalow. AE, MC, V. Free parking. **Amenities:** Restaurant; bar; 3 outdoor pools; tour service; car rental; massage; babysitting; laundry. *In room:* A/C, TV, safe.

Paraíso Escondido 🎫🎫 *Finds* This eclectic inn is hidden away on a shady street a couple of short blocks from the Adoquín and Playa Principal. A curious collection of Mexican folk art, masks, religious art, and paintings make this an exercise in Mexican magic realism, in addition to a tranquil place to stay. An inviting pool—surrounded by gardens, Adirondack chairs, and a fountain—affords a commanding view of the bay. The colonial-style rooms each have one double and one twin bed, a built-in desk, tile floors, a small bathroom, and a cozy balcony or terrace with French doors. The suites have much plusher decor than the rooms, with recessed lighting, desks set into bay windows, living areas, and large private balconies. The penthouse suite has a kitchenette, a tile chessboard inlaid in the floor, and murals adorning the walls—it is the owners' former apartment.

Calle Unión 10, 71980 Puerto Escondido, Oax. ⓒ **954/582-0444**. 25 units. $65 (£36) double; $120 (£66) suite; $150 (£83) penthouse suite. No credit cards. Free parking. **Amenities:** Restaurant; bar; outdoor pool. *In room:* A/C, TV.

INEXPENSIVE

Bungalows & Cabañas Acuario 🎫 Facing Zicatela Beach, this surfer's sanctuary offers cheap accommodations plus an on-site gym, surf shop, and Internet cafe. The two-story hotel and bungalows surround a pool shaded by great palms. Rooms are small and basic; bungalows offer basic kitchen facilities but don't have air-conditioning. The cabañas are more open and have hammocks. The adjoining retail area has public telephones, money exchange, a pharmacy, and a vegetarian restaurant. If you're traveling during low season, you can probably negotiate a better deal than the rates listed below once you're there.

Calle del Morro s/n, 71980 Puerto Escondido, Oax. © **954/582-0357.** Fax 954/582-1027. www.oaxaca-mio.com/bunacuario.htm. 40 units. High season $57 (£31) double, $69 (£38) double with A/C, $110 (£61) bungalow; 20% less in low season. No credit cards. Free parking. **Amenities:** Restaurant; Internet cafe; well-equipped gym; outdoor pool; Jacuzzi; tour desk. *In room:* No phone except in suite and 2 bungalows.

Hotel Arco Iris *R* *Value* Rooms at the Arco Iris occupy a three-story colonial-style house that faces Zicatela Beach. Each is simple yet comfortable, with a spacious terrace or balcony with hangers for hammocks to rent—all have great views, but the upstairs ones are better (12 units include kitchenettes). Beds come draped with mosquito nets, with bedspreads made using beautifully worked Oaxacan textiles. The restaurant/bar features one of the most popular happy hours in town, daily from 5:30 to 7:30pm, with live music during high season. Hotel Arco Iris is often packed.

Calle del Morro s/n, Playa Zicatela, 71980 Puerto Escondido, Oax. © **954/582-2344** and -1494. Fax 954/582-2963. www.puertoconnection.com/arco.html. 35 units. $55–$75 (£30–£41) double, $60–$80 (£33–£44) double with kitchen. Extra person $4 (£2.20). Rates 10%–20% higher at Easter and Christmas. MC, V. Ample free parking for cars and campers. **Amenities:** Restaurant; bar; outdoor pool; wading pool; TV/game room w/foreign channels; tour desk. *In room:* No phone.

Hotel Casa Blanca *R* *Value* If you want to be in the heart of the Adoquín, this is your best bet for excellent value and ample accommodations. The courtyard pool and adjacent *palapa* make great places to hide away and enjoy a margarita or a book from the hotel's exchange rack. The bright, simply furnished rooms offer a choice of bed combinations, but all have at least two beds and a fan. Some rooms have both air-conditioning and a minifridge. The best rooms have a balcony overlooking the action in the street below, but light sleepers should consider a room in the back. Some rooms accommodate up to five for $68 (£38). This is an excellent and economical choice for families.

Av. Pérez Gasga 905, 71980 Puerto Escondido, Oax. © **954/582-0168.** 21 units. High season $52 (£29) double, $95 (£52) double with A/C; low season $38 (£21) double, $85 (£47) double with A/C. MC, V. Limited street parking. **Amenities:** Outdoor pool; safe; money exchange. *In room:* TV, A/C (in some rooms), minifridge (in some rooms), fan, no phone.

Hotel Castillo de Reyes Proprietor Don Fernando has a knack for making his guests feel at home. Guests chat around tables on a shady patio near the office. Most of the bright, white-walled rooms have a special touch—perhaps a gourd mask or carved coconut hanging over the bed, plus over-the-bed reading lights. The rooms are shaded from the sun by palms and cooled by fans. The "castle" is on your left as you ascend the hill on Pérez Gasga, after leaving the Adoquín (you can also enter Pérez Gasga off Hwy. 200). This hotel is on one of Puerto's busiest streets, so traffic noise is a consideration.

Av. Pérez Gasga s/n, 71980 Puerto Escondido, Oax. ⓒ 954/582-0442. 18 units. High season $35 (£19) double; low season $25 (£14) double. No credit cards. Limited street parking. **Amenities:** Safe; money exchange. *In room:* Fans, no phone.

Hotel Flor de María Though not right on the beach, the Flor de María offers a welcoming place to stay. This cheery, three-story hotel faces the ocean, which you can see from the rooftop. Built around a garden courtyard, each room is colorfully decorated with beautiful *trompe l'oeil* still lifes and landscapes. Rooms have double beds with orthopedic mattresses, and views that vary between the ocean, courtyard, and exterior. The roof holds a small pool, a shaded hammock terrace, and an open-air bar (noon–8pm during high season) with cable TV—all in all, a great sunset spot. The hotel lies about .5km (one-third mile) from the Adoquín, 60m (197 ft.) up a cobblestone road from Marineros Beach on Calle Marinero at the eastern end of the beach.

Playa Marineros, 71980 Puerto Escondido, Oax. ⓒ **954/582-0536.** Fax 954/582-2617. 24 units. $45–$65 (£25–£36) double. Ask about off-season, long-term discounts. MC, V. Limited parking. **Amenities:** Restaurant; bar; small outdoor pool; Internet kiosk; small gym.

Rockaway Facing Playa Zicatela, this surfer's sanctuary offers very clean—and very cheap—accommodations geared for surfers. Every cabaña is equipped with a private bathroom, as well as ceiling fans and mosquito nets. The good-size swimming pool and *palapa* bar form a popular gathering spot. The cabañas in the older section do not have hot water; those in the newer section feature A/C, hot water, and cable TV.

Calle del Morro s/n, 71980 Puerto Escondido, Oax. ⓒ **954/582-0668.** Fax 954-582-2420. 14 units. High season $60 (£33) double, new rooms $80 (£44) double; low season $40 (£22) double, new rooms $60 (£33) double. No credit cards. Free parking. **Amenities:** Bar; outdoor pool. *In room:* A/C (in some), TV (in some), ceiling fans, mosquito nets, no phone.

WHERE TO DINE

In addition to the places listed below, a Puerto Escondido tradition is the *palapa* restaurants on Zicatela Beach, for early-morning surfer breakfasts or casual dining and drinking at night. One of the most popular is **Los Tíos,** offering very reasonable prices and surfer-size portions. After dinner, enjoy homemade Italian ice cream from **Gelateria Giardino.** It has two locations, on Calle del Morro at Zicatela Beach, and Pérez Gasga 609, on the Adoquín (© **954/582-2243**).

EXPENSIVE

Pascal ✿✿✿ *Finds* FRENCH   With an enchanted location on the edge of the bay, Pascal offers the only beachside terrace with views of the bobbing boats in front. Opened in 2006, it has quickly become one of the city's top restaurants. All of the French-inspired dishes are prepared by chef-owner Pascal on the outdoor grill using only fresh ingredients, and some of the specials include Chateaubriand, rack of lamb, fondue bourguignon, fish and seafood brochettes, and grilled lobster. The bouillabaisse tastes heavenly. Open only for dinner, Pascal offers candlelit tables amid towering palm trees, a centerpiece fountain, and live music weekends. Service is refined, and the cuisine matches the quality you would expect from a fine French restaurant. There's an enticing selection of French and international wines, as well.

Playa Principal s/n (off the Adoquín). © **954/103-0668.** Reservations recommended. Main courses $6–$25 (£3.30–£14). No credit cards. Daily 6pm–midnight.

MODERATE

Cabo Blanco INTERNATIONAL   People come to this beachside bar and grill for a good time and simple beach food, which includes grilled fish, shrimp, steaks, and ribs topped with a variety of flavorful sauces. Favorites are dill-Dijon mustard, wine-fennel, and Thai curry. A bonus is that Cabo Blanco turns into a rowdy Zicatela Beach bar, with special Monday night parties featuring an all-you-can-eat buffet plus dancing, and a Friday night reggae dance. The top-notch team of bartenders keeps the crowd well-served, if not always well-behaved.

Calle del Morro s/n. © **954/582-0337.** www.geocities.com/oaxiki/cabo_blanco_pe.html. Main courses $7–$15 (£3.85–£8.25). V. Dec–Apr daily 6pm–2am.

Restaurant Santa Fe ✿✿ *Finds* INTERNATIONAL   The Hotel Santa Fe's beachside restaurant sits under a welcoming *palapa,* with the gentle waves crashing just in front. The excellent fish and seafood selections include crayfish, red snapper, tuna, octopus, and giant shrimp prepared any way you like. More traditional dishes, such as Oaxacan-style enchiladas with mole, are also available. The restaurant offers numerous vegetarian and vegan selections, including chiles rellenos and breaded tofu served with salad and rice. Even if you don't plan to dine, this is a beautiful spot to come for a sunset cocktail and perhaps an hors d'oeuvre.

In the Hotel Santa Fe, Calle del Morro s/n. ✆ **954/582-0170**. Breakfast $4–$6 (£2.20–£3.35); main courses $5.50–$25 (£3–£14). AE, MC, V. Daily 7am–10:30pm.

INEXPENSIVE

Arte la Galería ✿ ITALIAN   At the east end of the Adoquín, La Galería offers a satisfying range of eats in a cool, creative setting. Dark-wood beams tower above, contemporary works by local artists grace the walls, and jazz music plays. Specialties include homemade pastas and brick-oven pizzas (the five-cheese pizza is especially delicious), but burgers and steaks are also available. Cappuccino and espresso, plus desserts such as apple empanadas, finish the meal. Continental and American breakfasts are available in the morning.

Av. Pérez Gasga s/n. ✆ **954/582-2039**. Breakfast $3–$5 (£1.65–£2.75); main courses $5–$18 (£2.75–£9.90). No credit cards. Daily 8am–11pm.

Cafecito ✿ (Value) FRENCH PASTRY/MEXICAN   Carmen started with a small bakery in Puerto, and when she opened this cafe years ago on Zicatela Beach, with the motto "Big waves, strong coffee!," it quickly eclipsed the bake shop, and now is her main business. But not to worry—it still features all the attractions of her early *patisserie,* with the added attraction of serving full meals all day long. This cafe/restaurant sits under a big *palapa* facing the beach. Giant shrimp dinners cost less than $10 (£5.50), and creative daily specials are always a sure bet. An oversize mug of cappuccino is $2.20 (£1.20), and a mango éclair—worth any price—is a steal at $1.20 (65p). Smoothies, natural juices, and a variety of coffee selections are available.

Calle del Morro s/n, Playa Zicatela. ✆ **954/582-0516**. Pastries $1–$2 (55p–£1.10); breakfast $3–$4.50 (£1.65–£2.50); main courses $3–$9 (£1.65–£4.95). No credit cards. Daily 6am–10pm.

El Jardín ✿✿ (Value) ITALIAN   This wonderful restaurant facing Zicatela Beach is generally packed. It's known for its generous use of fresh, healthy ingredients, including lots of olive oil, tomatoes, and Italian vinaigrette. Among the choices are delicious New York–style pizzas, vegetarian sandwiches, pastas, large salads, and crepes.

There's also a wide selection of fresh fish and seafood. Under a *palapa* roof, El Jardín's extensive menu includes fruit smoothies, Italian and Mexican coffees, herbal teas, and a complete juice bar. The restaurant makes its own tempeh, tofu, pastas, and whole-grain breads. The rich tiramisu is to die for.

Calle del Morro s/n, Playa Zicatela. ☎ 954/582-2315. Main courses $3–$10 (£1.65–£5.50). No credit cards. Daily 8–11pm.

Flor de María INTERNATIONAL This first-floor, open-air hotel dining room near the beach is particularly popular with locals. The menu changes daily but always includes fresh fish, grilled meats, and pastas. The restaurant sits in the Hotel Flor de María, just steps from the center of town and up a cobblestone road from Playa Marinero at the eastern end of the beach.

In Hotel Flor de María, Playa Marinero. ☎ 954/582-0536. Breakfast $2–$3.50 (£1.10–£1.95); main courses $5–$14 (£2.75–£7.70). No credit cards. Wed–Mon 8–11am and 6–9pm. Closed May–June and Sept–Oct.

Las Margaritas *Value* MEXICAN One of the tastiest Mexican restaurants in town, Las Margaritas lies off a busy street that's a short drive from the Adoquín. The casual, open-air terrace offers wood tables and chairs as well as an open kitchen, bar, and tortilla stand where you can watch authentic dishes being made. This is Mexican food prepared as though you were in a family's home, featuring dishes like *empanadas,* quesadillas, fish and seafood brochettes, steaks, and moles that explode with flavor.

8 Norte s/n (1 block from the market). ☎ 954/582-0212. Breakfasts $3–$4.50 (£1.65–£2.50); main courses $4–$12 (£2.20–£6.60). MC, V. Daily 8am–10pm.

WHAT TO SEE & DO IN PUERTO ESCONDIDO
BEACHES
Playa Principal, where small boats are available for fishing and tour services, and **Playa Marineros,** adjacent to the town center on a deep bay, are the best swimming beaches. Beach chairs and sun shades rent for about $5 (£2.75), which may be waived if you order food or drinks from the restaurants that offer them. **Playa Zicatela,** which has lifeguards and is known as the "Mexican Pipeline," adjoins Playa Marineros and extends southeast for several kilometers. The surfing part of Zicatela, with large curling waves, is about 4km (2½ miles) from the town center. Due to the size and strength of the waves, it's not a swimming beach, and only experienced surfers should attempt to ride Zicatela's powerful waves. Stadium-style lighting has been installed in both of these areas, in an attempt to crack down on

Ecotours & Other Adventurous Explorations

An excellent provider of ecologically oriented tour services is **Rutas de Aventura** ⭐, Hotel Santa Fe (© 954/582-0170; rutasdeaventura@gmail.com). Gustavo Boltjes speaks fluent English and offers kayak adventures, hiking excursions, and mountain-bike tours. He also leads waterfall hikes, camping trips, and agro-tourism adventures to learn about local farming and coffee production.

Turismo Dimar Travel Agency, on the landward side just inside the Adoquín (© **954/582-0737** or -2305; fax 954/582-1551; vww.viajesdimar.com; daily 8am–9pm), is another excellent source of information and can arrange all types of tours and travel. Manager Gaudencio Díaz Martinez speaks English and can arrange individualized tours or more organized ones, such as **Michael Malone's Hidden Voyages Ecotours.** Malone, a Canadian ornithologist, leads dawn and sunset trips in high season (winter) to **Manialtepec Lagoon,** a bird-filled mangrove lagoon about 20km (12 miles) northwest of Puerto Escondido. The tour ($40/£22) includes a stop on a secluded beach for a swim.

One of the most popular all-day tours offered by both companies is to **Chacahua Lagoon National Park,** about 65km (40 miles) west. It costs $45 (£25) with Dimar, $52 (£29) with Michael Malone. These are true ecotours—small groups

---

nighttime beach muggings. It has diminished the appeal of the Playa Principal restaurants—patrons now look into the bright lights rather than at the sea. Lifeguard service has recently been added to Playa Zicatela, although the lifeguards are known to go on strike.

Barter with one of the fishermen on the main beach for a ride to **Playa Manzanillo** and **Puerto Angelito,** two beaches separated by a rocky outcropping. Here, and at other small coves just west of town, swimming is safe and the overall pace is calmer than in town. You'll also find *palapas,* hammock rentals, and snorkeling equipment. The clear blue water is perfect for snorkeling. Local entrepreneurs cook fresh fish, tamales, and other Mexican dishes right at the beach. Puerto Angelito is also accessible by a road that's a short distance from town, so it tends to be busier. You can also take a cab to the cliff above **Playa Carrizalillo,** and descend one hundred odd stone stairs to a calm and secluded swimming beach. **Playa Bacocho** is on a

treading lightly. You visit a beautiful sandy spit of beach and the lagoon, which has incredible bird life and flowers, including black orchids. Locals provide fresh barbecued fish on the beach. If you know Spanish and get information from the tourism office, it's possible to stay overnight under a small *palapa*, but bring plenty of insect repellent.

An interesting and slightly out-of-the-ordinary excursion is **Aventura Submarina**, Av. Pérez Gasga 601A, in front of the tourism office (© **954/582-2353**). Jorge, who speaks fluent English and is a certified scuba instructor, guides individuals and small groups of qualified divers along the Coco trench just offshore. The price is $60 (£33) for a two-tank dive. This outfit offers a refresher scuba course at no extra charge. Jorge also arranges surface activities such as deep-sea fishing, surfing, and trips to lesser-known yet nearby swimming beaches. **Omar** (© **954/559-4406**) offers dolphin-watching tours in high season (winter).

Fishermen keep their colorful *pangas* (small boats) on the beach beside the Adoquín. A **fisherman's tour** around the coastline in a *panga* costs about $39 (£21), but a ride to Puerto Angelito beaches is only $5 (£2.75). Most hotels offer or will gladly arrange tours to meet your need.

shallow cove (dangerous for swimming) farther northwest and is best reached by taxi or boat rather than on foot. It's also the location of the Villa Sol Beach Club. A charge of $10 (£5.50) gives you access to pools, food and beverage service, and facilities.

SURFING

Zicatela Beach, 2.5km (1½ miles) southeast of Puerto Escondido's town center, is a world-class surf spot. A surfing competition in August and Fiesta Puerto Escondido, held for at least 3 days each November, celebrate Puerto Escondido's renowned waves. There is also a surfing exhibition and competition in February, for Carnevale. The tourism office can supply dates and details. Beginning surfers often start out at Playa Marineros before graduating to Zicatela's awesome waves, although you will see intermediate surfers out at **La Punta,** at the southernmost end of Playa Zicatela. The waves and strong currents make Zicatela dangerous for swimming.

NESTING RIDLEY TURTLES

The beaches around Puerto Escondido and Puerto Angel are nesting grounds for the endangered Ridley turtle. During the summer, tourists, on lucky occasions, can see the turtles laying eggs or observe the hatchlings trekking to the sea.

Escobilla Beach near Puerto Escondido seems to be the favored nesting grounds of the Ridley turtle. In 1991, the Mexican government established the Centro Mexicano la Tortuga, known locally as the **Turtle Museum.** On view are examples of all species of marine turtles living in Mexico, plus six species of freshwater turtles and two species of land turtles. The center (© **958/584-3376**) lies on **Mazunte Beach** 𝘧, near the town of the same name. Hours are Wednesday through Saturday from 10am to 4:30pm, and Sunday from 10am to 2:30pm; suggested donation is $3 (£1.65). If you come between July and September, ask to join an overnight expedition to Escobilla Beach to see mother turtles scuttle to the beach to lay their eggs. The museum is near a unique shop that sells excellent naturally produced soaps, shampoos, bath oils, and other personal-care products. All are made and packaged by the local community as part of a project to replace lost income from turtle poaching. Buses go to Mazunte from Puerto Angel about every half-hour, and a taxi ride is around $5.50 (£3). You can fit this in with a trip to Zipolite Beach (see "A Trip to Puerto Angel: Backpacking Beach Haven," below). Buses from Puerto Escondido don't stop in Mazunte; you can cover the 65km (40 miles) in a taxi or rental car.

The tourism cooperative at **Ventanilla** provides another chance to get up close to the turtles. The villagers here have created their own ecological reserve that encompasses a nearby lagoon, inhabited by crocodiles and dozens of species of birds, and a beach where sea turtles lay their eggs. A boat ride to see the crocs costs $4 (£2.25) and nothing on the menu at the restaurant is over $7 (£4). Turtles lay their eggs here year-round, although summer is the prime season, so there's always a possibility that a nest is about to hatch. Helping the locals release the eggs is free. Ventanilla is a $2 (£1.10) taxi ride from Mazunte or the nearby beaches, but if you're planning on staying after sunset, ask your driver to wait, since it's a long walk in the dark back to the main highway.

GUIDED WALKING TOURS

For local information and guided walking tours, visit the **Oaxaca Tourist Bureau** booth (© **954/582-0276;** ginainpuerto@yahoo.com).

It's just west of the pedestrian street. Ask for Gina, who speaks excellent English and is incredibly helpful. She provides information with a smile, and many say she knows more about Puerto Escondido than any other person. On her days off, Gina offers walking tours to the market and to little-known nearby ruins. Filled with history and information on native vegetation, a day with Gina promises fun, adventure, and insight into local culture.

A Mixtec ceremonial center was discovered in early 2000 just east of Puerto Escondido and is considered a major discovery. The site covers many acres with about 10 pyramids and a ball court, with the pyramids appearing as hills covered in vegetation. A number of large carved stones have been found. Situated on a hilltop, it commands a spectacular view of Puerto Escondido and the Pacific coast. The large archaeological site spans several privately owned plots of land and is not open to the public, although Gina has been known to offer a guided walking tour to it.

SHOPPING

During high season, businesses and shops are generally open all day. During low season, many close between 2 and 4pm.

The Adoquín holds a row of tourist shops selling straw hats, postcards, and T-shirts, plus a few excellent shops featuring Guatemalan, Oaxacan, and Balinese clothing and art. You can also get a tattoo or rent surfboards and boogie boards. Interspersed among the shops, hotels, restaurants, and bars are pharmacies and minimarkets. The largest of these is **Oh! Mar,** Av. Pérez Gasga 502. It sells anything you'd need for a day at the beach, plus phone (Ladatel) cards and Cuban cigars.

Also of interest is **Bazar Santa Fe** ⭐⭐, Hotel Santa Fe lobby, Calle del Morro s/n, Zicatela Beach (© 954/582-0170), a small shop that sells antiques, vintage Oaxacan embroidered clothing, jewelry, religious artifacts, and gourmet local coffee. At either location of **Bikini Brazil,** Playa Zicatela, Calle del Morro s/n (© **954/ 582-2333**), and on the Adoquín (© **954/582-0568**), you'll find the hottest bikinis under the sun imported from Brazil, land of the *tanga* (string bikini). Another cool beach shop on Playa Zicatela, Calle del Moro s/n, is **Trapoy y Harapos** (© **954/582-0759**), which sells bathing suits, sandals, and surfboards. The first surf shop in Puerto Escondido, **Central Surf** (© **954/582-2285;** www.central surfshop.com), on Zicatela Beach, Calle del Morro s/n, rents and sells surfboards, offers surf lessons, and sells related gear, including custom-made surf trunks. Nearby, the **360 Surf Shop** sells every-thing for your out-of-town surf needs, and sells, trades, and rents boards. They don't have a phone number, but you can e-mail them at **360@puertoconnection.com**. Board rentals usually go for about $10 to $20 (£5.50–£11) per day, with lessons available for $60 (£33) for 2 hours. In front of the Rockaway Resort on Zicatela Beach, there's a 24-hour **minisuper** (no phone) that sells the neces-sities: beer, suntan lotion, and basic food.

PUERTO ESCONDIDO AFTER DARK

Sunset watching is a ritual to plan your days around, and good look-out points abound. At Zicatela you can watch the sun descend behind the surfers, and at **La Galería,** located on the third floor of the Arco Iris hotel, you can catch up on local gossip while enjoying a sundowner. It has a nightly happy hour (with live music during high season) from 5:30 to 7:30pm. Other great sunset spots are the **Hotel Santa Fe,** at the junction of Zicatela and Marineros beaches, and the rooftop bar of **Hotel Flor de María.** For a more tranquil, romantic setting, take a cab or walk a half-hour or so west to the cliff-top lawn of the **Hotel Posada Real.**

Puerto's nightlife will satisfy anyone dedicated to late nights and good music. Most nightspots are open until 3am or until customers leave; none of them have phones. The Adoquín offers an ample selection of clubs. Favorites include **Wipeout,** a multilevel club that packs in the crowds until 4am, and **El Tubo,** an open-air beachside dance club just west of Pascal on the Adoquín.

On Zicatela Beach, **El Son y la Rumba** features live Latino jazz, by its house band, each night from 8 to 11pm. It switches over to DJs playing house music Wednesday through Saturday, after 11pm. The cover is $5 (£2.75), and it's located at Calle de Moro 7. Within walk-ing distance, **Bar Fly** sits upstairs overlooking the beach and features a DJ spinning Latin, retro, and electronic hits. It's open nightly from 9pm to 3am on Calle de Moro s/n. Don't miss **Cabo Blanco's** (see "Where to Dine," earlier in this chapter) Monday night dine-and-dance party (all you can eat), or its Friday reggae night. An added draw is the complimentary snacks with drink purchase, in the style of Mexico's cantina tradition. **Casa Babylon,** a few doors down, is a bohemian beach bar with a book exchange and table games. It's open nightly from 7pm until late, and has a hip surfer vibe.

There's a movie theater on Playa Zicatela, **PJ's Book Bodega and Music Shop.** It's a pretty simple setup consisting of a large screen and some beach chairs, and it serves up popcorn and movies nightly.

2 A Trip to Puerto Angel: Backpacking Beach Haven

Seventy-four kilometers (46 miles) southeast of Puerto Escondido and 50km (30 miles) northwest of the Bays of Huatulco lies the tiny fishing port of **Puerto Angel** (*pwer*-toh *ahn*-hehl). With its beautiful beaches, unpaved streets, and budget hotels, Puerto Angel is popular with the international backpacking set and those seeking an inexpensive and restful vacation. Repeated hurricane damage and the 1999 earthquake took its toll on the village, driving the best accommodations out of business, but Puerto Angel continues to attract visitors. Its small bay and several inlets offer peaceful swimming and good snorkeling. The village's way of life is slow and simple: Fishermen leave very early in the morning and return with their catch before noon. Taxis make up most of the traffic, and the bus from Pochutla passes every half-hour or so.

ESSENTIALS
GETTING THERE & DEPARTING
BY CAR   North or south from **Highway 200,** take coastal **Highway 175** inland to Puerto Angel. The road is well marked with signs to Puerto Angel. From Huatulco or Puerto Escondido, the trip should take about an hour.

BY TAXI   Taxis are readily available to take you to Puerto Angel or Zipolite Beach for a reasonable price (about $3/£1.65 to or from either destination), or to the Huatulco airport or Puerto Escondido (about $50/£28).

BY BUS   There are no direct buses from Puerto Escondido or Huatulco to Puerto Angel; however, numerous buses leave Puerto Escondido and Huatulco for Pochutla, 11km (7 miles) north of Puerto Angel. Take the bus to Pochutla, and then switch to a bus going to Puerto Angel. If you arrive in Pochutla from Huatulco or Puerto Escondido, you may be dropped at one of several bus stations that line the main street; walk 1 or 2 blocks toward the large

---

Tips Important Travel Note

Although car and bus hijackings along Highway 200 north to Acapulco have greatly decreased (thanks to improved security measures and police patrols), you're still wise to travel this road only during the day.

sign reading POSADA DON JOSE. The buses to Puerto Angel are in the lot just before the sign.

ORIENTATION

The town center is only about 4 blocks long, oriented more or less east-west. There are few signs in the village, and, off the main street, much of Puerto Angel is a narrow sand-and-dirt path. The navy base is toward the west end of town, just before the creek crossing toward Playa Panteón (Cemetery Beach).

Puerto Angel has several public (Ladatel) telephones that use widely available prepaid phone cards. The closest bank is **Bancomer** in Pochutla, which changes money Monday through Friday from 9am to 6pm, Saturday from 9am to 1pm. The *correo* **(post office),** open Monday through Friday from 9am to 3:30pm, is on the curve as you enter town.

BEACHES, WATERSPORTS & BOAT TRIPS

The golden sands and peaceful village life of Puerto Angel and the nearby towns are all the reasons you'll need to visit. Playa Principal, the main beach, lies between the Mexican navy base and the pier that's home to the local fishing fleet. Near the pier, fishermen pull their colorful boats onto the beach and unload their catch in the late morning while trucks wait to haul it off to processing plants in Veracruz. The rest of the beach seems light-years from the world of work and commitments. Except on Mexican holidays, it's relatively deserted. It's important to note that Pacific coast currents deposit trash on Puerto Angel beaches. The locals do a fairly good job of keeping it picked up, but the currents are constant.

Playa Panteón is the main swimming and snorkeling beach. Cemetery Beach, ominous as that sounds, is about a 15-minute walk from the center, straight through town on the main street that skirts the beach. The *panteón* (cemetery), on the right, is worth a visit—it holds brightly colored tombstones and equally brilliant blooming bougainvillea.

In Playa Panteón, some of the *palapa* restaurants and a few of the hotels rent snorkeling and scuba gear and can arrange boat trips, but they tend to be expensive. Check the quality and condition of gear—particularly scuba gear—that you're renting.

Playa Zipolite (see-poh-*lee*-teh) and its village are 6km (4 miles) down a paved road from Puerto Angel. Taxis charge about $3 (£1.65). You can catch a *colectivo* on the main street in the town center and share the cost.

Zipolite is well known as a good surf break and as a nude beach. Although public nudity (including topless sunbathing) is technically illegal, it's allowed here—this is one of only a handful of beaches in Mexico that permits it. This sort of open-mindedness has attracted an increasing number of young European travelers. Most sunbathers concentrate beyond a large rock outcropping at the far end of the beach. Police will occasionally patrol the area, but they are much more intent on drug users than on sunbathers. The ocean and currents here are quite strong (that's why the surf is so good!), and a number of drownings have occurred over the years—know your limits. There are places to tie up a hammock and a few *palapa* restaurants for a light lunch and a cold beer.

Hotels in Playa Zipolite are basic and rustic; most have rugged walls and *palapa* roofs. Prices range from $10 to $50 (£5.50–£28) a night.

Traveling north on Highway 175, you'll come to another hot surf break and a beach of spectacular beauty: **Playa San Agustinillo.** If you want to stay in San Agustinillo, there are no formal accommodations, but you'll see numerous signs for local guesthouses, which rent rooms for an average of $10 to $20 (£5.50–£11) a night, often with a home-cooked meal included. One of the pleasures of a stay in Puerto Angel is discovering the many hidden beaches nearby and spending the day. Local boatmen and hotels can give details and quote rates for this service.

You can stay in Puerto Angel near Playa Principal in the tiny town, or at Playa Panteón. Most accommodations are basic, older, cement-block style hotels, not meriting a full-blown description. Between Playa Panteón and town are several bungalow and guesthouse setups with budget accommodations.

3 Bahías de Huatulco

64km (40 miles) SE of Puerto Angel; 680km (422 miles) SE of Acapulco

Huatulco has the same unspoiled nature and laid-back attitude as its neighbors to the north, Puerto Angel and Puerto Escondido, but with a difference. In the midst of natural splendor, you'll also encounter indulgent hotels and modern roads and facilities.

Pristine beaches and jungle landscapes can make for an idyllic retreat from the stress of daily life—and when viewed from a luxury hotel balcony, even better. Huatulco is for those who want to enjoy the beauty of nature during the day, and then retreat to well-appointed comfort by night.

Undeveloped stretches of pure white sand and isolated coves await the promised growth of Huatulco, but it's not catching on as rapidly as Cancún, the previous resort planned by FONATUR, Mexico's Tourism Development arm. FONATUR development of the Bahías de Huatulco is an ambitious project that aims to cover 21,000 hectares (51,870 acres) of land, with over 16,000 hectares (39,520 acres) to remain ecological preserves. The small local communities have been transplanted from the coast into Crucecita. The area consists of three sections: **Santa Cruz, Crucecita,** and **Tangolunda Bay** (see "City Layout," below).

Though Huatulco has increasingly become known for its ecotourism attractions—including river rafting, rappelling, and hiking jungle trails—it has yet to develop a true personality. There's little shopping, nightlife, or even dining outside of the hotels, and what is available is expensive for the quality. However, the service in the area shines.

The opening of a new cruise-ship dock in Santa Cruz Bay in 2005 is changing the level of activity in Huatulco, providing the sleepy resort with an important business boost. The new dock handles up to two 3,000-passenger cruise ships at a time (passengers are currently ferried to shore aboard tenders). Also recently opened, but still being refined, is the new 20,000-hectare (49,400-acre) "ecoarchaeological" park, **El Botazoo,** at Punta Celeste, where there is a recently discovered archaeological site. Hiking, rappelling, and birdwatching are popular activities there. This new development is all being handled with ecological sensitivity in mind.

If you're drawn to snorkeling, diving, boat cruises, and simple relaxation, Huatulco nicely fits the bill. Nine bays encompass 36 beaches and countless inlets and coves. Huatulco's main problem has been securing enough incoming flights. It relies heavily on charter service from the United States and Canada.

ESSENTIALS
GETTING THERE & DEPARTING
BY PLANE **Click Mexicana** flights (© 01-800/112-5425 toll-free in Mexico; www.click.com.mx) connect Huatulco with Mexico City.

From Huatulco's international airport (airport code: HUX; © 958/581-9004 or -9005), about 20km (12 miles) northwest of the Bahías de Huatulco, private **taxis** charge $49 (£27) to Crucecita, $44 (£24) to Santa Cruz, and $49 (£27) to Tangolunda. **Transportes Terrestres**

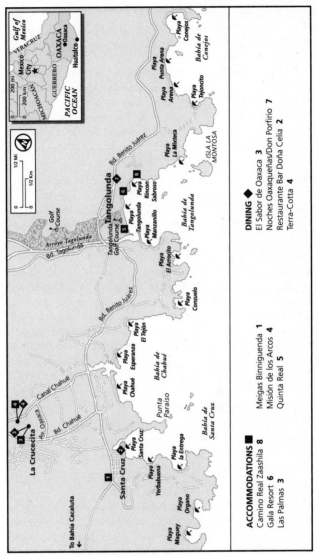

DINING ◆

El Sabor de Oaxaca **3**

Noches Oaxaqueñas/Don Porfirio **7**

Restaurante Bar Doña Celia **2**

Terra-Cotta **4**

ACCOMMODATIONS ■

Camino Real Zaashila **8**

Gala Resort **6**

Las Palmas **3**

Meigas Binniguenda **1**

Misión de los Arcos **4**

Quinta Real **5**

127

(*©* **958/581-9014**) *colectivos* fares are about $10 (£5.50) per person. When returning, make sure to ask for a taxi, unless you have a lot of luggage. Taxis to the airport run $42 (£23), but unless specifically requested, you'll get a Suburban, which costs $56 (£31).

Budget (*©* **800/527-0700** in the U.S., or 958/587-0010 or 958/581-9000) has an office at the airport that is open for flight arrivals. **Dollar** (*©* **958/587-1381**) also has rental offices downtown and offers one-way drop service for about $50 (£28) additional if you're traveling to Puerto Escondido. Because Huatulco is so spread out and has excellent roads, you may want to consider a rental car, at least for 1 or 2 days, to explore the area.

BY CAR   Coastal **Highway 200** leads to Huatulco (via Pochutla) from the north and is generally in good condition. The drive from Puerto Escondido takes just under 2 hours. The road is well maintained, but it's windy and doesn't have lights, so avoid travel after sunset. Allow at least 6 hours for the trip from Oaxaca City on mountainous **Highway 175.**

BY BUS   There are three bus stations in Crucecita, all within a few blocks, but none in Santa Cruz or Tangolunda. The **Gacela** and **Estrella Blanca** station, at the corner of Gardenia and Palma Real, handles service to Acapulco, Mexico City, Puerto Escondido, and Pochutla. The **Cristóbal Colón** station (*©* **958/587-0261**) is at the corner of Gardenia and Ocotillo, 4 blocks from the Plaza Principal. It serves destinations throughout Mexico, including Oaxaca, Puerto Escondido, and Pochutla. The **Estrella del Valle** station, on Jasmín between Sabali and Carrizal, serves Oaxaca.

VISITOR INFORMATION
The **State Tourism Office,** or Oficina del Turismo (*©* **958/ 581-0176;** fax 958/581-0177; www.baysofhuatulco.com.mx), has an information module in Tangolunda Bay, near the Grand Pacific hotel. It's open Monday to Friday from 8am to 5pm.

CITY LAYOUT
The overall resort area is called **Bahías de Huatulco** and includes nine bays. The town of Santa María de Huatulco, the original settlement in this area, is 27km (17 miles) inland. **Santa Cruz Huatulco,** usually called Santa Cruz, was the first developed area on the coast. It has a central plaza with a bandstand kiosk, which has been converted into a cafe that serves regionally grown coffee. It also has

an artisans' market on the edge of the plaza that borders the main road, a few hotels and restaurants, and a marina where bay tours and fishing trips set sail. **Juárez** is Santa Cruz's 4-block-long main street, anchored at one end by the Hotel Castillo Huatulco and at the other by the Meigas Binniguenda hotel. Opposite the Hotel Castillo is the marina, and beyond it are restaurants in new colonial-style buildings facing the beach. The area's banks are on Juárez. It's impossible to get lost and you can take in almost everything at a glance. This bay is the site of Huatulco's cruise-ship dock.

About 3km (2 miles) inland from Santa Cruz is **Crucecita,** a planned city that sprang up in 1985. It centers on a lovely grassy plaza. This is the residential area for the resorts, with neighborhoods of new stucco homes mixed with small apartment complexes. Crucecita has evolved into a lovely, traditional town where you'll find the area's best, and most reasonably priced, restaurants, plus some shopping and several less-expensive hotels.

Until other bays are developed, **Tangolunda Bay,** 5km (3 miles) east, is the focal point of development. Over time, half the bays will have resorts. For now, Tangolunda has an 18-hole golf course, as well as the Las Brisas, Quinta Real, Barceló Huatulco, Royal, Casa del Mar, and Camino Real Zaashila hotels, among others. Small strip centers with a few restaurants occupy each end of Tangolunda Bay. **Chahué Bay,** between Tangolunda and Santa Cruz, is a small bay with a beach club and other facilities under construction along with houses and a few small hotels.

GETTING AROUND

Crucecita, Santa Cruz, and Tangolunda are too far apart to walk, but **taxis** are inexpensive and readily available. Crucecita has taxi stands opposite the Hotel Grifer and on the Plaza Principal. Taxis are readily available through hotels in Santa Cruz and Tangolunda. The fare between Santa Cruz and Tangolunda is roughly $2.50 (£1.40); between Santa Cruz and Crucecita, $2 (£1.10); between Crucecita and Tangolunda, $2.50 (£1.40). To explore the area, you can hire a taxi by the hour (about $15/£8.25 per hour) or for the day.

There is **minibus service** between towns; the fare is 50¢ (30p). In Santa Cruz, catch the bus across the street from Castillo Huatulco; in Tangolunda, in front of the Grand Pacific; and in Crucecita, cater-cornered from the Hotel Grifer.

FAST FACTS: Bahías de Huatulco

Area Code The area code is **958**.

Banks All three areas have banks with ATMs, including the main Mexican banks, Banamex and Bancomer, and HSBC. They change money during business hours, Monday through Friday from 9am to 4pm. Banks line Calle Juárez in Santa Cruz, and surround the central plaza in Crucecita.

Drugstores **Farmacía del Carmen,** just off the central plaza in Crucecita (© 958/587-0878), is one of the largest drugstores in town. It's open Monday through Saturday from 8am to 10pm and Sunday from 8am to noon. **Farmacía La Clínica** (© 958/587-0591), Sabalí 1602, Crucecita, offers 24-hour service and delivery.

Emergencies **Police emergency** (© 060); **federal police** (© 958/587-0815); **transit police** (© 958/587-0186); and **Cruz Roja (Red Cross),** Bulevar Chahué 110 (© 958/587-1188).

Information **Oficina del Turismo,** the State Tourism Office (© 958/581-0176 or -0177; sedetur6@oaxaca.gob.mx) has an information module in Tangolunda Bay near the Campo de Golf. It's open weekdays, 8am to 5pm.

Internet Access Several Internet cafes are in Crucecita. One is at the cafe in the Misión de los Arcos, Av. Gardenia 902 (© 958/587-0165), which, in addition to paid service, is also a free wireless hot spot; another is on the ground-floor level of the **Hotel Plaza Conejo,** Av. Guamúchil 208, across from the main plaza (© 958/587-0054, or -0009; conejo3@mexico.com). It's about $1 (55p) per hour.

Medical Care **Dr. Ricardo Carrillo** (© 958/587-0687 or -0600) speaks English.

Post Office The *correo,* at Bulevar Chahué 100, Sector R, Crucecita (© 958/587-0551), is open Monday through Friday from 8am to 3pm, Saturday from 9am to 1pm.

WHERE TO STAY

Moderate- and budget-priced hotels in Santa Cruz and Crucecita are generally more expensive than similar hotels in other Mexican beach resorts. The luxury hotels have comparable rates, especially when they're part of a package that includes airfare. The trend here is toward all-inclusive resorts, which in Huatulco are an especially good option, given the lack of memorable dining and nightlife options. Hotels that are not oceanfront generally have an arrangement with a beach club at Santa Cruz or Chahué Bay, and offer shuttle service. Low-season rates apply August through November only. Parking is free at these hotels; the 17% tax is not included in the rack rates listed below.

EXPENSIVE

Camino Real Zaashila *Kids*   One of the original hotels in Tangolunda Bay, the Camino Real Zaashila sits on a wide stretch of sandy beach secluded from other beaches by small rock outcroppings. The calm water, perfect for swimming and snorkeling, makes it ideal for families. The white stucco building is Mediterranean in style and washed in colors on the ocean side. The boldly decorated rooms are large and have an oceanview balcony or terrace and a large bathroom with an Italian marble tub/shower combination. Each of the 41 club rooms on the lower levels has its own private plunge pool. The main pool is a free-form design that spans 500 feet of beach, with chaises built into the shallow edges. Well-manicured tropical gardens surround it and the guest rooms.

Bulevar Benito Juárez 5, Bahía de Tangolunda, 70989 Huatulco, Oax. © 800/ 722-6466 in the U.S., or 958/581-0460. Fax 958/581-0468. www.camino-zaashila.com. 120 units. High season $345 (£190) double, $381 (£210) club room; low season $234 (£129) double, $284 (£156) club room. AE, DC, MC, V. **Amenities:** 3 restaurants (1 Oaxacan); lobby bar w/live music; 2 large outdoor pools; outdoor whirlpool; lighted tennis court; beachside watersports center; kids' club; concierge; tour and travel agency services; room service; laundry service. *In room:* A/C, TV, minibar, safe.

Quinta Real *𝓡𝓡𝓡*   Double Moorish domes mark this romantic, relaxed hotel, known for its richly appointed cream-and-white decor and complete attention to detail. From the welcoming reception area to the luxurious beach club below, the staff emphasizes excellence in service. The small groupings of suites are built into the sloping hill to Tangolunda Bay and offer spectacular views of the ocean and golf course. Suites on the eastern edge of the resort sit above the highway, which generates some traffic noise. Interiors are elegant and comfortable, with stylish Mexican furniture, original art, wood-beamed ceilings, and marble tub/shower combinations with whirlpool tubs. Balconies have overstuffed seating areas and stone-inlay floors. Eight Grand Class Suites and the Presidential Suite have private pools. The most luxurious hotel in Huatulco, the Quinta Real is perfect for weddings, honeymoons, or small corporate retreats.

Bulevar Benito Juárez Lt. 2, Bahía de Tangolunda, 70989 Huatulco, Oax. ☏ **888/ 561-2817** in the U.S, or 958/581-0428, or -0430. Fax 958/581-0429. www.quintareal. com. 28 units. High season $390 (£215) Master Suite, $440 (£242) Grand Class Suite, $490 (£270) suite with private pool; low season $295 (£162) Master Suite, $345 (£190) Grand Class Suite, $395 (£217) suite with private pool. AE, MC, V. **Amenities:** Restaurant (breakfast, dinner); poolside restaurant (lunch); bar w/stunning view; beach club w/2 outdoor pools (1 for children); tennis court; concierge; tour desk; room service; in-room massage; laundry service; dry cleaning. *In room:* A/C, TV, minibar, hair dryer, safe.

MODERATE

Gala Resort ✿ (Kids) With all meals, drinks, entertainment, tips, and a slew of activities included in the price, the all-inclusive Gala is a value-packed experience. It caters to adults of all ages (married and single) who enjoy both activity and relaxation. An excellent— but often overcrowded—kids' activity program makes it a great option for families. Rooms have tile floors and Oaxacan wood trim, large tub/shower combinations, and ample balconies, all with views of Tangolunda Bay.

Bulevar Benito Juárez s/n, Bahía de Tangolunda, 70989 Huatulco, Oax. ☏ **958/581- 0000.** Fax 958/581-0220. www.gala-resort-huatulco.com. 290 units. High season $258–$320 (£142–£176) double, $402 (£221) junior suite, for children 12–17 $78 (£43), children 8–11 $54 (£30); low season $198–$258 (£109–£142) double, $299 (£164) junior suite, children 12–17 $60 (£33), children 8–11 $40 (£22). Children younger than 8 stay free in parent's room. Ask about special promotions. AE, MC, V. **Amenities:** 4 restaurants (buffet, a la carte); 4 bars; 5 outdoor pools, including a large free-form pool; 3 lighted tennis courts; full gym; complete beachside water-sports center. *In room:* A/C, TV, minibar, hair dryer, safe.

Hotel Meigas Binniguenda ✿ Huatulco's first hotel retains the charm and comfort that originally made it memorable. Rooms have Mexican-tile floors, foot-loomed bedspreads, and colonial-style fur-niture; French doors open onto tiny wrought-iron balconies over-looking Juárez or the pool and gardens. There's a section with newer rooms that have modern teak furnishings. A nice shady area sur-rounds the small pool in back of the lobby. The hotel is away from the marina at the far end of Juárez, only a few blocks from the water. It offers free transportation every hour to the beach club at Santa Cruz Bay.

Bulevar Santa Cruz 201, 70989 Santa Cruz de Huatulco, Oax. ☏ **958/587-0077** or -0078. Fax 958/587-0284. binniguenda@prodigy.net.mx. 165 units. Year-round $110 (£61) double. Children younger than 7 stay free in parent's room. AE, MC, V. **Amenities:** Large, *palapa*-topped restaurant and bar; small outdoor pool; shuttle to beach. *In room:* A/C, TV, safe.

INEXPENSIVE

Hotel Las Palmas   The central location and accommodating staff add to the appeal of the bright, basic rooms at Las Palmas. Located a half-block from the main plaza, it's connected to the popular El Sabor de Oaxaca restaurant (see "Where to Dine," below), which offers room service to guests. Rooms have tile floors, cotton textured bedspreads, tile showers, and cable TV.

Av. Guamúchil 206, 70989 Bahías de Huatulco, Oax. © 958/587-0060. Fax 958/587-0057. 25 units. High season $80 (£44) double; low season $45 (£25) double. AE, MC, V. **Amenities:** Currency exchange; safe. *In room:* A/C, TV.

Misión de los Arcos ★★ *Finds*   This exceptional hotel, just a block from the central plaza, is similar in style to the elegant Quinta Real—but at a fraction of the cost. The hotel is mostly white, accented with abundant greenery, giving it a fresh, inviting feel. Simple rooms continue the theme, washed in white, with cream and beige bed coverings and upholstery. Built-in desks, French windows, and minimal but interesting decorative accents give this budget hotel a real sense of style. At the entrance level, an excellent cafe offers high-speed Internet access, Huatulco's regionally grown coffee, tea, pastries, and ice cream. It's open from 8am to midnight. The adjacent Terra-Cotta restaurant (see below) serves breakfast, lunch, and dinner, and is equally stylish and budget-friendly. Although there's no pool, for $2.50 (£1.40) guests can use the Castillo Beach Club, at Chahué bay, open daily from 9am to 7pm. The hotel lies next door to La Crucecita's central plaza, close to all the shops and restaurants.

Gardenia 902, La Crucecita, 70989 Huatulco, Oax. © 958/587-0165. Fax 958/587-1904. www.misiondelosarcos.com. 13 units. High season $75 (£41) double, $80–$100 (£44–£55) suite; low season $50 (£28) double, $55–$75 (£30–£41) suite. Rates increase over Christmas and Easter holiday periods. AE, MC, V. Street parking. **Amenities:** Restaurant; nearby beach club; laundry service. *In room:* A/C, TV, Wi-Fi, safe.

WHERE TO DINE

El Sabor de Oaxaca ★★★ OAXACAN   This is the best place in the area to enjoy authentic, richly flavorful Oaxacan food, among the best of traditional Mexican cuisine. This colorful restaurant is a local favorite that also meets the quality standards of tourists. Among the most popular items are mixed grill for two, with a Oaxacan beef filet, tender pork tenderloin, chorizo (zesty Mexican sausage), and pork ribs; and the Oaxacan special for two, a generous sampling of the best of the menu, with tamales, Oaxacan cheese, pork mole, and more. If you're feeling adventurous, try the salty grilled *chapulines* (grasshoppers, a Oaxacan specialty). Generous breakfasts include eggs, bacon, ham, beans, toast, and fresh orange juice.

Av. Guamúchil 206, Crucecita. © **958/587-0060.** Fax 958/587-0057. Breakfast $4 (£2.25); main courses $6–$20 (£3.30–£11). AE, MC, V. Daily 7am–11pm.

Noches Oaxaqueñas/Don Porfirio ✦ SEAFOOD/OAXACAN

This dinner show presents the colorful, traditional folkloric dances of Oaxaca in an open-air courtyard reminiscent of an old hacienda (but in a modern strip mall). The dancers clearly enjoy performing traditional ballet under the direction of owner Celicia Flores Ramírez, wife of Don Willo Porfirio. The menu includes the *plato oaxaqueño,* a generous, flavorful sampling of traditional Oaxacan fare, with a tamal, a *sope* (a thick tortilla), Oaxacan cheese, grilled filet, pork enchilada, and a chile relleno. Other house specialties include grilled lobster, shrimp with mezcal, and spaghetti marinara with seafood. Meat lovers can enjoy American-style cuts or a juicy *arrachera* (skirt steak).

Bulevar Benito Juárez s/n (across from Royal Maeva), Tangolunda Bay. © **958/ 581-0001.** Main courses $10–$20 (£5.50–£11). AE, MC, V. Daily noon–11pm. Shows Tues, Thurs, and Sat from 8:30–10pm ($10/£5.50).

Restaurante Bar Doña Celia ✦ SEAFOOD   Doña Celia, an

original Huatulco resident, remains in business in the same area where she started her little thatch-roofed restaurant years ago. With outdoor tables fronting Santa Cruz, it offers fabulous seafood in picturesque surroundings. Among her specialties are *filete empapelado* (foil-wrapped fish baked with tomato, onion, and cilantro) and *filete almendrado* (fish filet covered with hotcake batter, beer, and almonds). The *ceviche* is terrific—one order is plenty for two—as is *platillo a la huatulqueño* (shrimp and young octopus fried in olive oil with chile and onion, served over white rice). There are also mouthwatering lobster selections, including lobster tacos. The restaurant is basic, but the food is the reason for its popularity.

Santa Cruz Bay. © **958/587-0128.** Breakfast $3.50–$6 (£1.95–£3.30); seafood $8–$30 (£4.40–£17). MC, V. Daily 8:30am–11pm.

Terra-Cotta ✦✦ *(Finds* INTERNATIONAL/MEXICAN   Located

inside the Hotel Misión de los Arcos, this stylish yet casual restaurant is delicious for breakfast, lunch, or dinner. Start the day in this whitewashed, Mediterranean setting with gourmet coffee, fruit salad, and an array of morning favorites, including specials such as

French toast stuffed with cream cheese and orange marmalade. Lunch and dinner share the same menu, which offers standards such as fajitas, baby back ribs, and gourmet tacos. Scrumptious desserts such as caramelized pineapple with coconut ice cream offer a sweet finish.

Gardenia 902, at the Hotel Misión de los Arcos, in front of La Crucecita's central plaza. ⓒ **958/587-0165.** Breakfast $1.50–$6 (85p–£3.30); lunch and dinner main courses $4–$14 (£2.20–£7.70). AE, MC, V. Daily 8am–10pm.

BEACHES, WATERSPORTS & OTHER THINGS TO DO

Attractions around Huatulco concentrate on the nine bays and their watersports. The number of ecotours and interesting side trips into the surrounding mountains is growing. Though it isn't a traditional Mexican town, the community of Crucecita is worth visiting. Just off the central plaza is the **Iglesia de Guadalupe,** with a large mural of Mexico's patron saint gracing the entire ceiling of the chapel. The image of the Virgin is set against a deep blue night sky, and includes 52 stars—a modern interpretation of Juan Diego's cloak.

You can dine in Crucecita for a fraction of the price in Tangolunda Bay, with the added benefit of some local color. Considering that shopping in Huatulco is generally poor, you'll find the best choices here, in the shops around the central plaza. They tend to stay open late, and offer a good selection of regional goods and typical tourist take-homes, including *artesanía,* silver jewelry, Cuban cigars, and tequila. A small, free trolley train takes visitors on a short tour of the town.

BEACHES

A section of the beach at Santa Cruz (away from the small boats) is an inviting sunning spot. Beach clubs for guests at non-oceanfront hotels are here. In addition, several restaurants are on the beach, and *palapa* umbrellas run down to the water's edge. For about $15 (£8.25) one-way, *pangas* from the marina in Santa Cruz will ferry you to **La Entrega Beach,** also in Santa Cruz Bay. There you'll find a row of *palapa* restaurants, all with beach chairs out front. Find an empty one, and use that restaurant for your refreshment needs. A snorkel equipment rental booth is about midway down the beach, and there's some fairly good snorkeling on the end away from where the boats arrive.

Between Santa Cruz and Tangolunda bays is **Chahué Bay.** The beach club has *palapas,* beach volleyball, and refreshments for an entrance fee of about $2.50 (£1.40). However, a strong undertow makes this a dangerous place for swimming.

Tangolunda Bay beach, fronting the best hotels, is wide and beautiful. Theoretically, all beaches in Mexico are public; however, nonguests at Tangolunda hotels may have difficulty entering the hotels to get to the beach.

BAY CRUISES & TOURS

Huatulco's major attraction is its coastline—a magnificent stretch of pristine bays bordered by an odd blend of cactus and jungle vegetation right at the water's edge. The only way to really grasp its beauty is to take a cruise of the bays, stopping at **Organo** or **Maguey Bay** for a dip in the crystal-clear water and a fish lunch at a *palapa* restaurant on the beach.

One way to arrange a bay tour is to go to the **boat-owners' cooperative** (© **958/587-0081**) in the red-and-yellow tin shack at the entrance to the marina. Prices are posted, and you can buy tickets for sightseeing, snorkeling, or fishing. Beaches other than La Entrega, including Maguey and San Agustín, are noted for offshore snorkeling. They also have *palapa* restaurants and other facilities. Several of these beaches, however, are completely undeveloped, so you will need to bring your own provisions. Boatmen at the cooperative will arrange return pickup at an appointed time. Prices run about $25 (£14) for 1 to 10 persons to La Entrega, and $50 (£28) for a trip to Maguey and Organo bays. The farthest bay is San Agustín; that all-day trip will run $100 (£55) in a private *panga*.

Another option is to join an organized daylong bay cruise. Any travel agency can easily make arrangements. Cruises are about $30 (£17) per person, with an extra charge of $5 (£2.75) for snorkeling-equipment rental and lunch. One excursion is on the *Tequila*, complete with guide, drinks, and on-board entertainment. Another, more romantic option is the *Luna Azul*, a 13m (43-ft.) sailboat that also offers bay tours and sunset sails.

Ecotours are growing in both popularity and number throughout the Bays of Huatulco. The mountain areas surrounding the Copalita River are also home to other natural treasures worth exploring, including the **Copalitilla Cascades.** Thirty kilometers (19 miles) north of Tangolunda at 395m (1,296 ft.) above sea level, this group of waterfalls—averaging 20 to 25m (66–82 ft.) in height—form natural whirlpools and clear pools for swimming. The area is also popular for horseback riding and rappelling.

An all-day **Coffee Plantation Tour** takes you into the mountains east of Huatulco, touring various coffee plantations. You'll learn how Oaxacan coffee is cultivated and learn about life on the plantations.

Lunch and refreshments are included. Cost for the day is $50 (£28); contact **Paraíso Tours** (www.paraisohuatulco.com) for reservations.

Guided **horseback riding** through the jungles and to Conejos and Magueyito beach makes for a wonderful way to see the natural beauty of the area. The ride lasts 3 hours, with departures at 9:45am and 1:45pm, and costs $35 to $45 (£19–£25). Contact **Caballo del Mar Ranch** (© 958/589-9387).

Another recommended guide for both **hiking** and **bird-watching** is Laura Gonzalez, of **Nature Tours Huatulco** (© 958/583-4047 or 589-0636; lauriycky@hotmail.com). Choices include a hike around Punta Celeste with views of the river, open sea, and forest, for sightings of terrestrial and aquatic birds. The 3½-hour tour can be made in the early morning or late afternoon, and costs $45 (£25). An 8-hour excursion to the Ventanilla Lagoons takes you by boat through a mangrove to view birds, iguanas, and crocodiles. The cost is $80 (£44), and lunch is included. Tours include transportation, binoculars, specialized bird guide, and beverages.

GOLF & TENNIS

The 18-hole, par-72 **Tangolunda Golf Course** (© 958/581-0037) is adjacent to Tangolunda Bay. It has tennis courts as well. The greens fee is $76 (£42), and carts cost $34 (£19). Tennis courts are also available at the **Barceló** hotel (© 958/581-0055).

SHOPPING

Shopping in the area is limited and unmemorable. It concentrates in the **Santa Cruz Market,** by the marina in Santa Cruz, and in the **Crucecita Market,** on Guamúchil, a half-block from the plaza. Both are open daily from 10am to 8pm (no phones). Among the prototypical souvenirs, you may want to search out regional specialties, which include Oaxacan embroidered blouses and dresses, and *barro negro,* pottery made from dark clay exclusively found in the Oaxaca region. Also in Crucecita is the Plaza Oaxaca, adjacent to the central plaza. Its clothing shops include **Poco Loco Club/Coconut's Boutique** (© 958/587-0279), for casual sportswear; and **Mic Mac** (© 958/587-0565), for beachwear and souvenirs. **Coconuts** (© 958/587-0057) has English-language magazines, books, and music.

HUATULCO AFTER DARK

There's a very limited selection of dance clubs around Huatulco—meaning that's where everyone goes. Huatulco seems to have the least consistent nightlife of any resort in Mexico, and clubs seem to change ownership—and names—almost annually. Check with your hotel concierge to see if any new places have opened; none of the places listed below have phones. The current hot spot is **Bar La Crema,** in Crucecita (about 4 blocks south of the *zócalo,* at the corner of Bugambilia and La Ceiba), with a lounge atmosphere and a mix of tunes. Nearby is **Café Dublin,** Carrizal 504 (1 block east and a half-block south from the *zócalo*), an Irish pub with a book exchange. Both bars open in the evening during high season and stay open as long as the management sees fit; hours are sporadic in low season. On the east side of the *zócalo* lies **Bar La Iguana,** playing rock music and featuring televised sports. The bar is typically open daily from noon to 4am during high season, with limited hours in low season.

La Papaya on Bulevar Chahué is a popular dance club open Thursday through Saturday into the wee hours. Each Wednesday, the Barceló Resort hosts its **Fiesta Mexicana** from 7 to 11pm, featuring folkloric dances, mariachi music, and a buffet of Mexican food and drinks.

5

Inland to Old Mexico: Taxco, Cuernavaca & Tepoztlán

It may seem as if the small towns in this region of Mexico are trying to capitalize on recent trends in travel toward spas and self-exploration, but in reality, they've helped define them. From the restorative properties of thermal waters and earth-based spa treatments to the mystical and spiritual properties of gemstones and herbs, the treasures and knowledge in these towns have existed for years—and, in some cases, for centuries.

This is only a sampling of towns south and west of Mexico City. They are fascinating in their diversity, history, and mystery, and make for a unique travel experience, either on their own or combined. They vary in character from mystical villages to sophisticated spa towns, with archaeological and colonial-era attractions in the mix. And with their proximity to Mexico City, all are within easy reach by private car or taxi—or by inexpensive bus—in under a few hours.

The legendary silver city of **Taxco,** on the road between Acapulco and Mexico City, is renowned for its museums, picturesque hillside colonial-era charm, and, of course, its silver shops. North of Taxco and southwest of Mexico City, over the mountains, are the venerable thermal spas at **Ixtapan de la Sal,** as well as their more modern counterparts in **Valle de Bravo.** Verdant **Cuernavaca,** known as the land of eternal spring, has gained a reputation for its exceptional spa facilities and its wealth of cultural and historic attractions. Finally, **Tepoztlán,** with its enigmatic charms and legendary pyramid, captivates the few travelers who find their way there.

1 Taxco: Cobblestones & Silver ★★

178km (110 miles) SW of Mexico City; 80km (50 miles) SW of Cuernavaca; 296km (184 miles) NE of Acapulco

In Mexico and around the world, the town of Taxco de Alarcón—most commonly known simply as Taxco (*tahs*-koh)—is synonymous with silver. The town's geography and architecture are equally precious: Taxco sits at nearly 1,515m (4,969 ft.) on a hill among hills, and almost any point in the city offers fantastic views.

Hernán Cortez discovered Taxco as he combed the area for treasure, but its rich caches of silver weren't fully exploited for another 2 centuries. In 1751, the French prospector Joseph de la Borda—who came to be known locally as José—commissioned the baroque Santa Prisca Church that dominates Taxco's *zócalo* (Plaza Borda) as a way of giving something back to the town. In the mid-1700s, Borda was considered the richest man in New Spain.

The fact that Taxco has become Mexico's most renowned center for silver design, even though it now mines only a small amount of silver, is the work of an American, William Spratling. Spratling arrived in the late 1920s with the intention of writing a book. He soon noticed the skill of the local craftsmen and opened a workshop to produce handmade silver jewelry and tableware based on pre-Hispanic art, which he exported to the United States in bulk. The workshops flourished, and Taxco's reputation grew.

Today, most of the residents of this town are involved in the silver industry in some way. Taxco is home to hundreds (some say up to 900) of silver shops and outlets, ranging from sleek galleries to small stands in front of stucco homes. You'll find silver in all of its forms here—the jewelry basics, tea sets, silverware, candelabras, picture frames, and napkin holders.

The tiny one-man factories that line the cobbled streets all the way up into the hills supply most of Taxco's silverwork. "Bargains" are relative, but nowhere else will you find this combination of diversity, quality, and rock-bottom prices. Generally speaking, the larger shops that most obviously cater to the tourist trade will have the highest prices—but they may be the only ones to offer "that special something" you're looking for. For classic designs in jewelry or other silver items, shop around, and wander the back streets and smaller venues.

You can get an idea of what Taxco is like by spending an afternoon, but there's much more to this picturesque town of 120,000 than just the Plaza Borda and the shops surrounding it. Stay overnight, wander its steep cobblestone streets, and you'll discover little plazas, fine churches, and, of course, an abundance of silversmiths' shops.

The main part of town is relatively flat. It stretches up the hillside from the highway, and it's a steep but brief walk up. White VW minibuses, called *combis,* make the circuit through and around town,

Taxco

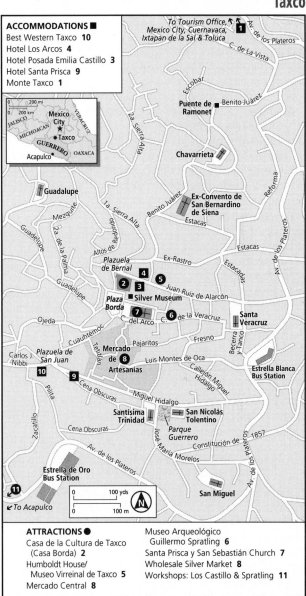

ACCOMMODATIONS ■
Best Western Taxco **10**
Hotel Los Arcos **4**
Hotel Posada Emilia Castillo **3**
Hotel Santa Prisca **9**
Monte Taxco **1**

To Tourism Office,
Mexico City, Cuernavaca,
Ixtapan de la Sal & Toluca **1**

Av. de los Plateros
C. de La Vista
Escobar
Puente de Ramonet
Benito Juárez
Chavarrieta
Reforma
2a. Sierra Alta
Guadalupe
1a. Sierra Alta
Mezquite
Benito Juárez
Ex-Convento de San Bernardino de Siena
Estacas
Estacas
Estacadas
Av. de los Plateros
Guadalupe
2a. de la Palma
Altos de Reme...
Plazuela de Bernal
Ex-Rastro
4 **5**
2
3
Juan Ruiz de Alarcón
Guadalupe
Ojeda
Plaza Borda
Silver Museum
7
C. del Arco
6
C. de la Veracruz
Santa Veracruz
Cuauhtémoc
Pajaritos
Fresno
Becerra y Tanco
Carlos J. Nibbi
Plazuela de San Juan
Mercado de Artesanías
8
Luis Montes de Oca
Callejón Miguel Hidalgo
Estrella Blanca Bus Station
10
9
Cena Obscuras
Teltilán
Pilita
Miguel Hidalgo
Zacatillo
Cena Obscuras
Santísima Trinidad
José María Morelos
San Nicolás Tolentino
Parque Guerrero
Constitución de 1857
Av. de los Plateros
Estrella de Oro Bus Station
11
To Acapulco
Av. de los Plateros
San Miguel

0   200 mi
0   200 km
Mexico City ★
JALISCO
MICHOACAN
GUERRERO
Taxco •
Acapulco •
VERACRUZ
OAXACA

0   100 yds
0   100 m
N

ATTRACTIONS ●
Casa de la Cultura de Taxco (Casa Borda) **2**
Humboldt House/ Museo Virreinal de Taxco **5**
Mercado Central **8**

Museo Arqueológico Guillermo Spratling **6**
Santa Prisca y San Sebastián Church **7**
Wholesale Silver Market **8**
Workshops: Los Castillo & Spratling **11**

picking up and dropping off passengers along the route, from about 7am until 9pm. These taxis are inexpensive (about 50¢/30p), and you should use them even if you arrive by car, because parking is practically impossible. Also, the streets are so narrow and steep that most visitors find them nerve-racking. Find a secured parking lot for your car, or leave it at your hotel and forget about it until you leave.

Warning: Self-appointed guides will undoubtedly approach you in the *zócalo* (Plaza Borda) and offer their services—they get a cut (up to 25%) of all you buy in the shops they take you to. Before hiring a guide, ask to see his SECTUR (Tourism Secretary) credentials. The Department of Tourism office on the highway at the north end of town can recommend a licensed guide.

ESSENTIALS
GETTING THERE & DEPARTING
BY CAR   From Mexico City, take Paseo de la Reforma to Chapultepec Park and merge with the Periférico, which will take you to Highway 95D on the south end of town. From the Periférico, take the Insurgentes exit and merge until you come to the sign for CUERNAVACA/TLALPAN. Choose either CUERNAVACA CUOTA (toll) or CUERNAVACA LIBRE (free). Continue south around Cuernavaca to the Amacuzac interchange, and proceed straight ahead for Taxco. The drive from Mexico City takes about 3½ hours.

From Acapulco you have two options: Highway 95D is the toll road through Iguala to Taxco, or you can take the old two-lane road (Hwy. 95) that winds more slowly through villages; it's in good condition.

BY BUS   From Mexico City, buses depart from the Central de Autobuses del Sur station (Metro: Taxqueña) and take 2 to 3 hours, with frequent departures.

Taxco has two bus stations. Estrella de Oro buses arrive at their own station on the southern edge of town. Estrella Blanca service, including Futura executive-class buses, and Flecha Roja buses arrive at the station on the northeastern edge of town on Avenida Los Plateros ("Avenue of the Silversmiths," formerly Av. Kennedy). Taxis to the *zócalo* cost around $2 (£1.10).

VISITOR INFORMATION
The **State of Guerrero Dirección de Turismo** (©/fax **762/622-2274**) has offices at the arches on the main highway at the north end of town (Av. de los Plateros 1), which is useful if you're driving into town. The office is open Monday through Friday from 8am to 3:30pm. To get there from the Plaza Borda, take a ZOCALO-ARCOS

combi and get off at the arch over the highway. As you face the arches, the tourism office is on your right.

CITY LAYOUT

The center of town is the tiny **Plaza Borda,** shaded by perfectly manicured Indian laurel trees. On one side is the imposing twin-towered, pink-stone **Santa Prisca Church;** whitewashed, red-tile buildings housing the famous silver shops and a restaurant or two line the other sides. Beside the church, deep in a crevice of the mountain, is the **wholesale silver market**—absolutely the best place to begin your silver shopping, to get an idea of prices for more standard designs. You'll be amazed at the low prices. Buying just one piece is perfectly acceptable, and buying in bulk can lower the per-piece price. One of the beauties of Taxco is that its brick and cobblestone streets are completely asymmetrical, zigzagging up and down the hillsides. The plaza buzzes with vendors of everything from hammocks and cotton candy to bark paintings and balloons.

FAST FACTS

The telephone area code is **762.** The main post office, Benito Juárez 6, at the City Hall building (☎ 762/622-8596), is open Monday through Saturday from 9am to 2:30pm. The older branch of the

Spanish & Art Classes in Taxco

The Taxco campus of the **Universidad Nacional Autónoma de México (UNAM;** ☎ 762/622-0124 for the Spanish school, or 622-3690 for the art school) sits on the grounds of the Hacienda del Chorrillo, formerly part of the Cortez land grant. Here, students learn silversmithing, Spanish, drawing, composition, and history under the supervision of UNAM instructors. Classes are small, and courses generally last 3 months. The school provides a list of prospective town accommodations that consist primarily of hotels. More reasonable accommodations for a lengthy stay are available, but best arranged once you're there. At many locations all over town, you'll find notices of furnished apartments or rooms for rent. For information about the school, contact either the Dirección de Turismo (tourist office) in Taxco (see "Visitor Information," above), or write the school directly at Hacienda del Chorrillo, 40200 Taxco, Gro.

post office (© **762/622-0501**), open Monday through Friday from 8am to 2:30pm, is on the outskirts, on the highway to Acapulco. It's in a row of shops with a black-and-white CORREO sign.

WHERE TO STAY
MODERATE

Best Western Taxco 𝍢𝍢   This is the newest and most modern hotel in the town center, with professional service and an international clientele. Rooms are smallish but very comfortable, with white tiles and bedspreads and Mexican architectural touches; some have windows (interior rooms do not), and the junior suite has a terrace with views of the surrounding hills. Near the Santa Prisca church, this hotel offers a quality Mexican restaurant and access to a nearby pool. The friendly staff will arrange in-room massages upon request.

Carlos J. Nibbi 2, Plazuela de San Juan, 40200 Taxco, Gro. © **762/627-6194.** Fax 762/622-3416. www.bestwesterntaxco.com. 23 units. $110 (£61) double weekdays; $120 (£66) double weekends; $160 (£88) junior suite weekdays; $190 (£105) junior suite weekends. AE, MC, V. Free parking. **Amenities:** Restaurant; access to outdoor pool and massage services; business center; laundry service. *In room:* A/C, TV, Wi-Fi.

Monte Taxco *(Overrated)*   This resort and country club sits atop a hill near the entrance to Taxco coming from Mexico City. A longtime landmark of the city, it offers golf and tennis, spa services, and access to the mountain's cable car. Colonial-style rooms are a bit dated but comfortable. Open weekends for dinner only, Toni's boasts the best city views of any restaurant in Taxco, and you can finish the night at the flashy dance club next door. You'll need to drive or take a taxi to reach the city center.

Fracc. Lomas de Taxco s/n, 40210 Taxco, Gro. © **762/622-1300.** Fax 762/622-1428. www.montetaxco.com.mx. 156 units. $170 (£94) double. AE, MC, V. Free parking. **Amenities:** Restaurant (w/spectacular city view; see review for Toni's, below); bar; dance club; heated outdoor pool; 9-hole golf course; 3 tennis courts; gym; spa services; travel desk; room service; laundry service. *In room:* A/C, TV.

INEXPENSIVE

Hotel los Arcos 𝍢   Los Arcos occupies a converted 1620 monastery. The handsome inner patio is bedecked with Puebla pottery and rustic furnishings surrounding a central fountain. Guest rooms are nicely but sparsely appointed, with natural tile floors and colonial-style furniture; the spacious junior suite has two levels. You'll feel immersed in colonial charm and blissful quiet. To find the hotel from the Plaza Borda, follow the hill down (with Hotel Agua

Escondida on your left) and make an immediate right at the Plazuela Bernal; the hotel is a block down on the left, opposite the Hotel Posada Emilia Castillo (see below).

Juan Ruiz de Alarcón 4, 40200 Taxco, Gro. ⓒ **762/622-1836.** Fax 762/622-7982. 21 units. $43 (£24) double; $50 (£28) triple; $56 (£31) quad; $62 (£34) junior suite. No credit cards. **Amenities:** Internet. *In room:* TV.

Hotel Posada Emilia Castillo *(Value* Each room in this delightful small hotel is simply but handsomely appointed with carved doors and furniture; the small tile bathrooms have showers only. Ask for an interior room, which are much quieter than those facing the street. A high-quality silver shop lies next to the colorful lobby. The hotel does not have parking but contracts with a local parking garage.

Juan Ruiz de Alarcón 7, 40200 Taxco, Gro. ⓒ/fax **762/622-1396.** www.hotelemilia castillo.com. 14 units. $45 (£25) double; $50 (£28) triple with TV. MC, V. From the Plaza Borda, go downhill a short block to the Plazuela Bernal and make an immediate right; the hotel is a block farther on the right, opposite the Hotel los Arcos (see above). **Amenities:** Internet. *In room:* TV.

Hotel Santa Prisca *(Value* The Santa Prisca, 1 block from the Plaza Borda on the Plazuela San Juan, is one of the older and best located hotels in town. Rooms are small but comfortable, with standard bathrooms (showers only), tile floors, wood beams, and a colonial atmosphere. For longer stays, ask for a room in the adjacent new addition, where the rooms are sunnier, quieter, and more spacious. There is a reading area in an upstairs salon overlooking Taxco, as well as a garden patio with fountains.

Cenaobscuras 1, 40200 Taxco, Gro. ⓒ **762/622-0080** or -0980. Fax 762/622-2938. 34 units. $50 (£28) double; $65 (£36) superior double; $74 (£41) junior suite. AE, MC, V. Limited free parking. **Amenities:** Dining-room-style restaurant and bar; room service; laundry service; safe.

WHERE TO DINE

Taxco gets a lot of day-trippers, most of whom choose to dine close to the Plaza Borda. Prices in this area are high for what you get. Just a few streets back, you'll find some excellent, simple *fondas* (taverns) or restaurants.

VERY EXPENSIVE

Toni's ⓡ STEAKS/SEAFOOD   High on a mountaintop, Toni's is an intimate, classic restaurant enclosed in a huge, cone-shaped *palapa* with a panoramic view of the city. Eleven candlelit tables sparkle with crystal and crisp linen, and piano music accompanies dinner. The menu, mainly shrimp or beef, is limited, but the food is quite good. Try tender, juicy prime roast beef, which comes with creamed spinach and baked potato. To reach Toni's, it's best to take a taxi. Note that it's open for dinner on weekends only.

In the Hotel Monte Taxco. © 762/622-1300. Reservations recommended. Main courses $15–$26 (£8.25–£14). AE, MC, V. Fri–Sat 7pm–1am.

MODERATE

Cafe Sasha 🕻🕻 INTERNATIONAL/VEGETARIAN   One of the cutest places to dine in town, Cafe Sasha is very popular with locals, and offers a great array of vegetarian options—such as falafel and vegetarian crepes, as well as Mexican and international classics. Try their Thai chicken curry or a hearty burrito. Open for breakfast, lunch, and dinner, it's also a great place for a cappuccino and pastry, or an evening cocktail. The music is hip, and the atmosphere is inviting and chic. Local artists often exhibit here, and there's live music on Sundays.

Calle Juan Ruiz de Alarcón 1, just down from Plazuela de Berna. No phone. www.cafesasha.com. Breakfast $2–$7 (£1.10–£3.85); main courses $5–$15 (£2.75–£8.25). No credit cards. Daily 8am–11:30pm.

El Adobe 🕻 MEXICAN   This charming restaurant is an eclectic Mexican mix of adobe, brick, and wood with decor that includes regional art, old black-and-white photos of Mexican and American entertainers, and some kitsch memorabilia. There are a number of romantic balcony tables lit with candles and lamps after dark. The hearty fare includes *cecina taxqueña* (thin strip steak served with guacamole), *pollo al adobe* (chicken with onions, green chile, and ham diced with grated cheese and cooked in aluminum foil), and enchiladas prepared anyway you want. A guitar player/singer performs weekend nights, and brunch is offered on Sundays.

Plazuela de San Juan 13. © 762/622-1416. Breakfast $3–$5 (£1.65–£2.75); main courses $5.50–$14 (£3–£7.70). MC, V. Daily 7:30am–11pm.

La Terraza Café-Bar INTERNATIONAL   One of two restaurants at the Hotel Agua Escondida (on the *zócalo*), the rooftop La Terraza is a scenic spot for a meal or a drink, with a great view of the church and tasty food. The menu is ample—you can get anything from breaded veal to grilled pork chops or chicken fajitas, and desserts include crepes, chocolate cake, and flan. Frosty margaritas and rich cappuccinos are also on order. During the day, cafe umbrellas shade the sun, but you can stargaze here at night.

Plaza Borda 4. © 762/622-1166. Main courses $4–$10 (£2.20–£5.50). MC, V. Daily noon–10pm.

Sotavento Restaurant Bar Galería &&& ITALIAN/INTERNA-
TIONAL   Paintings decorate the walls of this stylish restaurant,
which offers tables inside, on the balcony, or in the garden patio.
The extensive menu features Italian and Mexican dishes—try deli-
ciously fresh spinach salad and large pepper steak for a hearty meal,
or Spaghetti Barbara, with poblano peppers, onions, avocado, and
cream for a vegetarian option. Savory crepes are also available.

Benito Juárez 12, next to City Hall. *C* 762/627-1217. Main courses $4.50–$15
(£2.50–£8.25). MC, V. Tues–Sun 1pm–midnight. From the Plaza Borda, walk downhill beside the Hotel Agua Escondida, then follow the street as it bears left (don't
go right on Juan Ruiz de Alarcón) about 1 block; the restaurant is on the left just
after the street bends left.

Sr. Costilla's MEXICAN/INTERNATIONAL   The offbeat
decor at "Mr. Ribs" includes old photos of Mexican and international performers and a ceiling decked out with an assortment of
cultural curios (note the festive dangling skeletons). Several tiny
balconies hold minuscule tables that afford a view of the plaza and
church, and they fill up long before the large dining room does.
The broad menu features steaks, sandwiches, barbecue chicken,
shrimp, and spareribs, as well as desserts and an extensive selection
of drinks.

Plaza Borda 1 (next to Santa Prisca, above Patio de las Artesanías). *C*/fax **762/
622-3215.** Main courses $8–$22 (£4.40–£12). MC, V. Mon–Fri noon–midnight; Sat
9am–midnight; Sun 8am–8pm.

INEXPENSIVE
Restaurante Ethel MEXICAN   This family-run eatery opposite
the Hotel Santa Prisca, 1 block from the Plaza Borda, is simple and
cheap. It has colorful cloths on the tables and a tidy, homey atmosphere. The hearty *comida corrida* (food on the go) consists of soup
or pasta, meat (perhaps a small steak), dessert, and good coffee. Full
breakfasts, typical Mexican dishes, and rich *pozole* (a thick Mexican
soup) are offered, too.

Plazuela San Juan 14. *C* **762/622-0788.** Breakfast $5.50–$6 (£3–£3.30); main
courses $5.50–$7 (£3–£3.85); *comida corrida* (served 1–5pm) $5.80 (£3.20). No
credit cards. Daily 9am–9pm.

EXPLORING TAXCO
Shopping for jewelry and other items is the major pastime for
tourists. Prices for silver jewelry at Taxco's shops are about the best
in the world, and everything is available, from $1 (55p) trinkets to
artistic pieces costing hundreds of dollars.

In addition, Taxco is the home of some of Mexico's finest stone sculptors and is a good place to buy masks. However, beware of so-called "antiques"—there are virtually no real ones for sale.

SPECIAL EVENTS & FESTIVALS

January 18 marks the annual celebration in honor of Santa Prisca, with public festivities and fireworks displays. **Holy Week** 🎇🎇 in Taxco is one of the most poignant in the country, beginning the Friday a week before Easter with processions daily and nightly. The most riveting, on Thursday evening, lasts almost 4 hours and includes villagers from the surrounding area carrying statues of saints, followed by hooded members of a society of self-flagellating penitents, chained at the ankles and carrying huge wooden crosses and bundles of thorny branches. On Saturday morning, the Plaza Borda fills for the **Procession of Three Falls,** reenacting the three times Christ stumbled and fell while carrying the cross.

Taxco's **Silver Fair** starts the last week in November and continues through the first week in December. It includes a competition for silver works and sculptures among the top silversmiths. In late April to early May, **Jornadas Alarconianas** features plays and literary events in honor of Juan Ruiz de Alarcón (1572–1639), a world-famous dramatist who was born in Taxco—and for whom Taxco de Alarcón is named. Art exhibits, street fairs, and other festivities are part of the dual celebration.

SIGHTS IN TOWN

Casa de la Cultura de Taxco (Casa Borda)   Diagonally across from the Santa Prisca Church and facing Plaza Borda is the home José de la Borda built for his son around 1759. Now the Guerrero State Cultural Center, it houses a bookstore, classrooms, and exhibit halls where period clothing, engravings, paintings, and crafts are on display. The center also books traveling art exhibits, theatrical performances, music concerts, and dance events.

Plaza Borda 1. ⓒ **762/622-6617.** Fax 762/662-6634. Free admission. Tues–Sun 10am–5pm.

Humboldt House/Museo Virreinal de Taxco   Stroll along Ruiz de Alarcón (the street behind the Casa Borda) and look for the richly decorated facade of the Humboldt House, where the renowned German scientist and explorer Baron Alexander von Humboldt (1769–1859) spent a night in 1803. The museum houses 18th-century memorabilia pertinent to Taxco, most of which came from a secret room discovered during a recent restoration of the Santa Prisca Church. Signs with detailed information are in Spanish and English. As you enter, to the right are very rare *túmulos funerios* (painted funerary altars). The bottom two were painted in honor of Charles III of Spain; the top one, with a carved phoenix on top, was supposedly painted for the funeral of José de la Borda.

Another section presents historical information about Don Miguel Cabrera, Mexico's foremost 18th-century artist. Fine examples of clerical garments decorated with gold and silver thread hang in glass cases, and on the bottom level there's an impressive 17th-century carved wood altar of Dolores. Next to it, a small room is devoted to Humboldt and his sojourns through South America and Mexico.

Calle Juan Ruiz de Alarcón 12. © 762/622-5501. Admission $2 (£1.10) adults, $1.50 (85p) students and teachers w/ID. Tues–Sat 10am–6pm; Sun 10am–4pm.

Mercado Central   Located to the right of the Santa Prisca Church, behind and below Berta's, Taxco's central market meanders deep inside the mountain. Take the stairs off the street. In addition to a collection of wholesale silver shops, you'll find numerous food stands, always the best place for a cheap meal.

Plaza Borda. Shops daily 10am–8pm; food stands daily 7am–6pm.

Museo Arqueológico Guillermo Spratling   A plaque in Spanish explains that most of the collection of pre-Columbian art displayed here, as well as the funds for the museum, came from William Spratling (1900–67). You'd expect this to be a silver museum, but it's not—for Spratling silver, go to the Spratling Ranch Workshop (see "Nearby Attractions," below). The entrance floor and the one above display a good collection of pre-Columbian statues and implements in clay, stone, and jade. The upper floor holds changing exhibits.

Calle Porfirio A. Delgado 1. © 762/622-1660. Admission $2.50 (£1.40) adults, free for children younger than 13; free to all Sun. Tues–Sat 9am–5pm; Sun 9am–3pm. Leaving Santa Prisca Church, turn right and right again at the corner; continue down the street, veer right, then immediately left. The museum will be facing you.

Santa Prisca y San Sebastián Church 🎯🎯   This is Taxco's centerpiece parish church; it faces the pleasant Plaza Borda. José de la Borda, a French miner who struck it rich in Taxco's silver mines, funded the construction. Completed in 1758, it's one of Mexico's most impressive baroque churches. The ultracarved facade is eclipsed by the interior, where the intricacy of the gold-leafed saints and cherubic angels is positively breathtaking. The paintings by Miguel Cabrera, one of Mexico's most famous colonial-era artists, are the pride of Taxco. The sacristy (behind the high altar) contains more Cabrera paintings.

Guides, both children and adults, will approach you outside the church offering to give a tour. Make sure the guide's English is passable, and establish whether the price is per person or per tour.

Plaza Borda. (2) 762/622-0184. Free admission. Daily 10am–8pm.

NEARBY ATTRACTIONS

The impressive **Grutas de Cacahuamilpa** (2), known as the Cacahuamilpa Caves or Grottoes, are less than a half-hour north of Taxco. Hourly guided tours run daily at the caverns, which are truly sensational and well worth the visit. To see them, you can join a tour from Taxco (see above) or take a *combi* from the Flecha Roja terminal in Taxco; the one-way fare is $3 (£1.65), and admission to the caves is $3 (£1.65). For more information, see "Sights near Tepoztlán," later in this chapter.

Los Castillo   Don Antonio Castillo was one of hundreds of young men to whom William Spratling taught silversmithing in the 1930s. He was also one of the first to branch out with his own shops and line of designs, which over the years have earned him a fine reputation. Castillo has shops in several Mexican cities. Now, his daughter Emilia creates her own noteworthy designs, including decorative pieces with silver fused onto porcelain. Emilia's work is for sale on the ground floor of the Posada de los Castillo, just below the Plazuela Bernal.

8km (5 miles) south of town on the Acapulco Hwy. Also at Plazuela Bernal, Taxco. (2) 762/622-1016 or -1988 (workshop). Free admission. Workshop Mon–Fri 8am– 2pm and 3–6pm; open to groups at other hours by appointment only.

Spratling Ranch Workshop   William Spratling's hacienda-style home and workshop on the outskirts of Taxco still bustles with busy hands reproducing unique designs. A trip here will show you what distinctive Spratling work was all about, for the designs crafted today show the same fine work. Although the prices are higher than at other outlets, the designs are unusual and considered collectible. There's no store in Taxco, and unfortunately, most of the display cases hold only samples. With the exception of a few jewelry pieces, most items are by order only. Ask about U.S. outlets.

10km (6¼ miles) south of town on the Acapulco Hwy. (2) 762/622-0026. Free admission. Mon–Sat 9am–5pm. The *combi* to Iguala stops at the ranch; fare is 70¢ (40p).

TAXCO AFTER DARK

Bar Acerto (© 762/622-0064) is the most enticing place overlooking the square for cocktails, conversation, and people-watching, all of which continue until 11pm daily. Taxco's popular, modern dance club, **Windows,** sits high up the mountain in the **Hotel Monte Taxco** (© 762/622-1300). The whole city is on view, and music runs the gamut from Latin pop to '80s hits. For a $5 (£2.75) cover, you can dance away Friday or Saturday night from 10pm to 3am.

Completely different in tone is **Berta's** (© 762/622-0172), next to the Santa Prisca Church. Opened in 1930 by a lady named Berta, who made her fame on a drink of the same name (tequila, soda, lime, and honey), it's the traditional gathering place of the local gentry and more than a few tourists. Spurs and old swords decorate the walls. Grab a seat on the balcony overlooking the plaza and church. A Berta (the drink, of course) costs about $5 (£2.75), rum, the same. It's open daily from 11am to 8pm.

La Concha Nostra (© 762/622-7944) has a local, edgy feel and features live rock music Saturday nights for a $3 (£1.65) cover. It's located upstairs inside the Hotel Casa Grande at Plazuela de San Juan 7, and is open nightly until 1am. The gay-friendly **Aztec Disco** (© 762/627-3833) features drag shows and dancing. It's located on Av. de los Plateros 184, and is open from 10pm until late.

2 Cuernavaca: Land of Eternal Spring 🌟🌟🌟

102km (63 miles) S of Mexico City; 80km (50 miles) N of Taxco

Often called the "land of eternal spring," Cuernavaca is known these days as much for its rejuvenating spas and spiritual sites as it is for its perfect climate and flowering landscapes. Spa services are easy to find, but more than that, Cuernavaca exudes a sense of deep connection with its historical and spiritual heritage. Its palaces, walled villas, and elaborate haciendas are home to museums, spas, and extraordinary guesthouses.

Wander the traditional markets and you'll see crystals, quartz, onyx, and tiger's eye, in addition to tourist trinkets. These stones come from the Tepozteco Mountains—for centuries considered an energy source—which cradle Cuernavaca to the north and east. This area is where Mexico begins to narrow, and several mountain ranges converge. East and southeast of Cuernavaca are two volcanoes, also potent symbols of earth energy: Ixtaccihuatl (the Sleeping Woman) and the recently active Popocatépetl (the Smoking Mountain).

Cuernavaca, capital of the state of Morelos, is also a cultural treasure, with a past that closely follows the history of Mexico. So divine are the landscape and climate that both the Aztec ruler Moctezuma II and French Emperor Maximilian built private retreats here. Today, the roads between Mexico City and Cuernavaca are jammed almost every weekend, when city residents seek the same respite. Cuernavaca even has a large American colony, plus many students attending the numerous language and cultural institutes.

Emperor Charles V gave Cuernavaca to Hernán Cortez as a fief, and in 1532 the conquistador built a palace (now the Museo de Cuauhnáhuac), where he lived on and off for half a dozen years before returning to Spain. Cortez introduced sugar cane cultivation to the area, and African slaves were brought in to work in the cane fields, by way of Spain's Caribbean colonies. His sugar hacienda at the edge of town is now the impressive Hotel de Cortez.

After Mexico gained independence from Spain, powerful landowners from Mexico City gradually dispossessed the remaining small landholders, imposing virtual serfdom on them. This condition led to the rise of Emiliano Zapata, the great champion of agrarian reform, who battled the forces of wealth and power, defending the small farmer with the cry of *"¡Tierra y Libertad!"* (Land and Liberty!) during the Mexican Revolution of 1910.

Today, Cuernavaca's popularity has brought an influx of wealthy foreigners and industrial capital. With this commercial growth, the city has also acquired the less desirable byproducts of increased traffic, noise, and air pollution—although still far, far less than nearby Mexico City, which you may be escaping.

ESSENTIALS
GETTING THERE & DEPARTING
BY CAR   From Mexico City, take Paseo de la Reforma to Chapultepec Park and merge with the Periférico, which will take you to Highway 95D, the toll road on the far south of town that goes to Cuernavaca. From the Periférico, take the Insurgentes exit and continue until you come to signs for Cuernavaca/Tlalpan. Choose either the CUERNAVACA CUOTA (toll) or CUERNAVACA LIBRE (free) road on the right. The free road is slower and very windy, but is more scenic.

BY BUS   *Important note:* Buses to Cuernavaca depart directly from the Mexico City airport. The trip takes an hour. The Mexico City Central de Autobuses del Sur exists primarily to serve the Mexico

Cuernavaca

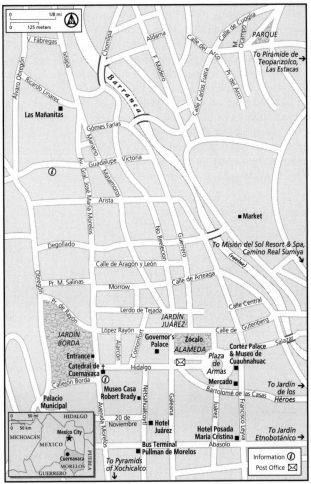

City–Cuernavaca–Taxco–Acapulco–Zihuatanejo route. Pullman de Morelos has two stations in Cuernavaca: downtown, at the corner of Abasolo and Netzahualcóyotl (© **777/318-0907** or 312-6063), 4 blocks south of the center of town; and Casino de la Selva (© **777/312-9473**), less conveniently located at Plan de Ayala 14, near the railroad station.

Autobuses Estrella Blanca (© 777/312-2626; www.estrellablanca. com.mx) depart from the Central del Sur with 4 buses daily from Mexico City. They arrive in Cuernavaca at Av. Morelos Sur 329, between Arista and Victoria, 6 blocks north of the town center. Here, you'll find frequent buses to Toluca, Chalma, Ixtapan de la Sal, Taxco, Acapulco, the Cacahuamilpa Caves, Querétaro, and Nuevo Laredo.

Estrella de Oro (© 777/312-3055; www.estrelladeoro.com.mx), Morelos 900, serves Iguala, Chilpancingo, Acapulco, and Taxco.

Estrella Roja (© 777/318-5934; www.estrellaroja.com.mx), a second-class station at Galeana and Cuauhtemotzin in Cuernavaca, about 8 blocks south of the town center, serves Cuautla, Yautepec, Oaxtepec, and Izúcar de Matamoros.

VISITOR INFORMATION

Cuernavaca's **Municipal Tourist Office** is at Av. Morelos Sur 278, between Jalisco and Tabasco (© 777/314-3920; www.cuernavaca. gob.mx), half a block north of the Estrella de Oro bus station and about a 15- to 20-minute walk south of the cathedral. The **Morelos State Tourism Office** is located on Av. Morelos Sur 187 (© 777/ 314-1880; www.morelostravel.com). Both are open Monday through Friday from 9am to 5pm. There's also a **City Tourism kiosk** (© 777/329-4404), on Morelos beside the El Calvario Church. It's open daily from 9am to 5pm.

CITY LAYOUT

In the center of the city are two contiguous plazas. The smaller and more formal, across from the post office, has a Victorian gazebo (designed by Gustave Eiffel, of Eiffel Tower fame) at its center. This is the **Alameda.** The larger, rectangular plaza with trees, shrubs, and benches is the **Plaza de Armas.** These two plazas are known collectively as the *zócalo* and form the hub for strolling vendors selling balloons, baskets, bracelets, and other crafts from surrounding villages. It's all easygoing, and one of the great pleasures of the town is hanging out at a park bench or table in a nearby restaurant. On Sunday afternoons, orchestras play in the gazebo. At the eastern end of the Alameda is the **Cortez Palace,** the conquistador's residence, now the Museo de Cuauhnáhuac.

Note: The city's street-numbering system is extremely confusing. It appears that the city fathers, during the past century or so, imposed a new numbering system every 10 or 20 years. An address given as "no. 5" may be in a building that bears the number "506," or perhaps "Antes no. 5" (former no. 5).

FAST FACTS: Cuernavaca

American Express The local representative is **Viajes Marín**, Edificio las Plazas, Loc. 13 (𝄐 **777/314-2266** or 318-9901; fax 777/312-9297). It's open daily from 9am to 7pm.

Area Code The telephone area code is **777**.

Banks Bank tellers (9am to 3 or 5pm, depending on the bank), ATMs, and *casas de cambio* change money. The closest bank to the *zócalo* is **Bancomer,** Matamoros and Lerdo de Tejada, cater-cornered to Jardín Juárez (across López Rayón from the Alameda). ATMs at banks generally remain open until 6pm Monday through Friday and a half-day on Saturday.

Drugstore **Farmacias del Ahorro** (𝄐 **777/322-2277**) offers hotel delivery service, but you must ask the front desk of your hotel to place the order, because the pharmacy requires the name of a hotel employee. It has 12 locations around the city, but the individual pharmacies have no phone. They are open daily from 7am to 10pm.

Elevation Cuernavaca sits at 1,533m (5,028 ft.).

Hospital **Hospital Inovamed,** Calle Cuauhtémoc 305, Col. Lomas de la Selva (𝄐 **777/311-2482,** -2483, or -2484).

Internet Access **MarkSoft** Internet, Otilio Montano, Col. Altavista (www.marksoftsolutions.com), serves coffee and Internet access for $3 (£1.65) per 15 minutes. You can also try **Café Internet Net-Conn,** Morelos Norte 360-A, Col. Carolina (𝄐 **777/317-9496**), which offers high-speed access for $2.50 (£1.40) per hour, as well as color laser printers, Web cams, scanners, and other equipment. It's open Monday through Saturday from 8am to 11pm, closed Sunday.

Population Cuernavaca has 400,000 residents.

Post Office The *correo* (𝄐 **777/312-4379**) is on the Plaza de Armas, next door to Café los Arcos. It's open Monday through Friday from 8am to 6pm, Saturday from 10am to 2pm.

Spanish Lessons Cuernavaca is known for its Spanish-language schools. Generally, the schools will help students find lodging with a family or provide a list of places to stay. Rather than make a long-term commitment in a family living situation, try it for a week, then decide. Contact the **Universidad Internacional,** San Jerónimo 304 (Apdo. Postal 1520), 62000 Cuernavaca, Morelos (𝄐 **800/574-1583** in the U.S., or 777/317-1087;

www.spanish.com.mx); **Instituto de Idioma y Cultura en Cuernavaca** (© 777/317-8947; fax 777/317-0455); or **Universal Centro de Lengua y Comunicación Social A.C. (Universal Language School)**, J. H. Preciado 171 (Apdo. Postal 1-826, 62000 Cuernavaca, Morelos; © **777/318-2904** or 312-4902; www.universalspanish.com). Note that the whole experience, from classes to lodging, can be quite expensive; the school may accept credit cards for the class portion.

WHERE TO STAY
EXPENSIVE

Camino Real Sumiya 🕭🕭   About 11km (7 miles) south of Cuernavaca, this unusual resort, whose name means "the place of peace, tranquillity, and longevity," was once the home of Woolworth heiress Barbara Hutton. Using materials and craftsmen from Japan, she constructed the estate in 1959 for $3.2 million (£1.8 million) on 12 wooded hectares (30 acres). The main house, a series of large connected rooms and decks, overlooks the grounds and contains restaurants and the lobby. Sumiya's charm rests in its relaxing atmosphere, which is best midweek (escapees from Mexico City tend to fill it on weekends). The guest rooms, which cluster in three-story buildings bordering manicured lawns, are simple in comparison to the striking Japanese architecture of the main house. Rooms have subtle Japanese accents, with austere but comfortable furnishings and scrolled wood doors. Hutton built a Kabuki-style theater and exquisite Zen meditation garden, which are now used only for special events. The theater contains vividly colored silk curtains and gold-plated temple paintings protected by folding cedar and mahogany screens. Strategically placed rocks in the garden represent the chakras, or energy points of the human body.

Interior Fracc. Sumiya s/n, Col. José Parres, 62550 Jiutepec, Mor. © **01-800/ 901-2300** in Mexico, or 777/329-9888. Fax 777/329-9889. www.camino real.com/sumiya. 163 units. $180 (£99) double; $385 (£212) suite. Low-season packages and discounts available. AE, DC, MC, V. Free parking. From the freeway, take the Atlacomulco exit and follow signs to Sumiya. Ask directions in Cuernavaca if you're coming from there, as the route is complicated. **Amenities:** 2 restaurants; poolside snack bar; outdoor pool; golf privileges nearby; 10 tennis courts; business center; concierge; room service; convention facilities w/simultaneous translation capabilities. *In room:* A/C, TV, Wi-Fi, minibar, hair dryer, iron, safe, ceiling fan.

Las Mañanitas   This has been Cuernavaca's most renowned luxury lodging for years and is also a popular weekend dining spot for affluent visitors from Mexico City. Guest rooms are formal in style, with gleaming polished molding and brass accents, large bathrooms, and rich fabrics. Rooms in the original mansion, called terrace suites, overlook the restaurant and inner lawn; the large rooms in the patio section each have a secluded patio; and those in the luxurious, expensive garden section each have a patio overlooking the pool and emerald lawns. Sixteen rooms have fireplaces, and the hotel also has a heated pool in the private garden. The hotel is one of only two in Mexico associated with the prestigious Relais & Châteaux chain. Transportation to and from the Mexico City airport can be arranged through the hotel for $140 (£77) each way. The restaurant overlooking the peacock-filled gardens is one of the country's premier dining places (see "Where to Dine," below). It's open to nonguests for all meals.

Ricardo Linares 107 (5½ long blocks north of the Jardín Borda), 62000 Cuernavaca, Mor. © 777/362-0000. Fax 777/318-3672. www.lasmananitas.com.mx. 32 units. Weekday $215–$325 (£118–£179) double; weekend $250–$350 (£138–£193) double. Rates include breakfast. AE, MC, V. Free valet parking. **Amenities:** Restaurant; outdoor pool; concierge; room service; laundry service. *In room:* TV, hair dryer.

Misión Del Sol Resort & Spa ✦✦✦ (Finds)   This adults-only hotel and spa offers an experience that rivals any in North America or Europe—and is an exceptional value. You feel a sense of peace from the moment you enter the resort, which draws on the mystical wisdom of the ancient cultures of Mexico, Tibet, Egypt, and Asia. Guests and visitors are encouraged to wear light-hued clothes to contribute to the harmonious flow of energy.

Architecturally stunning adobe buildings that meld with the natural environment house the guest rooms, villas, and common areas. Streams border the extensive gardens. Such group activities as reading discussions, a chess club, and painting workshops take place in the salon, where films are shown on weekend evenings. Spacious rooms are designed according to Feng-Shui principles; each looks onto its own garden or stream and has three channels of ambient music. Some have air-conditioning. Bathrooms are large, with sunken tubs, and the dual-headed showers have river rocks set into the floor, as a type of reflexology treatment. Beds contain magnets for restoring proper energy flow. Villas feature two separate bedrooms, plus a living/dining area and a meditation room. The spa has a menu of 32 services, with an emphasis on water-based treatments. Elegant relaxation areas are interspersed among the treatment rooms and whirlpool.

Av. General Diego Díaz González 31, Col. Parres, 62550 Cuernavaca, Mor. ⓒ **01-800/999-9100** toll-free inside Mexico, or 777/321-0999. Fax 777/320-7981. www.misiondelsol.com.mx. 42 units, plus 12 villas. $243 (£134) deluxe double; $502 (£276) two-bedroom villa (up to 4 persons); $595 (£327) three-bedroom villa (up to 6 persons). Special spa and meal packages available. AE, MC, V. Free parking. Children younger than 13 not accepted. **Amenities:** Restaurant; 2 tennis courts; well-equipped gym; extensive spa services; basketball; volleyball; daily meditation, yoga, and Tai Chi classes. *In room:* Safe.

MODERATE

Hotel Posada María Cristina ⓐⓐ   The María Cristina's high walls conceal many delights: a small swimming pool, lush gardens with fountains, a good restaurant, and patios. Guest rooms vary in size; all are exceptionally clean and comfortable, with firm beds and colonial-style furnishings. Bathrooms have inlaid Talavera tiles and skylights. Suites are only slightly larger than normal rooms; junior suites have Jacuzzis. La Calandria, the handsome little restaurant on the first floor, overlooks the gardens and serves excellent meals based on Mexican and international recipes. Even if you don't stay here, consider having a meal. The popular Sunday brunch ($16/£8.80 per person) features live classical music. The hotel lies half a block from the Palacio de Cortez.

Bulevar Juárez 300, Col. Centro (Apdo. Postal 203), 62000 Cuernavaca, Mor. ⓒ 777/318-2981. Fax 777/312-9126 or 777/318-2981. www.maria-cristina.com. 20 units. $130 (£72) double; $135–$220 (£74–£121) suite or cabaña. AE, MC, V. Free parking. **Amenities:** Restaurant; bar; outdoor pool; concierge; tour desk. *In room:* A/C, TV, hair dryer, ceiling fan.

INEXPENSIVE

Hotel Juárez   Low rates and a prime location (downtown, 1 block from the Casa Borda) make the Juárez a good choice for those intent on exploring the town's cultural charms. Each of the simple rooms is old-fashioned but well kept.

Netzahualcóyotl 19, 62000 Cuernavaca, Mor. ⓒ **777/314-0219.** 12 units. $35 (£19) double. No credit cards. Limited street parking. From the Cathedral, go east on Hidalgo, then turn right on Netzahualcóyotl. The hotel is 1 block down on the left. **Amenities:** Outdoor pool; tour desk. *In room:* TV.

WHERE TO DINE
VERY EXPENSIVE

Restaurant Las Mañanitas MEXICAN/INTERNATIONAL Las Mañanitas has set the standard for sumptuous, leisurely dining in Cuernavaca, filling with wealthy families from Mexico City on weekends and holidays. The setting is exquisite and the service superb, although the food is more standard than special. Tables stand on a shaded terrace with a view of gardens, strolling peacocks, and softly playing violinists or a trio playing romantic boleros. Diners have the option of ordering drinks and making their menu selections from chairs in the garden, waiting to take their seats at their tables when their meals are served. The cuisine is Mexican with an international flair, drawing on seasonal fruits and vegetables and offering a full selection of fresh seafood, certified Angus beef, lamb chops, baby back ribs, and free range chicken, but in standard preparations. Try the zucchini flower soup, filet of red snapper in curry sauce, and black-bottom pie, the house specialty.

In Las Mañanitas hotel, Ricardo Linares 107 (5½ long blocks north of the Jardín Borda). ⓒ 777/362-0019. Fax 777/318-3672. www.lasmananitas.com.mx. Reservations recommended. Main courses $19–$39 (£10–£21). AE, MC, V. Daily 8–11am, 1–5pm, and 7–11pm.

MODERATE

Casa Hidalgo ✿✿✿ GOURMET MEXICAN/INTERNATIONAL   In a beautifully restored colonial building across from the Palacio de Cortez, this is a relatively recent addition to Cuernavaca dining. The food is more sophisticated and innovative than that at most places in town. Specialties include chilled mango and tequila soup, smoked rainbow trout, and the exquisite Spanish-inspired filet Hidalgo—breaded and stuffed with serrano ham and *manchego* cheese. There are always daily specials, and bread is baked on the premises. Tables on the balcony afford a view of the action in the plaza below. The restaurant is accessible by wheelchair.

Calle Hidalgo 6. ⓒ 777/312-2749. www.casahidalgo.com. Reservations recommended on weekends. Main courses $14–$20 (£7.70–£11). AE, MC, V. Mon–Thurs 1:30–11pm; Fri–Sat 1:30pm–midnight; Sun 1:30–10pm.

Restaurant La India Bonita ✿✿ MEXICAN   Cuernavaca's oldest restaurant is housed among the interior patios and portals of the restored home—known as Casa Mañana—of former U.S. Ambassador Dwight Morrow. The beautiful setting features patio tables amid trickling fountains, palms, and flowers. Specialties include *mole poblano* (chicken with a sauce of bitter chocolate and fiery chiles) and the signature *La India Bonita* plate with steak, enchiladas, rice, and beans. There are also several daily specials. A breakfast mainstay is *desayuno Maximiliano,* a gigantic platter of chicken enchiladas with an assortment of sauces.

Morrow 15 (between Morelos and Matamoros), Col. Centro, 2 blocks north of the Jardín Juárez. ⓒ 777/318-6967 or 312-5021. Breakfast $4–$7 (£2.20–£3.85); main courses $7–$16 (£3.85–£8.80). AE, MC, V. Tues–Thurs 8am–10pm; Fri 8am–11pm; Sat 9am–11pm; Sun–Mon 9am–5pm.

INEXPENSIVE

La Universal *Value* MEXICAN/PASTRIES   This is a busy place, partly because of its great location (overlooking both the Alameda and Plaza de Armas), partly because of its traditional Mexican specialties, and partly because of its reasonable prices. It's open to the street and has many outdoor tables, usually filled with older men discussing the day's events or playing chess. These tables are perfect for watching the parade of street vendors and park life. The specialty is a Mexican grilled sampler plate, including *carne asada,* enchilada, pork cutlet, green onions, beans, and tortillas, for $12 (£6.60). A full breakfast special ($5/£2.75) is served Monday through Friday from 9:30am to noon. Live music is played weekdays from 3 to 5pm and again from 8 to 10pm.

Guerrero 2. © **777/318-6732** or -5970. Breakfast $5–$8 (£2.75–£4.40); main courses $9–$14 (£4.95–£7.70); *comida corrida* $8.90 (£4.90). AE, MC, V. Daily 9:30am–1am.

EXPLORING CUERNAVACA

On weekends, the whole city (including the roads, hotels, and restaurants) fills with people from Mexico City. This makes weekends more hectic, but also more fun. You can spend 1 or 2 days sightseeing pleasantly enough. If you've come on a day trip, you may not have time to make all the excursions listed below, but you'll have enough time to see the sights in town. Also notable is the traditional *mercado* **(public market)** adjacent to the Cortez Palace. It's open daily from 10am to 10pm, and the colorful rows of stands are a lively place for testing your bargaining skills as you purchase pottery, silver jewelry, crystals, and other trinkets. Note that the Cuauhnáhuac museum is closed on Monday.

Catedral de Cuernavaca *Moments*   As you enter the church precincts and pass down the walk, try to imagine what life in Mexico was like in the old days. Construction on the church, also known as the *Catedral de Asunción de María,* began in 1529, a mere 8 years after Cortez conquered Tenochtitlán (Mexico City) from the Aztec, and was completed in 1552. The churchmen could hardly trust their safety to the tenuous allegiance of their new converts, so they built a fortress as a church. The skull and crossbones above the main door are a symbol of the Franciscan order, which had its monastery here. The monastery is still here, in fact, and open to the public; it's on the northwest corner of the church property. Also visible on the exterior walls of the main church are inlaid rocks, placed there in memory of the men who lost their lives during its construction.

Once inside, wander through the sanctuaries and the courtyard, and pay special attention to the impressive frescoes painted on the walls, in various states of restoration. The frescoes date from the 1500s and have a distinct Asian style.

The main church sanctuary is stark, even severe, with an incongruous modern feeling (it was refurbished in the 1960s). Frescoes on these walls, discovered during the refurbishing, depict the persecution and martyrdom of St. Felipe de Jesús and his companions in Japan. No one is certain who painted them. In the churchyard, you'll see gravestones marking the tombs of the most devout—or wealthiest—of the parishioners. Being buried on the church grounds was believed to be the most direct route to heaven.

At the corner of Hidalgo and Morelos (3 blocks southwest of the Plaza de Armas). ✆ **777/318-4590.** Free admission. Daily 8am–2pm and 4–7pm.

Jardín Borda   Across Morelos Street from the cathedral lies the Jardín Borda (Borda Gardens). José de la Borda, the Taxco silver magnate, ordered a sumptuous vacation house built here in the late 1700s. When he died in 1778, his son Manuel inherited the land and transformed it into a botanical garden. The large enclosed garden next to the house was a huge private park, laid out in Andalusian style, with kiosks and an artificial pond. Maximilian took it over as his private summer house in 1865. He and Empress Carlota entertained lavishly in the gardens and held frequent concerts by the lake.

The gardens were completely restored and reopened in 1987 as the Jardín Borda Centro de Artes. In the gateway buildings, several galleries hold changing exhibits and large paintings showing scenes from the life of Maximilian and from the history of the Borda Gardens. One portrays the initial meeting between Maximilian and La India Bonita, a local maiden who became his lover.

On your stroll through the gardens, you'll see the little man-made lake on which Austrian, French, and Mexican nobility rowed small boats in the moonlight. Ducks have taken the place of dukes, however. There are rowboats for rent. The lake is now artfully adapted as an outdoor theater (see website for performance information), with seats for the audience on one side and the stage on the other. A cafe serves refreshments and light meals, and a weekend market inside the *jardín* sells arts and crafts.

Av. Morelos Sur 271, at Hidalgo. ✆ **777/318-1044.** Fax 777/318-3706. www. arte-cultura-morelos.gob.mx. Admission $3 (£1.65) adult, $1.50 (85p) children; free Sun. Tues–Sun 10am–5:30pm.

Jardín Etnobotánico y Museo de Medicina Tradicional y Herbolaria 𝕲𝕲   This museum of traditional herbal medicine, in the south Cuernavaca suburb of Acapantzingo, occupies a former resort residence built by Maximilian, the Casa del Olvido. During his brief reign, the Austrian-born emperor came here for trysts with La India Bonita, his Cuernavacan lover. The building was restored in 1960, and the house and gardens now preserve the local wisdom of folk medicine. The shady gardens are lovely to wander through, and you shouldn't miss the 200 orchids growing near the rear of the property.

Matamoros 14, Acapantzingo. 𝓒 777/312-5955, 312-3108, or 314-4046. www. inah.gob.mx. Free admission. Daily 9am–5pm. Take a taxi, or catch *combi* no. 6 at the mercado on Degollado. Ask to be dropped off at Matamoros near the museum; turn right on Matamoros and walk 1½ blocks; the museum will be on your right.

Museo Casa Robert Brady 𝕲𝕲   This private home and garden turned museum contains more than 1,300 works of exceptional art. Among them are pre-Hispanic and colonial pieces; oil paintings by Frida Kahlo and Rufino Tamayo; popular Mexican art; and handicrafts from America, Africa, Asia, and India. Robert Brady, an Iowa native with a degree in fine arts from the Art Institute of Chicago, assembled the collections. He lived in Venice for 5 years before settling in Cuernavaca in 1960. The wildly colorful rooms remain exactly as Brady left them when he died here in 1986. Admission includes a guide in Spanish; English and French guides are available if requested in advance.

Calle Netzahualcóyotl 4 (between Hidalgo and Abasolo). 𝓒 777/318-8554. Fax 777/ 314-3529. www.bradymuseum.org. Admission $3 (£1.65). Tues–Sun 10am–6pm.

Museo de Cuauhnáhuac   The museum is in the Cortez Palace, the former home of the greatest of the conquistadors, Hernán Cortez. Construction started in 1530 on the site of a Tlahuica Indian ceremonial center and was finished by the conquistador's son Martín. The palace later served as the legislative headquarters for the state of Morelos.

In the east portico on the upper floor is a large Diego Rivera mural commissioned by Dwight Morrow, U.S. ambassador to Mexico in the 1920s. It depicts the history of Cuernavaca from the coming of the Spaniards to the rise of Zapata (1910). On the lower level, the excellent bookstore is open daily from 11am to 8pm. Tour guides in front of the palace offer their services in the museum, and for other sights in Cuernavaca, for about $10 (£5.50) per hour.

Make sure you see official SECTUR (Tourism Secretary) credentials before hiring one of these guides. This is also a central point for taxis in the downtown area.

In the Cortez Palace, Leyva 100. ℂ **777/312-8171**. www.morelostravel.com/cultura/museo7.html. Admission $3.70 (£2.05); free Sun. Tues–Sun 9am–6pm.

ACTIVITIES & EXCURSIONS
GOLF

With its perpetually springlike climate, Cuernavaca is an ideal place for golf. The **Tabachines Golf Club and Restaurant,** Km 93.5 Carr. Mexico-Acapulco (ℂ **777/314-3999**), the city's most popular course, is open for public play. Percy Clifford designed this 18-hole course, surrounded by beautifully manicured gardens blooming with bougainvillea, gardenias, and other flowers. The elegant restaurant is a popular place for breakfast, lunch, and especially Sunday brunch. Greens fees are $75 (£41) during the week and $190 (£105) on weekends. American Express, Visa, and MasterCard are accepted. It's open Tuesday through Sunday from 7am to 6pm; tee times are available from 7am to 2pm.

Also in Cuernavaca is the **Club de Golf Hacienda San Gaspar,** Avenida Emiliano Zapata, Col. Cliserio Alanis (ℂ **777/319-4424;** www.sangaspar.com), an 18-hole golf course designed by Joe Finger. It's surrounded by more than 3,000 trees and has two artificial lagoons, plus beautiful panoramic views of Cuernavaca, the Popocatépetl and Ixtaccihuatl volcanoes, and the Tepozteco Mountains. Greens fees are $75 (£41) on weekdays, $130 (£72) on weekends (discounted after 2pm); carts cost an additional $28 (£15) for 18 holes, and a caddy is $17 (£9.35) plus tip. American Express, Visa, and MasterCard are accepted. Additional facilities include a gym with whirlpool and sauna, pool, four tennis courts, and a restaurant and snack bar. It's open Wednesday through Monday from 7am to 7pm.

LAS ESTACAS

Either a side trip from Cuernavaca or a destination on its own, Las Estacas, Km 6.5 Carretera Tlaltizapán–Cuautla, Morelos (ℂ **777/312-4412** or -7610 in Cuernavaca, or 734/345-0350; www.lasestacas.com), is a natural water park. Its clear spring waters reputedly have healing properties. In addition to the crystal-clear rivers, Las Estacas has two pools, wading pools for children, horseback riding, and a *balneario* (traditional-style spa), open daily from 8am to 6pm. Several restaurants serve such simple food as quesadillas, fruit with yogurt, sandwiches, and *tortas*. Admission is $20 (£11) for adults, $12 (£6.60) for children under 1.2m (4 ft.) tall. A small, basic hotel charges $120 to $150 (£66–£83) for a double room; rates include the entrance fee to the *balneario* and breakfast. Cheaper lodging options are available, including a trailer and camping park; you can rent an adobe or straw hut with two bunk beds for $30 (£17). Visit the website for more information. MasterCard and Visa are accepted. On weekends, the place fills with families. Las Estacas is 36km (22 miles) east of Cuernavaca. To get there, take Highway 138 to Yautepec, then turn right at the first exit past Yautepec.

PYRAMIDS OF XOCHICALCO☆

This beautiful ceremonial center provides clues to the history of the whole region. Artifacts and inscriptions link the site to the mysterious cultures that built Teotihuacán and Tula, and some of the objects found here would indicate that residents were also in contact with the Mixtec, Aztec, Maya, and Zapotec. The most impressive building in Xochicalco is the Pirámide de la Serpiente Emplumada (Pyramid of the Plumed Serpent), with its magnificent reliefs of plumed serpents twisting around seated priests. Underneath the pyramid is a series of tunnels and chambers with murals on the walls. There is also an observatory, where from April 30 to August 15 you can follow the trajectory of the sun as it shines through a hexagonal opening. The pyramids (© **777/314-3920** for information) are 36km (22 miles) southwest of Cuernavaca. They're open daily from 9am to 5pm. Admission is $3 (£1.65).

CUERNAVACA AFTER DARK

Cuernavaca has a number of cafes right off the Jardín Juárez where people gather to sip coffee or drinks until the wee hours—check out La Universal (see "Where to Dine," earlier in this chapter). Band concerts are held in the Jardín Juárez on Thursday and Sunday evenings. **La Plazuela,** a short, pedestrian-only stretch across from the Cortez Palace, features cafes, kitsch stores, and live-music bars. It's geared toward a 20-something, university crowd.

3 Tepoztlán ☆☆

72km (45 miles) S of Mexico City; 45km (28 miles) NE of Cuernavaca

Tepoztlán is one of the strangest and most beautiful towns in Mexico. Largely undiscovered by foreign tourists, it occupies the floor of a broad, lush valley whose walls were formed by bizarrely shaped mountains that look like the work of some abstract expressionist giant. The mountains are visible from almost everywhere in town; even the municipal parking lot boasts a spectacular view.

Tepoztlán remains small and steeped in legend and mystery—it lies adjacent to the alleged birthplace of Quetzalcoatl, the Aztec serpent god—and comes about as close as you're going to get to an unspoiled, magical mountain hideaway. Eight chapels, each with its own cultural festival, dot this traditional Mexican village. Though the town stays tranquil during the week, escapees from Mexico City descend in droves on the weekends, especially Sunday. Most Tepoztlán residents, whether foreigners or Mexicans, tend to be mystically or artistically oriented—although some also appear to be just plain disoriented.

Aside from soaking up the ambience, two things you must do are climb up to the Tepozteco pyramid and hit the weekend folkloric market. In addition, Tepoztlán offers a variety of treatments, cures, diets, massages, and sweat lodges. Some of these are available at hotels; for some, you have to ask around. Many locals swear that the valley possesses mystical curative powers.

If you have a car, Tepoztlán provides a great starting point for traveling this region of Mexico. Within 90 minutes are Las Estacas, Taxco, las Grutas de Cacahuamilpa, and Xochicalco (some of the prettiest ruins in Mexico). Tepoztlán lies 20 minutes from Cuernavaca and only an hour south of Mexico City (that is, an hour once you're able to get out of Mexico City), which—given its lost-in-time feel—seems hard to believe.

ESSENTIALS
GETTING THERE & DEPARTING
BY CAR From Mexico City, the quickest route is Highway 95 (the toll road) to Cuernavaca; just before the Cuernavaca city limits, you'll see the clearly marked turnoff to Tepoztlán on 95D and Highway 115. The slower, free federal Highway 95D, direct from Mexico City, is also an option, and may be preferable if you're departing from the western part of the city. Take 95D south to Km 71, where the exit to Tepoztlán on Highway 115 is clearly indicated.

BY BUS From Mexico City, buses to Tepoztlán run regularly from the Terminal de Sur and the Terminal Poniente. The trip takes an hour.

In addition, you can book round-trip transportation to the Mexico City airport through **Marquez Sightseeing Tours** (© 777/315-5875; www.tourbymexico.com/marqueztours) and some hotels. The round-trip cost is about $200 (£110).

Cooking Classes in Tepoztlán

An engaging cooking school called **Cocinar Mexicano** offers weeklong programs in Mexican cuisine. The founder, Magda Bogin, conducts class from her large, sunny outdoor kitchen, tiled in blue-and-white Talavera. Participants study recipes typical of the festival that coincides with their visit. During the Day of the Dead workshop, for example, students learn to make tamales, the traditional dish that families bring to the gravesites of deceased love ones. For other festivals, the focus is mole, a typical fiesta food often made with chocolate and chiles that's arguably the most complex dish in Mexican cuisine. Cost for the class is $1,895 (£1,042), which includes round-trip transportation from Mexico City and most meals but not airfare or accommodations. Frommer's readers receive a $100 (£55) discount. For more information, visit www.cocinarmexicano.com.

WHERE TO STAY

The town gets very busy on the weekends, so if your stay will include Friday or Saturday night, make reservations well in advance. In addition to the choices noted below, consider two other excellent options just outside of town. **Casa Bugambilia** ⟨⟨⟨, Callejón de Tepopula 007, Valle de Atongo (© **739/395-0158;** www.casa bugambilia.com), is an 11-room hotel property 3km (1¾ miles) outside of Tepoztlán. Don't confuse this hotel with Posada Bugambilia, a modest hotel in town. The spacious rooms are elegantly furnished with high-end, carved Mexican furniture, and every room has a fireplace. Doubles average $180 to $250 (£99–£138). **Las Golondrinas** ⟨⟨⟨, Callejón de Términas 4 (© **739/395-0649;** http://homepage.mac.com/marisolfernandez/LasGolondrinas), is a three-bedroom B&B in the area behind Ixcatepec church; it's so off the beaten track that even cabdrivers have trouble finding the place. But owner Marisol Fernández has imbued the house with her tranquil, down-to-earth charm; the guest rooms open onto a wraparound terrace that overlooks the garden, a small pool, and the Tepozteco Mountains beyond. Doubles cost $120 (£66), including breakfast.

Hotel Nilayam ⟨ Formerly Hotel Tepoztlán, this holistic-oriented retreat lies in a colonial building, but the decor has been brightened up considerably. Stays here encourage self-exploration: The gracious, helpful staff offers complete detox programs and a full array of services, including body and facial treatments, reflexology, hot stone and shiatsu massages, and yoga, Tai-Chi, and meditation. The hotel has a great view of the mountain, and the restaurant features a creative menu of vegetarian cuisine. Spa packages are available.

Industrias 6, 62520 Tepoztlán, Mor. ⓒ **739/395-0503.** Fax 739/395-0522. www. nilayam.net. 35 units. $120 (£66) double. AE, MC, V. Free parking. **Amenities:** Restaurant; outdoor pool; spa services; private *temazcal* (pre-Hispanic sweat lodge). *In room:* TV.

Posada del Tepozteco 🌟🌟 This property looks out over the town and down the length of the spectacular valley; the views from just about anywhere are superb. Rooms are tastefully furnished in colonial style. All but the least expensive have terraces and views. All suites have small whirlpool tubs. The grounds are exquisitely landscaped, and the atmosphere is intimate and romantic.

Paraíso 3 (2 blocks from the town center), 62520 Tepoztlán, Mor. ⓒ **739/395-0010.** Fax 739/395-0323. www.posadadeltepozteco.com. 21 units. $120–$175 (£66–£96) double; $200–$366 (£110–£201) suite. MC, V. Free parking. **Amenities:** Restaurant w/stunning view; small outdoor pool.

WHERE TO DINE

In addition to the two choices listed below, El Chalchi restaurant at the **Hotel Nilayam** (see above) offers some of the best vegetarian fare in the area. It's 3 blocks from the main square, with main courses priced around $6 (£3.30).

El Ciruelo Restaurant Bar 🌟 GOURMET MEXICAN This upscale restaurant surrounded by beautiful flowering gardens and adobe walls offers a sampling of Tepoztlán's essence. The service is positively charming, and the food divine. House specialties include

---

⟨Moments⟩ Tepoznieves: A Taste of Heaven

Don't leave town without a stop at **Tepoznieves,** Av. 5 de Mayo 21 (ⓒ **739/395-3813**), the sublime local ice-cream shop. The store's slogan, "nieve de dioses" (ice cream of the gods), doesn't exaggerate. Almost 200 types of ice cream and sorbet, made only with natural ingredients, come in flavors familiar (vanilla, bubble gum), exotic (tamarind, rose petal, mango studded with chile piquin), and off-the-wall (beet, lettuce, corn). It's open daily 8am to 9pm.

chalupas of goat cheese, chicken with *huitlacoche,* and a regional treat: milk-based gelatin with brown sugar.

Zaragoza 17, Barrio de la Santísima, in front of the church. © **739/395-1203.** Dinner $6–$20 (£3.30–£11). AE. Sun 1–7pm; Mon–Thurs 1–6pm; Fri–Sat 1–11pm.

Restaurant Axitla 🌟🌟🌟 *(Finds* GOURMET MEXICAN/INTERNATIONAL   Axitla is not only the best restaurant in Tepoztlán, but also one of the finest in Mexico for showcasing the country's cuisine. Gourmet Mexican delicacies are made from scratch using the freshest local ingredients. Specialties include chicken breast stuffed with wild mushrooms in a *chipotle chile* sauce, *chiles en nogada,* pepper steak, grilled octopus, and exceptional mole. There are also excellent steaks and fresh seafood. And, if the food isn't enough—and believe me, it is—the enchanted setting will make your meal even more memorable. The restaurant lies at the base of the Tepozteco Pyramid (about a 10-min. walk from the town center), surrounded by 1.2 hectares (about 3 acres) of junglelike gardens that encompass a creek and lily ponds. The views of the Tepozteco Mountains are magnificent. Memo and Laura, the gracious owners, speak excellent English and are marvelous sources of information about the area.

Av. del Tepozteco, at the foot of the trail to the pyramid. © **739/395-0519.** Lunch and dinner $8–$15 (£4.40–£8.25). MC, V. Wed–Sun 10am–7pm.

EXPLORING TEPOZTLAN

Tepoztlán's **weekend folkloric market** is one of the best in central Mexico. More crafts are available on Saturdays and Sundays, but the market also opens on Wednesdays. Vendors sell all kinds of ceramics, from simple fired-clay works resembling those made with pre-Hispanic techniques, to the more commercial versions of majolica and pseudo-Talavera. There are also puppets, carved wood figures, and some textiles, especially thick wool Mexican sweaters and jackets made out of *jerga* (a coarse cloth). Very popular currently is the "hippie"-style jewelry that earned Tepoztlán its fame in the '60s and '70s. The market is also remarkable for its variety of food stands selling fruits and vegetables, spices, fresh tortillas, and indigenous Mexican delicacies.

The other primary activity is hiking up to **Tepozteco pyramid.** The climb is steep and fairly strenuous, although perfectly doable in a few hours and not dangerous. In fact, you'll see folks across three generations doing the hike. Dense vegetation shades the trail (actually a long natural staircase), which is beautiful from bottom to top.

Once you arrive at the pyramid you are treated to remarkable views and, if you are lucky, a great show by a family of *coatis* (tropical raccoons), who visit the pyramid most mornings to beg for food; they especially love bananas. The pyramid is a Tlahuica construction that predates the Náhuatl (Aztec) domination of the area. It was the site of important celebrations in the 12th and 13th centuries. The main street in Tepoztlán, Avenida 5 de Mayo, takes you to the path that leads you to the top of the Tepozteco. The 2km winding rock trail begins where the name of Avenida 5 de Mayo changes to Camino del Tepozteco. The hike takes about an hour each way, but if you stop and take in the scenery and really enjoy the trail, it can take up to 2 hours each way. Water and drinks are available at the top. The trail is open daily from 9am to 5:30pm and, while the hike is free, the pyramid costs $3 (£1.65) to enter.

Also worth visiting is the **former convent Domínico de la Navidad.** The entrance to the Dominican convent lies through the religious-themed "Gate of Tepoztlán," constructed with beads and seeds, just east of the main plaza. Built between 1560 and 1588, the convent is now a museum open Tuesday through Sunday from 10am to 5pm.

SIGHTS NEAR TEPOZTLAN

Many nearby places are easily accessible by car. One good tour service is **Marquez Sightseeing Tours,** located in Cuernavaca (© 777/ 315-5875; www.tourbymexico.com/marqueztours). Marquez has four- and seven-passenger vehicles, very reasonable prices, and a large variety of set tours. The dependable owner, Arturo Marquez Diaz, speaks better-than-passable English and will allow you to design your own tour, including to archaeological sites and museums. He also offers transportation to and from Mexico City airport for approximately $200 (£110).

Two tiny, charming villages, **Santo Domingo Xocotitlán** and **Amatlán,** are only a 20-minute drive from Tepoztlán and can be reached by minibuses, which depart regularly from the center of town. There is nothing much to do in these places except wander around absorbing the marvelous views of the Tepozteco Mountains and drinking in the magical ambience.

Las Grutas de Cacahuamilpa ⓕ, the Cacahuamilpa Caves or Grottoes, are an unforgettable system of caverns with a wooden illuminated walkway for easy access. As you pass from chamber to chamber, you'll see spectacular illuminated rock formations, including stalactites, stalagmites, and twisted rock formations with names like Dante's head, the champagne bottle, the tortillas, and Madonna with child. Admission for 2 hours is $3 (£1.65); a guide for groups, which can be assembled on the hour, costs an additional $8 (£4.40). The caverns are open daily from 10am to 7pm (last tickets sold at 5pm), and lie 90 minutes from Tepoztlán and 30 minutes from Taxco.

About 40 minutes southeast of Tepoztlán is **Las Estacas,** an ecological resort with a cold-water spring that is said to have curative powers. The ruins of **Xochicalco** (see "Cuernavaca," earlier in this chapter) and the colonial town of **Taxco** (earlier in this chapter) are easily accessible from Tepoztlán.

Appendix:
Useful Terms & Phrases

Most Mexicans are very patient with foreigners who try to speak their language; it helps a lot to know a few basic phrases. I've included simple phrases for expressing basic needs, followed by some common menu items.

ENGLISH-SPANISH PHRASES

English	Spanish	Pronunciation
Good day	**Buen día**	Bwehn *dee*-ah
Good morning	**Buenos días**	*Bweh*-nohs *dee*-ahs
How are you?	**¿Cómo está?**	*Koh*-moh eh-*stah*
Very well	**Muy bien**	Mwee byehn
Thank you	**Gracias**	*Grah*-syahs
You're welcome	**De nada**	Deh *nah*-dah
Goodbye	**Adiós**	Ah-*dyohs*
Please	**Por favor**	Pohr fah-*bohr*
Yes	**Sí**	See
No	**No**	Noh
Excuse me	**Perdóneme**	Pehr-*doh*-neh-meh
Give me	**Déme**	*Deh*-meh
Where is . . . ?	**¿Dónde está . . . ?**	*Dohn*-deh eh-*stah*
the station	**la estación**	lah eh-stah-*syohn*
a hotel	**un hotel**	oon oh-*tehl*
a gas station	**una gasolinera**	*oo*-nah gah-soh-lee-*neh*-rah
a restaurant	**un restaurante**	oon res-tow-*rahn*-teh
the toilet	**el baño**	el *bah*-nyoh

English	Spanish	Pronunciation
a good doctor	**un buen médico**	oon bwehn *meh*-dee-coh
the road to . . .	**el camino a/hacia . . .**	el cah-*mee*-noh ah/*ah*-syah
To the right	**A la derecha**	Ah lah deh-*reh*-chah
To the left	**A la izquierda**	Ah lah ees-*kyehr*-dah
Straight ahead	**Derecho**	Deh-*reh*-choh
I would like	**Quisiera**	Key-*syeh*-rah
I want	**Quiero**	*Kyeh*-roh
to eat	**comer**	koh-*mehr*
a room	**una habitación**	*oo*-nah ah-bee-tah-*syohn*
Do you have . . . ?	**¿Tiene usted . . . ?**	Tyeh-neh oo-*sted*
a book	**un libro**	oon *lee*-broh
a dictionary	**un diccionario**	oon deek-syoh-*nah*-ryoh
How much is it?	**¿Cuánto cuesta?**	*Kwahn*-toh *kweh*-stah
When?	**¿Cuándo?**	*Kwahn*-doh
What?	**¿Qué?**	Keh
There is (Is there . . . ?)	**(¿)Hay (. . . ?)**	Eye
What is there?	**¿Qué hay?**	Keh eye
Yesterday	**Ayer**	Ah-*yer*
Today	**Hoy**	Oy
Tomorrow	**Mañana**	Mah-*nyah*-nah
Good	**Bueno**	*Bweh*-noh
Bad	**Malo**	*Mah*-loh
Better (best)	**(Lo) Mejor**	(Loh) Meh-*hohr*
More	**Más**	Mahs
Less	**Menos**	*Meh*-nohs

English	Spanish	Pronunciation
No smoking	**Se prohibe fumar**	Seh proh-*ee*-beh foo-*mahr*
Postcard	**Tarjeta postal**	Tar-*heh*-tah poh-*stahl*
Insect repellent	**Repelente contra insectos**	Reh-peh-*lehn*-teh *cohn*-trah een-*sehk*-tohs

MORE USEFUL PHRASES

English	Spanish	Pronunciation
Do you speak English?	**¿Habla usted inglés?**	*Ah*-blah oo-*sted* een-*glehs*
Is there anyone here who speaks English?	**¿Hay alguien aquí que hable inglés?**	Eye *ahl*-gyehn ah-*kee* keh *ah*-bleh een-*glehs*
I speak a little Spanish.	**Hablo un poco de español.**	*Ah*-bloh oon *poh*-koh deh eh-spah-*nyohl*
I don't understand Spanish very well.	**No (lo) entiendo muy bien el español.**	Noh (loh) ehn-*tyehn*-doh mwee byehn el eh-spah-*nyohl*
The meal is good.	**Me gusta la comida.**	Meh *goo*-stah lah koh-*mee*-dah
What time is it?	**¿Qué hora es?**	Keh *oh*-rah ehs
May I see your menu?	**¿Puedo ver el menú (la carta)?**	*Pweh*-doh vehr el meh-*noo* (lah *car*-tah)
The check, please.	**La cuenta, por favor.**	Lah *kwehn*-tah pohr fah-*bohr*
What do I owe you?	**¿Cuánto le debo?**	*Kwahn*-toh leh *deh*-boh
What did you say?	**¿Mande?** (formal) **¿Cómo?** (informal)	*Mahn*-deh *Koh*-moh

English	Spanish	Pronunciation
I want (to see) . . .	**Quiero (ver)** . . .	*kyeh*-roh (vehr)
a room	**un cuarto** or	oon *kwar*-toh,
	una habitación	*oo*-nah ah-bee-tah-*syohn*
for two persons	**para dos personas**	*pah*-rah dohs pehr-*soh*-nahs
with (without) bathroom	**con (sin) baño**	kohn (seen) *bah*-nyoh
We are staying here only . . .	**Nos quedamos aquí solamente** . . .	Nohs keh-*dah*-mohs ah-*kee* soh-lah-*mehn*-teh
one night.	**una noche.**	*oo*-nah *noh*-cheh
one week.	**una semana.**	*oo*-nah seh-*mah*-nah
We are leaving . . .	**Partimos (Salimos)** . . .	Pahr-*tee*-mohs (sah-*lee*-mohs)
tomorrow.	**mañana.**	mah-*nya*-nah
Do you accept . . . ?	**¿Acepta usted . . . ?**	Ah-*sehp*-tah oo-sted
traveler's checks?	**cheques de viajero?**	*cheh*-kehs deh byah-*heh*-roh
Is there a laundromat . . . ?	**¿Hay una lavandería . . . ?**	Eye *oo*-nah lah-*bahn*-deh-*ree*-ah
near here?	**cerca de aquí?**	*sehr*-kah deh ah-*kee*
Please send these clothes to the laundry.	**Hágame el favor de mandar esta ropa a la lavandería.**	*Ah*-gah-meh el fah-*bohr* deh mahn-*dahr* eh-stah *roh*-pah a lah lah-*bahn*-deh-*ree*-ah

NUMBERS

1	**uno** (*ooh*-noh)	17	**diecisiete** (dyeh-see-*syeh*-teh)
2	**dos** (dohs)	18	**dieciocho** (dyeh-*syoh*-choh)
3	**tres** (trehs)	19	**diecinueve** (dyeh-see-*nweh*-beh)
4	**cuatro** (*kwah*-troh)		
5	**cinco** (*seen*-koh)	20	**veinte** (*bayn*-teh)
6	**seis** (sayes)	30	**treinta** (*trayn*-tah)
7	**siete** (*syeh*-teh)	40	**cuarenta** (kwah-*ren*-tah)
8	**ocho** (*oh*-choh)	50	**cincuenta** (seen-*kwen*-tah)
9	**nueve** (*nweh*-beh)	60	**sesenta** (seh-*sehn*-tah)
10	**diez** (dyehs)	70	**setenta** (seh-*tehn*-tah)
11	**once** (*ohn*-seh)	80	**ochenta** (oh-*chehn*-tah)
12	**doce** (*doh*-seh)	90	**noventa** (noh-*behn*-tah)
13	**trece** (*treh*-seh)	100	**cien** (syehn)
14	**catorce** (kah-*tohr*-seh)	200	**doscientos** (do-*syehn*-tohs)
15	**quince** (*keen*-seh)	500	**quinientos** (kee-*nyehn*-tohs)
16	**dieciséis** (dyeh-see-*sayes*)	1,000	**mil** (meel)

TRANSPORTATION TERMS

English	Spanish	Pronunciation
Airport	**Aeropuerto**	Ah-eh-roh-*pwehr*-toh
Flight	**Vuelo**	*Bweh*-loh
Rental car	**Arrendadora de autos**	Ah-*rehn*-da-doh-rah deh *ow*-tohs
Bus	**Autobús**	Ow-toh-*boos*
Bus or truck	**Camión**	Ka-*myohn*
Lane	**Carril**	Kah-*reel*
Nonstop (bus)	**Directo**	Dee-*rehk*-toh
Baggage (claim area)	**Equipajes**	Eh-kee-*pah*-hehss
Intercity	**Foraneo**	Foh-rah-*neh*-oh
Luggage storage area	**Guarda equipaje**	*Gwar*-dah eh-kee-*pah*-heh
Arrival gates	**Llegadas**	Yeh-*gah*-dahss
Originates at this station	**Local**	Loh-*kahl*
Originates elsewhere	**De paso**	Deh *pah*-soh

English	Spanish	Pronunciation
Are seats available?	Hay lugares disponibles?	Eye loo-*gah*- rehs dis-pohn-*ee*-blehss
First class	Primera	Pree-*meh*-rah
Second class	Segunda	Seh-*goon*-dah
Nonstop (flight)	Sin escala	Seen ess-*kah*-lah
Baggage claim area	Recibo de equipajes	Reh-*see*-boh deh eh-kee-*pah*-hehss
Waiting room	Sala de espera	*Sah*-lah deh ehss-*peh*-rah
Toilets	Sanitarios	Sah-nee-*tah*-ryohss
Ticket window	Taquilla	Tah-*kee*-yah

Index

See also Accommodations and Restaurant indexes, below.

GENERAL INDEX

Acapulco, 2, 49–81
    accommodations, 56–64
    activities, 70–77
    beaches, 70–72
    climate, 55
    consulates, 55
    getting around, 54
    Internet access, 55–56
    layout of, 53–54
    medical care, 55
    nightlife, 78–81
    restaurants, 64–70
    safety, 56
    shopping, 77–78
    tourist police, 56
    traveling to and from, 52–53
    visitor information, 53
Acapulco Ballet Folklórico, 78
Acapulco Historical Museum, 75–76
Accommodations. See also Accommodations Index and specific destinations
    out-of-the-ordinary, 35
Active vacations, 35–37
AeroMexico Vacations, 33
Airport security, 29–30
Air travel, 29–30
    within Mexico, 37–38
Alaska Airlines Vacations, 34
Alebrijes, 79
Amatlán, 169
American Airlines Vacations, 33, 34
American Express, 11
    Acapulco, 55
    Cuernavaca, 155
    Ixtapa/Zihuatanejo, 86
AMTAVE, 36
Año Nuevo, 13
Apple Vacations, 34
Archaeological Conservancy, 36
Art classes, 143
Art galleries, 78

Ash Wednesday, 13
Assumption of the Virgin Mary, 15
ATMs (automated teller machines), 10
Auto insurance, 32, 40

Baby-O, 79–80
Bahías de Huatulco, 2, 105, 125–138
    accommodations, 130–133
    beaches and outdoor activities, 135–137
    getting around, 129
    Internet access, 130
    layout of, 128–129
    medical care, 130
    nightlife, 137–138
    restaurants, 133–135
    shopping, 137
    traveling to and from, 126, 128
    visitor information, 128
Banks and ATMs, 10, 86, 110, 130, 155
Beaches. See also entries starting with "Playa"
    Acapulco, 70–72
    Bahías de Huatulco, 135–136
    Ixtapa/Zihuatanejo, 98–99
    Puerto Angel, 124–125
    Puerto Escondido, 117–119
Bird-watching, 72, 100, 126, 137
Boating (boat rentals), 73, 100
Boat tours and cruises, 36
    Acapulco, 72–73
    Bahías de Huatulco, 136
    Ixtapa/Zihuatanejo, 100
    Puerto Angel, 124–125
Bribes and scams, 23–24
Bullfights, 75
Bungee jumping, 79
Business hours, 42
Bustamante, Sergio, 78
Bus travel
    to the Mexican border, 33
    within Mexico, 41

Calendar of events, 13–16
Candlemass, 13
Carlos 'n' Charlie's
    Acapulco, 80
    Ixtapa, 104
Carnaval, 13
Car rentals, 39–40
Car travel
    to Mexico, 30–32
    within Mexico, 38–40
    returning to the United States, 32–33
Casa de la Cultura de Taxco (Casa
    Borda), 148
Casa Marina, 102
Chacahua Lagoon National Park,
    118–119
Chahué Bay, 129, 135
Children, families with, 24–25
Christine, 104
Christmas, 16
Christmas Posadas, 16
Cinco de Mayo, 14
Classic Vacations, 34
Climate, 12–13
Coco Cabaña Collectibles, 102
Coffee Plantation Tour, 136–137
Constitution Day, 13
Consulates, 43–44, 55
Continental Airlines Vacations, 33
Continental Vacations, 34
Cooking classes, 166
Copalitilla Cascades, 136
Corpus Christi, 14
Coyuca Lagoon, 72
Credit cards, 12
Crime, 22–23
Crucecita, 126, 129
Cruise lines, 33
Cuernavaca, 2, 151–164
    accommodations, 156–158
    activities and excursions, 163–164
    exploring, 160–163
    Internet access, 155
    layout of, 154
    nightlife, 164
    restaurants, 158–160
    traveling to and from, 152–154
    visitor information, 154
Culinary Adventures, 36
Currency, 8–9
Customs allowances, 6–8

Day of the Dead, 15–16
Delta Vacations, 33, 34
Dentists, 42
Día de la Candelaria, 13
Día de la Constitución, 13
Día de la Marina, 14
Día de la Raza, 15
Día de la Santa Cruz, 14
Día de Reyes, 13
Día de San Pedro, 14
Diarrhea, travelers' (turista), 19
Dietary red flags, 19–20
Disabilities, travelers with, 26
Doctors, 42. See also Hospitals
Documents needed for entry, 5–6
    car documents, 30–32
Dolphins, swimming with, 76–77
Dolphin shows, 76
Dolphin-watching tours, 119
Domínico de la Navidad, former
    convent, 169
Drug laws, 42
Drugstores, 42–43, 55, 87,
    110, 130, 155

Ecotours and adventure trips,
    118–119
El Botazoo, 126
Electricity, 43
Elevation sickness, 20
El Mirador (Acapulco), 70
Embassies and consulates, 43–44, 55
Emergencies, 44
Entry requirements, 5–6
    car documents, 30–32
Escobilla Beach, 120

Families with children, 24–25
Feast of San Isidro, 14
Feast of the Virgin of Guadalupe, 16
Festival of the Radishes (Festival de
    los Rábanos), 16
Fishing
    Acapulco, 73
    Ixtapa/Zihuatanejo, 100
    Puerto Escondido, 117
FMT (Mexican Tourist Permit), 6
Food of the Gods Festival
    (Oaxaca), 15
Fuerte de San Diego, 75
Funjet Vacations, 34–35

Galería Espacio Pal Kepenyes, 78
Gasoline, 38
Gay and lesbian travelers, 25, 151
Gelateria Giardino, 115
GOGO Worldwide Vacations, 35
Golf, 74, 101, 137, 163
Gran Noche Mexicana, 78
Grutas de Cacahuamilpa,
  150, 169–170
Guelaguetza Dance Festival, 14–15

Handicrafts, 102
Health concerns, 18–22
Health insurance, 17–18
High-altitude hazards, 20
Highway 200, 53, 84
Holy Cross Day, 14
Holy Week, 14
Horseback riding
  Acapulco, 74–75
  Bahías de Huatulco, 137
  Ixtapa/Zihuatanejo, 101–102
Hospitals, 21, 55, 87, 110
Huatulco, 105, 125–138. See also
  Bahías de Huatulco
Humboldt House/Museo Virreinal de
  Taxco, 148–149
Hurricane season, 13

Iglesia de Guadalupe, 135
Independence Day, 15
Insurance, 17–18
  auto, 32, 40
Internet access, 44
Isla Ixtapa, 99
Ixtapa/Zihuatanejo, 2, 82–104
  accommodations, 87–94
  activities, 97–102
  climate, 86
  getting around, 86
  hospitals, 87
  Internet access, 87
  layout of, 85
  nightlife, 103–104
  restaurants, 94–97
  shopping, 102–103
  traveling to and from, 82–84
  visitor information, 85

Juárez, Benito, Birthday, 14

Kayaking, 100

Labor Day, 14
La Entrega Beach, 135
La Fuente, 103
Language, 44
La Punta, 119
Las Estacas, 163–164, 170
Legal aid, 44
Liquor laws, 44–45
Los Castillo, 150
Los Morros de Los Pericos islands,
  99–100
Lost documents, 6
Lost-luggage insurance, 18

Mágico Mundo Marino, 70
Maguey Bay, 136
Mail, 45
Mambo Café, 80
Mandara, 80
Manialtepec Lagoon, 118
Mazunte Beach, 120
Medical insurance, 17–18
Mercado Central (Taxco), 149
Mexicana Vacations (MexSeaSun
  Vacations), 35
Mexican tourist offices, 5
Mexican Tourist Permit (FMT), 6
Mexico Art Tours, 36
Mexico Travel Net, 35
Money matters, 8–12
Mosquitoes and gnats, 20
Mountain climbing, 35
Museo Arqueológico Guillermo
  Spratling, 149
Museo de Arqueología de la Costa
  Grande, 97–98
Museo Histórico de Acapulco, 75–76

National parks and nature reserves,
  35–36
National Silver Fair, 16
Navy Day, 14
New Year's Day, 13
New Year's Eve, 16
Nightlife
  Acapulco, 78–81
  Cuernavaca, 164
  Ixtapa/Zihuatanejo, 103–104

Nightlife *(cont.)*
    Puerto Escondido, 122
    Taxco, 151
Nude beach, 125
Nuestra Señora de la Soledad, cathedral, 70

Oaxaca Reservations/Zapotec
Tours, 36–37
Olmedo, Dolores, home of, 76
Organo Bay, 136

Package tours, 33–35
Palladium, 81
Parasailing, 73, 100
Parque Acuático el CICI, 76
Passports, 45
Pepe's Piano Bar, 81
Petacalco Beach, 101
Pets, 46
Pie de la Cuesta, 71–72
Playa Bacocho, 118–119
Playa Caleta, 70, 71
Playa Caletilla, 70, 71
Playa Carrizalillo, 118
Playa Condesa, 71
Playa Escobilla, 120
Playa Hornitos, 71
Playa Hornos, 71
Playa Icacos, 71
Playa la Angosta, 70
Playa Larga, 99, 102
Playa La Ropa, 98
    accommodations, 90–92
    restaurant, 96
Playa las Cuatas, 99
Playa Las Gatas, 98
Playa Linda, 99, 101
Playa Madera, 98
    accommodations, 88–90
    restaurant, 96
Playa Majahua, 99
Playa Manzanillo, 71, 118
Playa Marineros, 109, 117
Playa Mazunte, 120
Playa Municipal, 98
Playa Palmar, 99
Playa Panteón, 124
Playa Paraíso, 71
Playa Principal, 109, 117
Playa Puerto Marqués, 71

Playa Quieta, 99
Playa Revolcadero, 71
Playa San Agustinillo, 125
Playa Vista Hermosa, 99
Playa Zicatela, 109, 117–119
Playa Zihuatanejo. *See* Ixtapa/
    Zihuatanejo
Playa Zipolite, 124–125
Plaza Bahía, 77
Plaza Condesa, 77–78
Pleasant Mexico Holidays, 35
Police, 46
Post offices, 56, 87, 110, 124,
    130, 143, 144, 155
Pozole, 69
Puerto Angel, 2, 123–125
Puerto Angelito, 118
Puerto Escondido, 2, 105–122
    accommodations, 111–114
    getting around, 110
    Internet access, 110
    layout of, 109
    nightlife, 122
    restaurants, 115–117
    Ridley turtles, 120
    safety, 110
    shopping, 121–122
    sights and activities, 117–121
    traveling to and from, 106, 108
    visitor information, 108–109
Puerto Marqués, 71
Punta del Guitarrón, 71
Punta Diamante, 71
Pyramids of Xochicalco, 164

Restaurants. *See* Restaurant Index
    and specific destinations
Restrooms, 46
Revolcadero Beach, 71
Revolution Day, 16
Ridley turtles, 120
Roqueta Island, 71, 72–73

Safety, 22–24
St. Peter and St. Paul's Day, 14
Salon Q, 81
Sanborn's, 77
Santa Cruz Bay, 126
Santa Cruz Huatulco, 128–129
Santa Prisca y San Sebastián Church,
    149–150
Santo Domingo Xocotitlán, 169

Scams, 23–24
Scorpions, 20–21
Scuba diving, 35, 73, 101
Seasons, 12–13
Seniors, 27
Señor Frog's, 104
Shopping
    Acapulco, 77–78
    Bahías de Huatulco, 137
    Ixtapa/Zihuatanejo, 102–103
    Puerto Escondido, 121–122
Smoking, 46–47
Snorkeling, 35, 98, 99, 118, 124, 135
Spanish schools and classes,
    143, 155–156
Spratling Ranch Workshop, 150
Students, 28
Sun exposure, 19
Surf-and-sports shops, 121
Surfing, 125
    Ixtapa/Zihuatanejo, 101
    Puerto Escondido, 117, 119
Swimming, Acapulco, 71–72

Tangolunda Bay, 126, 129, 136
Taxco, 2, 139–151
    accommodations, 144–145
    exploring, 147–150
    layout of, 143
    nightlife, 151
    restaurants, 145–147
    traveling to and from, 142
    visitor information, 142–143
Taxis, 40–41
Telephones, 47–48
Tennis, 74, 101, 137
Tepoznieves, 167
Tepozteco pyramid, 168–169
Tepoztlán, 164–170
    exploring, 168–169
    restaurants, 167–168
    traveling to and from, 165
Three Kings Day, 13
Time zone, 48
Tipping, 48
Toll roads, 38–39
Transportation, 37–41
Traveler's checks, 11
Travel insurance, 17–18
Trek America, 37
Trip-cancellation insurance, 17
Tropical illnesses, 21–22

Turista (travelers' diarrhea), 19
Turtle Museum, 120
Turtles, 120

United Vacations, 33
Universidad Nacional Autónoma de
    México (UNAM), 143
US Airways Vacations, 34

Ventanilla, 120
Visitor information, 2, 4–5
Viva Zapatos, 103

Water, drinking, 48
Water-skiing, 73
Watersports. See also specific sports
    Acapulco, 73
    Ixtapa/Zihuatanejo, 99–101
    Puerto Angel, 124
Women travelers, 27–28

Zen, 104
Zicatela Beach, 109, 117–119
Zihuatanejo. See Ixtapa/Zihuatanejo

ACCOMMODATIONS
Amuleto, 90
Apartamentos Amueblados Valle, 88
Barceló Ixtapa, 92–93
Best Western Posada Real, 111
Best Western Taxco, 144
Bungalows & Cabañas Acuario,
    112–113
Bungalows Ley, 88–89
Calinda Beach, 61
Camino Real Acapulco Diamante,
    57–58
Camino Real Sumiya, 156
Camino Real Zaashila, 131
Casa Bugambilia, 166
Casa Kau-Kan, 92
Casa Yal'ma Ka'an, 58
Fairmont Pierre Marqués, 58–59
Fiesta Americana Villas Acapulco,
    59–60
Gala Resort, 132
Hotel Arco Iris, 113

Hotel Caleta, 62
Hotel Casa Blanca, 113
Hotel Castillo de Reyes, 114
Hotel Costa Linda, 63
Hotel Elcano, 60
Hotel Flor de María, 114
Hotel Juárez, 158
Hotel Las Palmas, 133
Hotel los Arcos, 144–145
Hotel Los Flamingos, 63–64
Hotel Meigas Binniguenda, 132
Hotel Mirador Acapulco, 63
Hotel Misión, 64
Hotel Nilayam, 166–167
Hotel Posada Emilia Castillo, 145
Hotel Posada María Cristina, 158
Hotel Santa Fe, 111–112
Hotel Santa Prisca, 145
Hyatt Regency Acapulco, 60–61
La Casa Que Canta, 90–91
Las Brisas Ixtapa, 93
Las Golondrinas, 166
Las Mañanitas, 156–157
Misión de los Arcos, 133
Misión Del Sol Resort & Spa, 157–158
Monte Taxco, 144
NH Krystal Ixtapa, 93–94
Paraíso Escondido, 112
Posada Citlali, 88
Posada del Tepozteco, 167
Quinta Real, 131–132
Rockaway, 114
Sand's Acapulco, 61–62
The Tides Zihuatanejo, 91–92
Villas Miramar, 89–90
Villas San Sebastián, 92

RESTAURANTS

Arte la Galería, 116
Baikal, 65
Beccofino, 96–97
Cabo Blanco, 115
Cafecito, 116
Cafe Sasha, 146
Casa Hidalgo, 159
Casa Nova, 66
Casa Puntarenas, 95
Coconuts, 94
El Adobe, 146
El Amigo Miguel, 69
El Cabrito, 68
El Chalchi, 167
El Ciruelo Restaurant Bar, 167–168
El Jardín, 116–117
El Olvido, 67
El Sabor de Oaxaca, 133–134
Flor de María, 117
Golden Cookie Shop, 97
Ika Tako, 68
Kau-Kan, 94–95
La Perla, 96
La Sirena Gorda, 95
Las Margaritas, 117
La Terraza Café-Bar, 146
La Universal, 160
Mariscos Pipo, 70
Mezzanotte Acapulco, 66
Noches Oaxaqueñas/Don Porfirio, 134
Nueva Zelanda, 95–96
100% Natural, 68–69
Pascal, 115
Restaurante Axitla, 168
Restaurante Bar Doña Celia, 134
Restaurante Ethel, 147
Restaurant La India Bonita, 159
Restaurant Las Mañanitas, 158–159
Restaurant Santa Fe, 115–116
Ruben's, 97
Sotavento Restaurant Bar Galería,
    147
Sr. Costilla's, 147
Su Casa/La Margarita, 67
Terra-Cotta, 134–135
Toni's, 145–146
Villa de la Selva, 96
Zibu, 66–67

FROMMER'S® COMPLETE TRAVEL GUIDES

Alaska
Amalfi Coast
American Southwest
Amsterdam
Argentina & Chile
Arizona
Atlanta
Australia
Austria
Bahamas
Barcelona
Beijing
Belgium, Holland & Luxembourg
Belize
Bermuda
Boston
Brazil
British Columbia & the Canadian
   Rockies
Brussels & Bruges
Budapest & the Best of Hungary
Buenos Aires
Calgary
California
Canada
Cancún, Cozumel & the Yucatán
Cape Cod, Nantucket & Martha's
   Vineyard
Caribbean
Caribbean Ports of Call
Carolinas & Georgia
Chicago
China
Colorado
Costa Rica
Croatia
Cuba
Denmark
Denver, Boulder & Colorado Springs
Edinburgh & Glasgow
England
Europe
Europe by Rail
Florence, Tuscany & Umbria

Florida
France
Germany
Greece
Greek Islands
Hawaii
Hong Kong
Honolulu, Waikiki & Oahu
India
Ireland
Israel
Italy
Jamaica
Japan
Kauai
Las Vegas
London
Los Angeles
Los Cabos & Baja
Madrid
Maine Coast
Maryland & Delaware
Maui
Mexico
Montana & Wyoming
Montréal & Québec City
Moscow & St. Petersburg
Munich & the Bavarian Alps
Nashville & Memphis
New England
Newfoundland & Labrador
New Mexico
New Orleans
New York City
New York State
New Zealand
Northern Italy
Norway
Nova Scotia, New Brunswick &
   Prince Edward Island
Oregon
Paris
Peru
Philadelphia & the Amish Country

Portugal
Prague & the Best of the Czech
   Republic
Provence & the Riviera
Puerto Rico
Rome
San Antonio & Austin
San Diego
San Francisco
Santa Fe, Taos & Albuquerque
Scandinavia
Scotland
Seattle
Seville, Granada & the Best of
   Andalusia
Shanghai
Sicily
Singapore & Malaysia
South Africa
South America
South Florida
South Pacific
Southeast Asia
Spain
Sweden
Switzerland
Tahiti & French Polynesia
Texas
Thailand
Tokyo
Toronto
Turkey
USA
Utah
Vancouver & Victoria
Vermont, New Hampshire & Maine
Vienna & the Danube Valley
Vietnam
Virgin Islands
Virginia
Walt Disney World® & Orlando
Washington, D.C.
Washington State

FROMMER'S® DAY BY DAY GUIDES

Amsterdam
Chicago
Florence & Tuscany

London
New York City
Paris

Rome
San Francisco
Venice

PAULINE FROMMER'S GUIDES! SEE MORE. SPEND LESS.

Hawaii

Italy

New York City

FROMMER'S® PORTABLE GUIDES

Acapulco, Ixtapa & Zihuatanejo
Amsterdam
Aruba
Australia's Great Barrier Reef
Bahamas
Big Island of Hawaii
Boston
California Wine Country
Cancún
Cayman Islands
Charleston
Chicago
Dominican Republic

Dublin
Florence
Las Vegas
Las Vegas for Non-Gamblers
London
Maui
Nantucket & Martha's Vineyard
New Orleans
New York City
Paris
Portland
Puerto Rico
Puerto Vallarta, Manzanillo &
   Guadalajara

Rio de Janeiro
San Diego
San Francisco
Savannah
St. Martin, Sint Maarten, Anguilla &
   St. Bart's
Turks & Caicos
Vancouver
Venice
Virgin Islands
Washington, D.C.
Whistler

Frommer's® Cruise Guides

Alaska Cruises & Ports of Call

Cruises & Ports of Call

European Cruises & Ports of Call

Frommer's® National Park Guides

Algonquin Provincial Park
Banff & Jasper
Grand Canyon

National Parks of the American West
Rocky Mountain
Yellowstone & Grand Teton

Yosemite and Sequoia & Kings
Canyon
Zion & Bryce Canyon

Frommer's® Memorable Walks

London
New York

Paris
Rome

San Francisco

Frommer's® With Kids Guides

Chicago
Hawaii
Las Vegas
London

National Parks
New York City
San Francisco

Toronto
Walt Disney World® & Orlando
Washington, D.C.

Suzy Gershman's Born to Shop Guides

France
Hong Kong, Shanghai & Beijing
Italy

London
New York

Paris
San Francisco

Frommer's® Irreverent Guides

Amsterdam
Boston
Chicago
Las Vegas

London
Los Angeles
Manhattan
Paris

Rome
San Francisco
Walt Disney World®
Washington, D.C.

Frommer's® Best-Loved Driving Tours

Austria
Britain
California
France

Germany
Ireland
Italy
New England

Northern Italy
Scotland
Spain
Tuscany & Umbria

The Unofficial Guides®

Adventure Travel in Alaska
Beyond Disney
California with Kids
Central Italy
Chicago
Cruises
Disneyland®
England
Florida
Florida with Kids

Hawaii
Ireland
Las Vegas
London
Maui
Mexico's Best Beach Resorts
Mini Mickey
New Orleans
New York City

Paris
San Francisco
South Florida including Miami &
the Keys
Walt Disney World®
Walt Disney World® for
Grown-ups
Walt Disney World® with Kids
Washington, D.C.

Special-Interest Titles

Athens Past & Present
Best Places to Raise Your Family
Cities Ranked & Rated
500 Places to Take Your Kids Before They Grow Up
Frommer's Best Day Trips from London
Frommer's Best RV & Tent Campgrounds
   in the U.S.A.

Frommer's Exploring America by RV
Frommer's NYC Free & Dirt Cheap
Frommer's Road Atlas Europe
Frommer's Road Atlas Ireland
Great Escapes From NYC Without Wheels
Retirement Places Rated

Frommer's® PhraseFinder Dictionary Guides

French

Italian

Spanish

I don't speak sign language.

A hotel can close for all kinds of reasons.
Our Guarantee ensures that if your hotel's undergoing construction, we'll let you know in advance. In fact, we cover your entire travel experience. See www.travelocity.com/guarantee for details.

travelocity
You'll never roam alone.